I0160392

THE
SEARCH FOR THE NEXT
MICKEY MANTLE

FROM TOM TRESH TO BRYCE HARPER

BARRY SPARKS

SUNBURY
P R E S S ®

Mechanicsburg, PA USA

Published by Sunbury Press, Inc.
Mechanicsburg, Pennsylvania

SUNBURY
P R E S S
www.sunburypress.com

Copyright © 2022 by Barry Sparks.
Cover Copyright © 2022 by Sunbury Press, Inc.

Sunbury Press supports copyright. Copyright fuels creativity, encourages diverse voices, promotes free speech, and creates a vibrant culture. Thank you for buying an authorized edition of this book and for complying with copyright laws by not reproducing, scanning, or distributing any part of it in any form without permission. You are supporting writers and allowing Sunbury Press to continue to publish books for every reader. For information contact Sunbury Press, Inc., Subsidiary Rights Dept., PO Box 548, Boiling Springs, PA 17007 USA or legal@sunburypress.com.

For information about special discounts for bulk purchases, please contact Sunbury Press Orders Dept. at (855) 338-8359 or orders@sunburypress.com.

To request one of our authors for speaking engagements or book signings, please contact Sunbury Press Publicity Dept. at publicity@sunburypress.com.

FIRST SUNBURY PRESS EDITION: November 2022

Set in Adobe Garamond | Interior design by Crystal Devine | Cover by Darleen Sedjro | Edited by Lawrence Knorr.

Publisher's Cataloging-in-Publication Data
Names: Sparks, Barry, author.
Title: The search for the next Mickey Mantle : from Tom Tresh to Bryce Harper / Barry Sparks.
Description: First trade paperback edition. | Mechanicsburg, PA : Sunbury Press, 2022.
Summary: Unbelievably high, and often unrealistic, expectations come with being labeled "the next Mickey Mantle." But once an organization or the media utters or writes that phrase, it becomes an albatross for most players. The expectation is that the player will become one of the greatest players in the game, not an average player, or even a star, but a superstar of the brightest magnitude. Few are able to rise to that level.
Identifiers: ISBN 978-1-62006-955-4 (softcover).
Subjects: SPORTS & RECREATION / General | SPORTS & RECREATION / Baseball / General | SPORTS & RECREATION / Baseball / History.

Product of the United States of America
0 1 1 2 3 5 8 13 21 34 55

Continue the Enlightenment!

Cover photo: National Baseball Hall of Fame Library, Cooperstown, N.Y.
Topps® trading cards used courtesy of The Topps Company, Inc.

To my wife, Ann, a patient listener and a
source of constant encouragement.

CONTENTS

Introduction   1

CHAPTERS

1   The Curse of Talent and the Burden of Potential   5

2   Mickey Mantle: The Gold Standard   9

3   Tom Tresh: The First Next Mickey Mantle   24

4   Joe Pepitone: The Player Who Was His Own Worst Enemy   36

5   Roger Repoz: The Quick Starter   52

6   Rick Reichardt: The $200,000 Bonus Baby   60

7   Bobby Murcer: The Other Oklahoma Kid   75

8   Steve Whitaker: The Hot-Tempered Slugger   91

9   Bill Robinson: The Black Mickey Mantle   100

10 Tony Solaita: The Powerful Samoan   111

11 Ron Blomberg: The Often-Injured Jewish Hero   121

12 Clint Hurdle: The Can't-Miss Kid   131

13 Kirk Gibson: The Hard-Nosed Impact Player   142

14 Jay Buhner: The Underappreciated Prospect   159

15 Gregg Jefferies: The Wunderkind   169

16 Ruben Rivera: The Colossal Mystery   185

17 Mike Trout: The Complete Package   197

18 Bryce Harper: The Teen Destined to be a Star   212

Appendix (season-by-season records of each player)   227
Endnotes   234
Acknowledgments   245
Bibliography   247
Index   250
About the Author   253

INTRODUCTION

What baseball team wouldn't want a player of
Mickey Mantle's caliber?
—LONG-TIME BASEBALL SCOUT

After appearing in 14 World Series in 16 seasons from 1949-1964, the New York Yankees dynasty ended in 1965 when they finished sixth in the American League with a 77-85 record. It was no aberration. In 1966, the decades-old juggernaut fell with a thud into the basement of the 10-team American League. The club closed with a 70-89 record, 26.5 games behind the Baltimore Orioles. It marked the first time since 1912 the team occupied last place. The Yankees would not finish in first place again until 1976, when they captured the American League East title.

In the summer of 1965, Cleveland Indians manager Birdie Tebbetts said, "All the Yankees need is one great player. If there isn't anyone, the Yankees need to worry."[1]

Of course, it wasn't that simple. There were a multitude of reasons for the Yankees' decline. Finding a superstar to replace the fading Mickey Mantle wouldn't be easy, but it would be easier than fixing an array of problems. The club had searched for the "next Mickey Mantle" since switch-hitting Tom Tresh won the American League Rookie of the Year Award in 1962. Tresh was the first in a long line of candidates to potentially fill Mantle's shoes, a Herculean task.

Mantle won the American League Most Valuable Player Award in 1962 after placing second to teammate Roger Maris in the MVP voting in 1960 and 1961. At age 30, Mantle had battled injuries throughout his career, and the club wasn't sure how much longer it could count on him to be productive. Despite any optimism the club could muster, the Yankee superstar entered the latter part of his career.

There was plenty of pressure on the Yankees' front office to produce the 'next Mickey Mantle.' After more than 40 years of continuous superstars—Ruth, Gehrig, DiMaggio, and Mantle—fans weren't ready for it to end. A team with a superstar is a team with hope, charisma, and an attendance magnet. Touting a potential superstar is a way to sell fans on a brighter future.

The Yankees and the New York media, particularly in the 1960s and early 1970s, unfairly hung "the next Mickey Mantle" label on many players, all of whom fell short of his standards. Tresh, Joe Pepitone, Roger Repoz, Bobby Murcer, Steve Whitaker, Bill Robinson, Tony Solaita, and Ron Blomberg were victims of the hype.

In 1965 when Mantle and Maris were both injured, the Yankees called up 25-year-old, left-handed hitting outfielder Roger Repoz from Toledo. Plagued by strikeouts and a low batting average most of his minor league career, Repoz led the International League in home runs when he was summoned to the majors. Johnny Johnson, director of the Yankees farm system, proclaimed, "The next Yankee star is Roger Repoz. There is no doubt about it."[2] In 127 games over three seasons with New York, Repoz tallied 12 home runs and batted .240.

Cleveland Indians manager Birdie Tebbetts offered another observation, "There is a myth that you put a player in a Yankee uniform, and he becomes great. But you have to put the right player in the uniform. The Yankees are having trouble getting that kind of player because the other clubs are building themselves up."[3] Implementing the major league amateur draft in 1965 almost guaranteed the Yankees wouldn't be able to turn their fortunes around quickly. Before the draft, the club flooded the country with its savvy scouts and used its power and prestige to sign a host of talented players. Under the amateur draft, however, teams selected players in the inverse order of their finish. It was an effort to introduce parity and end bidding wars. It didn't favor the Yankees.

In 1967, Jack Mann, author of *The Decline and Fall of the New York Yankees*, wrote, "the Yankees are in this mess because of 10 years, maybe 20 years, of bad management. Not stupid management, but short-sighted management, the failure to recognize the game of baseball was changing into a system of controlled mediocrity, to which the Yankee method could no longer be superior, or even equal."[4]

Arrogance had cost the Yankees. When bonus players became the rage in the 1950s, the Yankees shunned them for the most part. The club preferred to sign players relatively cheaply. They counted on the aura of pinstripes to offset their subpar bonus offers. Bobby Murcer, who idolized Mantle growing up in Oklahoma, signed with the Yankees for $10,000, even though the Los Angeles Dodgers offered him $20,000. He dreamed of playing for the Yankees and figured a string of World Series checks would make up the difference.

The Yankees signed Roger Repoz for $4,000 and Steve Whitaker for $5,500. After Tony Solaita signed for a modest $1,000 bonus, he joked, "I signed for a steak dinner, and I had to leave the tip."[5] On the flip side, the club offered Rick Reichardt more money than the Los Angeles Angels did in 1964 ($200,000), but the youngster passed up the offer to sign with the California club. The New Yorkers also inked Ron Blomberg for $75,000 in 1972.

Even though the Yankees had Elston Howard, the 1963 American League Most Valuable Player, they had been slow to scout and sign Black players. That reluctance cost them a wealth of talent.

The Yankees weren't the only team to drag their feet in this area. Most American League teams were guilty, to varying degrees, of the same practice. The National League was much quicker in scouting and signing Black players. From 1949, when Jackie Robinson of the Brooklyn Dodgers was voted Most Valuable Player, through 1967, 14 of the 19 National League MVPs and 11 of the 19 batting champs were Black.

Injuries also plagued the Yankees. To compound matters, the club insisted that some of its players play through their injuries or management failed to treat the injuries properly. Arm injuries rendered promising pitchers Jim Bouton and Bill Stafford ineffective. After winning 39 games in 1963 and 1964, Bouton won just 16 more in six seasons. Stafford won 28 games in 1961 and 1962 but only 12 more in the next five seasons.

From 1966 through 1970, the Yankees' star power was greatly diminished. Whitey Ford, Mickey Mantle, Roger Maris, Bobby Richardson, Tony Kubek, Tom Tresh, Clete Boyer, Elston Howard, Ralph Terry, and Al Downing were traded or retired.

Even though the Yankees still won in the early 1960s, the fledging New York Mets started to cut into their attendance in 1962. Attendance slipped by 250,000 in 1962 and another 200,000 in 1963. The gate for 1963 was 1.3 million, the lowest since 1945. In 1972, attendance dipped below one million.

Would a player of Mickey Mantle's caliber solve the Yankees' woes? Perhaps not, but the potential upside fueled a relentless search. Other teams also scoured the country for a five-tool player (one who could hit for average, hit for power, run, field and throw) who defied description. A player you could build a team around and forge a dynasty. A player who could command attention and fill a stadium. It was a search that would go on for more than 50 years.

CHAPTER 1

THE CURSE OF TALENT AND THE BURDEN OF POTENTIAL

The worse curse in life is unlimited potential.
—KEN BRETT, FORMER MAJOR LEAGUE PITCHER

To better understand the players' challenges in this book, you must understand the psychology of high expectations and the pressure accompanying them. Baseball is a "bright-spotlight, heavy-pressure, big-dollar sport in which far more dreams are crushed than cashed in," according to Bob Tewksbury, former major league pitcher and mental skills coach for several major league teams.[1] Being successful in a sport of failure is extremely difficult. It requires tremendous talent, dedication, a strong work ethic, the ability to adjust, confidence, resiliency, and more.

No baseball prospect ever asked to be labeled "the next Mickey Mantle." The label comes with unbelievably high and often unrealistic expectations. But once an organization or media utters or writes the phrase, it becomes an albatross for most players. The expectation is that the player will become one of the greatest players in the game, not an average player or even a star, but a superstar of the brightest magnitude. Although the comparison to Mantle is flattering, most players try to dismiss it quickly.

H.A. Dorfman and Karl Kuehl, authors of *The Mental Game of Baseball: A Guide to Peak Performance*, write that there's a difference between a player's expectations and the expectations of others for that player. The latter expectations can damage the player's game and his view of himself as a performer and person. Typically, too much is expected too soon of a young prospect.

Boston's Fred Lynn, who won the Rookie of the Year Award and the Most Valuable Player Award in 1975, said, "I had high expectations of myself, but what expectations other people put on you, those can be difficult to live up to."[2]

Excessively high expectations rarely result in high-level performance. When expectations are high, so is the pressure to meet those expectations. When expectations undermine a player's confidence, he tends to doubt his ability when things don't go as planned.

Tewksbury writes, "True confidence is the realization that when things are challenging, you know that you have the internal resources not only to cope with those times but to overcome them with time, effort and persistence."[3] According to Dr. Patrick Cohn, founder of Peak Performance Sports, high expectations lead to increased pressure and other negative consequences, such as:

- Reduced confidence
- Anxiety
- Fear of failure
- Overthinking
- Inability to move past mistakes
- Negative thinking
- Under-performance

In trying to meet the high expectations of others, athletes will typically try harder, compounding the pressure. Players often lose sight of establishing realistic goals for themselves. Dorfman and Kuehl emphasize that goals serve the individual; expectations serve others. While players can adjust their goals, they rarely can adjust the expectations of others.

Mickey Mantle faced higher expectations and more pressure than perhaps any player in baseball history. As a 19-year-old rookie in 1951, he was expected to replace Yankee legend Joe DiMaggio under the greatest blaze of publicity since Babe Ruth reported to the Polo Grounds in 1920. Yankee coach Bill Dickey said, "Mantle is the greatest prospect I've ever seen in my life."[4]

When Mantle arrived to spring training in 1952 after his rookie season, he said, "I know now that I can't be what the writers made me out to be last spring. I felt like I had to get a base hit every time I came to the plate."[5] Players have to learn that they can't please everybody.

Mantle was expected to become the greatest player of all time. In 1956, former Yankee Jerry Coleman preposterously proposed that "Mantle had the potential to bat .400 and hit 80 homers."[6] As a former major leaguer, Coleman had to know that feat was humanly impossible.

Kansas City Royals scout Bill Fischer projected that 18-year-old Clint Hurdle would hit for a high average and knock 25 to 40 home runs a year. Hurdle slugged 32 home runs and batted .259 in an 11-year major league career. He adjusted his goals based on his abilities, but the fans, media, and the Royals never changed their expectations.

The Yankees' Tom Tresh wasn't a natural home run hitter, but some expected him to hit 40 homers a season. Trying to meet those expectations, he swung harder, changed his batting stance, and threw off his timing. He lost confidence as his batting average declined.

Mired in a deep slump early in his career, Yankee outfielder Bill Robinson admitted he became a head case. "I started to press. I couldn't relax. I couldn't sleep. The slump got to me. My teammates told me I was trying too hard. That didn't help. It was on my mind all the time."[7]

The relentless booing also bothered Robinson, who said he tried to hit a home run every at-bat to impress the fans. "The boos really tore me up when I was with the Yankees," he said. "All the ballplayers hear them, and I couldn't take it."[8]

Fans seem to delight in heckling and booing players who are not living up to expectations. Every weak grounder, strike out, or pop-up with men on base unleashes a torrent of dissatisfaction. In reviewing Hurdle's early failings, Jim Hawkins of the *Detroit Press* wrote, "The fans haven't forgiven him for being human."[9]

The media often piles on, declaring the player a flop, disappointment, or underachiever. The player is always saddled with the responsibility for his failure, even though the team may have rushed him to the majors, misjudged his talent, tinkered endlessly with his batting style, or mishandled him psychologically.

High expectations and pressure can handicap a player's development. Rick Reichardt, who signed with the Los Angeles Angels in 1964 for a $200,000 bonus (equal to $1.7 million today), appeared in just 57 minor league games before making his major league debut. Although he played a full season at Triple-AAA before rejoining the Angels at the end of 1965, he regretted not playing more games in the minors and gaining more experience. Eager for him to succeed, the Angels overloaded him with advice, and he ended up confused and frustrated.

Detroit Tigers manager Sparky Anderson said Kirk Gibson was the only player he had ever managed who had the chance of being another Mickey Mantle. The comparison to Mantle haunted Gibson, who asked Sparky to refrain from making the comparison. Anderson agreed and said, "That was the worst thing I could have done to him. All it did was burden him. I set him back who knows how long, probably a couple of years."[10]

Detroit hitting coach Gates Brown said, "The comparison to Mickey Mantle hurt Kirk. He tried to live up to that, and it hurt him."[11]

Unfortunately, most of the players in this book did not have the benefit of a sports psychologist. They could have benefited greatly, especially since Tewksbury maintains that 90 percent of baseball is mental.

Although Chicago Cubs owner Philip K. Wrigley hired baseball's first sports psychologist, Coleman Griffith, in 1938, the experiment was short-lived. For decades, baseball teams have psychologically ignored their players. Several teams, however, hired mental training consultants in the 1980s. That movement gained more traction in 1989 with the publication of *The Mental Game of Baseball: A Guide to Peak Performance* by Dorfman and Kuehl. Today, nearly every major league team employs a sports psychologist or mental skills coach.

According to *Sports Illustrated*, "They (mental skills coaches) instruct players on everything from meditation to goal-setting to managing anxiety."[12]

According to Peak Performance Sports, the goal of sports psychology is to "teach athletes how to be more confident, improve focus, stay composed under pressure, practice more efficiently and develop better pre-performance routines."[13]

All the players tabbed 'the next Mickey Mantle' had to battle what sportswriter Bob Hertzel called "the curse of talent and the burden of potential."[14] It undoubtedly made their journey more difficult.

CHAPTER 2

MICKEY MANTLE
outfielder NEW YORK YANKEES

MICKEY MANTLE
THE GOLD STANDARD

*He should lead the league in everything. With his combination of
speed and power, he should win the Triple Crown every year. In fact,
he should do anything he wants to.*
—NEW YORK YANKEES MANAGER CASY STENGEL

Before the start of the 1951 season, it was rumored that Yankee great Joe
DiMaggio would announce his retirement before the end of the year. Joe
D had majestically reigned over the baseball world since 1936. Graceful,
cold, and aloof, he was a God-like figure many felt could never be replaced. The Yankees, however, believed 19-year-old Mickey Mantle was
the future.

The muscular 5-11, 190-pounder was a rare switch-hitter with power
from both sides, blazing speed, and the ability to win a batting title. His

experience was limited, his talent was raw, and his potential was off the charts.

Yankee scout Tom Greenwade signed him the day he graduated from high school in Commerce, Oklahoma, for $1,105, plus a $410 monthly salary to play the rest of the season with the Class D Independence Yankees. He batted .313 in 89 games. The following season, he was promoted to Class C Joplin, Missouri, in the Western Association. He attracted plenty of attention as he batted .383, won the league batting title and was named the Most Valuable Player. Despite his success at the plate, he was a mistake-prone shortstop, committing 55 errors. He was better suited for the outfield or first base.

New York sportswriters and the Yankees' publicity machine kicked into overdrive when Mantle arrived in Phoenix for spring training camp in 1951. In the first game, the Oklahoma native slugged a home run right-handed. In the next at-bat, he blasted a home run left-handed. Several days later, he easily beat all the Yankees in a foot race. That was enough fodder for reams of copy.

Yankee catcher Ralph Houk remembered the first time he saw Mantle in Phoenix. "He hit the ball so hard it was unreal. Each time up, he seemed to hit the ball harder than the time before. It got so that batting practice and Mickey's in-game at-bats were the most exciting parts of the day."[1]

No rookie stirred up a commotion and extravagant publicity like Mantle. Soon, hyperbole ran rampant. According to some writers, Mantle was a combination of Joe DiMaggio at the plate, Ty Cobb on the bases, and Tris Speaker in the outfield.

Veteran baseball men thought the teenager was special. Yankee great Bill Dickey said, "Mantle is the greatest prospect I've seen in my time, and I go back quite a way."[2] Yankee coach Tommy Henrich, who was helping Mantle learn to play the outfield, said, "Mantle is a rare youngster. He has great potential. He's one of the finest-looking kids I have ever seen."[3]

Cleveland Indians manager Al Lopez commented, "He's one of those once-in-a-lifetime boys."[4] Mantle was good, but just how good? Veteran observers reminded those heaping praise on the youngster that he had a lot to learn and hadn't played a game in the major leagues yet.

It was originally thought Mantle would be assigned to Class-AAA Kansas City in the American Association after spring training. But the more he produced and impressed, the more manager Casey Stengel considered keeping him on the Yankees to open the 1951 season. No Yankee had jumped from Class C to the big club. In 30 exhibition games, Mantle batted .402 with 31 RBI, nine homers, a triple, and seven doubles.

Stengel talked the Yankees' front office into keeping Mantle. On Opening Day, April 17, 1951, the teenager was in the starting lineup, patrolling right field and batting third. Playing in front of 44,000 fans at Yankee Stadium, Mantle collected his first major league hit, a single off Boston's Bill Wight in the sixth inning, as New York won 5-0.

The shy, quiet and introverted Mantle had stepped onto one of the world's biggest stages under the greatest blaze of publicity since Babe Ruth reported to the Polo Grounds in 1920, according to *Baseball Digest*. New York City, his teammates, the horde of media, the massive crowds, and the attention he received awed the country boy, who grew up in Commerce, Oklahoma (population 3,000). All that, minus the exorbitant expectations, would have been enough to overwhelm any young player.

The expectations, however, were like a tight uniform he wore every day. He was expected to succeed Joe DiMaggio, who said he would be willing to move to right field or left field to make room for Mantle because he "can't miss being a great one."[5] He also was expected to help lead the Yankees to their third consecutive American League pennant.

Mickey played well in the first month of the season. On May 16, he was batting .316 with four home runs and 26 RBI. The rookie's biggest problem was strikeouts. It concerned Stengel and frustrated Mantle, who often berated himself after fanning. He displayed his temper by kicking a water cooler, tossing his bat and helmet, or disgustedly heading toward the bench. Striking out was a bigger sin in the 1950s than today.

In a Memorial Day doubleheader against the Boston Red Sox, Mantle, whose average was rapidly declining, went 0-for-5, striking out five times as the Yankees lost both games. After the fifth strikeout, Mickey, frustrated and discouraged, returned to the dugout and told Stengel, "Put somebody in there who can hit. I can't."[6]

After hitting .303 in May, he slipped to .228 in June. His strikeout rate increased, his power declined, and he failed to drive in runners. The Yankees were in a pennant race and couldn't afford Mantle to be unproductive. On July 15, Stengel informed his young prospect that he was being shipped to Class-AAA Kansas City. At the time, Mantle was hitting .260 and had struck out 52 times in 69 games. The manager encouraged Mantle, telling him he hadn't lost faith in him and would be back.

Although heartbroken and afraid he had missed his opportunity, Mickey tried to look on the positive side. "It's all right. I'd rather play every day in the minors than sit on the Yankee bench. Nobody has to tell me I have a lot to learn about outfielding and hitting."[7]

Mantle arrived in Kansas City and immediately went into a deep slump. Depressed and convinced he couldn't play, he called his father in Oklahoma and asked him to come to get him. His father, Mutt, drove 150 miles to his hotel room. When he arrived, he got Mickey's suitcase and started stuffing his clothes in it.

"What are you doing?" asked Mickey, who thought his father would try to talk him out of returning home.

"I'm taking you home," replied his father with a tear in his eye. The father and son had spent countless hours working on his switch-hitting, refining his skills, and discussing baseball. "You can work in the mines with me. I thought I raised a man. You're nothing but a coward. If you're going to give up on yourself, you might as well come home with me instead of wasting everyone's time."[8]

Mantle begged his father not to take him home. Mutt and Mickey talked throughout the night, and the following morning, Mutt headed back to Oklahoma alone.

"That was the turning point of my career," he said. "I stayed, and things turned around for me. As I look back, going down to Kansas City was probably the best thing I could have done. My confidence was shot, and I needed to build it back up in the minor leagues."[9]

In 40 games with Kansas City, Mickey batted .361 with 11 homers and 50 RBI. The Yankees recalled him on August 24. When he rejoined the club, Stengel said, "I told you you'd be back."[10]

When he returned to New York, he felt a different kind of pressure. For the third time in two years, the Oklahoma draft board notified Mickey that he was scheduled for a physical examination. Due to news reports and concerns from Oklahoma residents, another physical examination was requested to clear up his draft status.

His draft board classified him 4F in December 1950. The classification made him ineligible to serve in the military. Osteomyelitis, a bone disease he suffered after being kicked in the left ankle in a high school football game, was believed to be the cause of the 4F classification. With the Korean conflict underway, Mantle's draft status proved very unpopular. Critics maintained that if he could play professional sports, he could serve in the military. As a result, he was booed loudly and regularly. He received hate mail and death threats. Mickey said he would be glad to serve if he was physically fit.

After an exhaustive three-day exam at Fort Sill, doctors verified he still suffered from osteomyelitis in his left leg. He was declared 4F for the third time. Some critics, however, still were not satisfied.

New York trailed Cleveland by two games when he rejoined the team. In the final five weeks of the 1951 season, he slammed six homers, drove in 20 runs, and lifted his average to .267. The Yankees won 98 games and finished five games ahead of the Indians. With 13 round-trippers and 65 RBI, Mantle had a respectable rookie season. Teammate Gil McDougald, however, earned the 1951 American League Rookie of the Year honor.

Appearing in his first World Series added another layer of pressure for the rookie, who just a year ago was competing in Class C. Mantle was in right field when the World Series against the New York Giants opened in Yankee Stadium. After going 0-for-3 in the opening loss, his career was forever altered in Game 2.

With the Yankees leading 2-0, Willie Mays led off the top of the fifth inning. Mays smacked a line drive to right center. Center fielder Joe DiMaggio ran to his left, and Mantle raced to his right. The ball was more in Mantle's territory, but at the last second, Joe D called for the ball. Mantle suddenly felt his right leg give way and fell to the ground. Joe caught the ball and ran to Mickey, asking him what had happened. In pain, Mantle started to say he thought he had broken his right knee, but he passed out. He had to be carried off the field on a stretcher.

Neither DiMaggio nor Mantle was sure of what happened. Observers speculated that Mantle had stepped in a sprinkler hole covered by a wooden trapdoor that gave slightly if stepped on.

The following day, Mantle's knee was swollen, and he was on crutches. He was admitted to Lenox Hill Hospital, where Yankee physician Dr. Sidney Gaynor performed surgery on his knee to repair torn ligaments. The outfielder would never play baseball pain-free again. Mutt Mantle accompanied his son to the hospital. Mickey leaned on his father's shoulder for support when he got out of the cab. Mutt collapsed to the sidewalk and was admitted to the hospital, too. The two shared a hospital room.

Doctors examined Mutt and determined he had advanced Hodgkin's disease and needed immediate treatment. The prognosis was bleak. Doctors thought he would be dead in a matter of months. It was heartbreaking news for Mickey.

The Yankees beat the Giants in six games for their third consecutive World Series title. Mantle turned 20 years old ten days after the series ended. It had been a pressure-packed season of highs and lows. Perhaps no other rookie ever faced more pressure, considering the on-and-off-the-field events.

Reflecting on Mantle's rookie season, former Yankee Bobby Brown said, "Mickey Mantle as a rookie in 1951 had the most raw talent of anyone I had ever seen—then and now. I don't believe anyone ever came into baseball who could run faster, hit from both sides of the plate with such power, and throw as well as anyone. He was terrific in every phase of the game."[11]

When Mantle arrived at spring training in 1952, he believed he would greatly benefit from the year's experience and there would be less pressure. "I know now that I can't be what the writers made me out to be last spring," he said. "I felt I had to get a base hit every time I came to bat. I think I began to worry right from Opening Day."[12]

He said his high number of strikeouts (74) resulted from being over-anxious, pressing, and swinging at bad pitches.

During the off-season, he worked to get his knee back into shape. He wore a full-length brace that locked at the knee and then a modified brace that allowed him to bend at the knee. He performed a series of exercises daily. When he reported to spring training, he walked with a limp; his knee wasn't at full strength, nor could he run at full speed.

DiMaggio announced his retirement in December 1951. But Mantle wasn't the only candidate to take over the center fielder's position. Jackie Jensen, Bob Cerv, and Gene Woodling also were contenders.

In early March, Mutt Mantle was admitted to a Denver hospital with advanced-stage cancer. He died on May 6, 1952, at the age of 40. Mickey was devastated. He returned to Commerce, Okla., for the funeral. He would always harbor a fear of dying young.

When Mantle rejoined the Yankees, he returned to his right-field position. But on May 20, Stengel moved him to center field and batted him third in the lineup. Mickey responded by rapping four hits to raise his average to .315. He would remain a fixture in center field for years to come.

Mickey was now more comfortable at the plate and in the outfield. He delivered under pressure, slammed towering home runs, and played like a veteran. He sparked the club in the stretch drive for the pennant. He batted .340 as New York won 20 of 24 games to edge the Indians by two games. Mantle finished his sophomore season with 23 homers (12 right-handed and 11 left-handed), a .311 batting average (third in the league), 87 RBI, and 94 runs scored. On the downside, he fanned 111 times, erasing Frank Crosetti's team record of 105 in 1937.

At the end of September, Mantle received another call to report for an Army physical exam. Army regulations had now changed. Anyone who had been successfully treated for osteomyelitis in the past two years was now eligible for induction. *The Miami* (Oklahoma) *News-Record* called it the Mickey Mantle ruling.

With his draft status uncertain, Mantle prepared for the 1952 World Series against the Brooklyn Dodgers. The 20-year-old enjoyed a magnificent series as he rapped 10 hits in 29 at-bats (.345) and slugged a pair of homers as the Yankees edged the Dodgers in seven games. After the series, Dodgers star Jackie Robinson said, "It was that Mantle, that Mickey Mantle killed us. If it hadn't been for him, I think this would have been a very different series."[13]

In November, Mantle was declared unfit for military service once again. His right knee was the reason for his 4F status, not his osteomyelitis. The issue was finally closed.

Two weeks later, the Yankee slugger finished third in the American League Most Valuable Player voting. He placed behind pitchers Bobby Shantz of the Philadelphia A's (24-7) and Allie Reynolds of the Yankees (20-8). Shantz garnered 16 first-place votes, while Reynolds collected four and Mantle three.

At the start of spring training in 1953, Joe DiMaggio said, "In a couple of years, Mickey Mantle may become one of the greatest stars baseball has known."[14] The switch-hitter created a buzz as he batted .412 with a .784 slugging percentage in the exhibition season. Despite his impressive display, he said, "Too much is expected of me. After all, I'm only 21."[15] Expectations soared after the fourth game of the season when the Yankee slugger bashed a historic home run off southpaw Chuck Stobbs in Griffith Stadium in Washington, D.C., on April 17. Mantle rocketed the second pitch over the 405-foot left field fence. It nicked the scoreboard and left the ballpark. Observers couldn't believe how far the ball traveled. Yankees' PR man Red Patterson decided to measure the blast. He announced the home run traveled 565 feet. Questions about his methods and the veracity of the distance abounded, but Patterson turned the home run into a PR man's dream. Everyone in baseball talked about it. Requests to appear on television and radio overwhelmed Mantle, who became a legend almost overnight.

Dick Young, a New York *Daily News* columnist, wrote, "The Mickey Mantle immortality legend is 10 percent physical, 20 percent potential, and 70 percent the figment of Red Patterson's fertile imagination . . . Mantle hasn't led the league in anything yet."[16] Yankee coach Bill Dickey said, "I've seen Babe, Gehrig, and Foxx. Frankly, I never thought I would see their likes again. But now I've changed my mind. For sheer power, Mickey Mantle ranks with the best of them. I think he may eventually be rated as the tops of all time."[17]

Seven-time National League home run champ Ralph Kiner recently traded from the Pirates to the Cubs, said, "I honestly believe Mickey Mantle has a chance to become the greatest player of all time because he has two terrific assets—power and speed—most of the greats had one or the other, but not both."[18]

The debate was no longer whether Mantle would become a great player or a Hall of Famer but whether he would become the greatest player of all time. The Yankees started talking about the possibility of him winning a batting title and perhaps the Triple Crown.

From May 24 to June 11, Mickey hit safely in 16 consecutive games and raised his average to .353. Late in the summer, he tore a left thigh muscle and suffered strained ligaments in his right knee in September. The Yankees rolled to 99 wins and their fifth consecutive World Series appearance.

Mantle's right knee bothered him in the 1953 World Series against the Brooklyn Dodgers. It severely hampered him when he batted left-handed as he fanned eight times in 16 at-bats. He struck out four times in Game 3 against right-hander Carl Erskine. Although he batted .208 (5-for-28), he contributed two timely home runs. His two-run shot in the bottom of the eighth in Game 2 broke a 2-2 tie and propelled the Yankees to a 4-2 win. In Game 5, he clouted a grand slam in the top of the third that helped push New York to a 6-0 lead. The Yankees defeated the Dodgers in six games to wrap up their fifth consecutive World Championship.

During the off-season, Mantle had surgery on his right knee to re-move floating cartilage. In January, he underwent a second surgery on his leg to remove a cyst. Doctors told the Yankees he wouldn't be able to play until May, but he was in the Opening Day lineup. When he entered May batting under .200, the team admitted it had let him play too soon. Fans booed every time Mantle struck out, left a runner stranded on base, or displayed his temper. His performance failed to match the abundant publicity he received.

Joe Trimble of the *New York Daily News* wrote, "The general con-clusion around the league is that Mickey Mantle hasn't lived up to his potential, that he has been overrated, and the 'tape measure philosophy' which causes him to try for a homer every time up has hurt him."[19]

After 62 games, the 22-year-old Mantle had 11 homers and batted in the .280s. It spurred Bob Addie of the *Washington Post* to write, "The Yankees tried to shove Mickey Mantle down the public's throat, but it didn't work."[20] Addie expressed the sentiments of many other writers and fans.

Mantle had performed adequately in his career but far from sensa-tionally. An occasional mammoth homer was a reminder of his potential. Behind closed doors, the Yankees' front office was irritated with his under-performance. They were convinced he had the ability but perhaps not the desire for greatness. His carousing nightlife and excessive drinking with Yankee teammates Whitey Ford and Billy Martin were also of concern.

Mantle turned in a respectable year in 1954, batting .300, knocking 27 homers, and driving in 100 runs (102) for the first time. He led the league in runs scored with 129 and strikeouts with 107. It was far from what the Yankees were expecting. Although New York won 103 games, it finished second to Cleveland, winning 111 games. The Yankees' streak of five consecutive World Championships ended.

When Mickey arrived in spring training in 1955, he predicted he would have his best season. Entering his fifth season, there was palpable pressure on him to prove the hype was legitimate.

Stengel said he had to cut down on his strikeouts, harness his temper and fully develop his abilities. "Nothing is beyond him. Nothing. He could be the number one player in our league."[21]

DiMaggio observed, "If Mantle doesn't come up big this year, I'm afraid he never will. Five years is long enough for anybody."[22]

On May 13, the Yankee slugger provided another reminder of his awesome potential. He clubbed three home runs, two left-handed and one right-handed, against Detroit. It was the first time an American Leaguer homered from both sides of the plate in a game. The outburst gave him 10 homers for the season.

He had shortened his swing and stopped swinging for the fences on every pitch. He bashed eight home runs in May and batted .340. Still, he was a favorite target of the boobirds. Some were still upset by his 4F status, while others jeered his frequent strikeouts and temper tantrums.

An *Associated Press* writer commented, "Nobody could live up to Mickey Mantle's billing. When he got off to an unimpressive start, then was stymied by injuries and ailments, the fans felt let down. They haven't recovered from it. They still are expecting too much."[23]

The 23-year-old secured his first home run title with a strong September. He clouted 12 four-baggers to finish with 37. Guz Zernial of the Kansas City Athletics placed second with 30. Six National Leaguers, however, cleared the fences 40 or more times, including 51 by Willie Mays.

Hobbled by a pulled muscle in his right thigh, Mantle was limited to three pinch-hitting appearances in the season's final two weeks. He finished 1955 batting .306 with 99 RBI and a league-leading 113 walks. He also led the league in on-base percentage (.431), slugging percentage (.611), and on-base percentage plus slugging (1.1042).

The Yankees, winners of 96 games, returned to the World Series in 1955 to face the Brooklyn Dodgers. Mantle's injury limited him to 10 at-bats. He started Games 3 and 4 and pinch-hit in Game 7. He went 2-for-10 as the Dodgers finally defeated the Yankees.

Mantle finished fifth in the voting for the American League Most Valuable Player Award. Teammate Yogi Berra earned his second consecutive MVP. Mickey, however, topped Berra in every offensive category except RBI, where Berra held a 108 to 99 edge. Other top vote-getters were Al Kaline, Al Smith, and Ted Williams. Mantle's Wins Above Replacement (WAR) of 9.6 was tops in the league and more than twice Berra's 4.5.

Stengel reminded fans that Mantle was only 24 and had not yet reached his peak. Considering his osteomyelitis and bum knee, the manager said his star had performed admirably and had not disappointed him. Privately, Stengel was frustrated by Mantle's failure to dedicate himself to optimizing his talents.

Entering his sixth season, Mantle paled in comparison to Joe DiMaggio. In his first five seasons, Mantle led the league in homers once and scored once. He hit more than 30 homers once and drove in more than 100 runs once. His best performances were 37 homers, 102 RBI, and a .311 batting average. By comparison, Joe D earned an MVP award, led the league in homers once, runs scored once, and won two batting titles in his first five seasons. His best performances were 46 homers, 167 RBI, and a .381 batting average.

Baseball writers and veteran observers believed Mantle was due to break out in 1956.

In spring training, Joe Reichler of the *Associated Press* wrote, "Mickey Mantle seems ready for the stardom that has been predicted for him. It will be no surprise if he captured the 1956 Triple Crown."[24]

Shirley Povich of the *Washington Post* wrote, "This is Mickey Mantle's year. This is the one when he'll burst into full magnificence, hit more and longer home runs than anybody else, lead the league in batting, perhaps, and certainly get more extra-base hits than anybody else."[25]

Former Yankee Jerry Coleman said, "Mantle has the potential to bat .400 and hit 80 homers,"[26] while former Boston Brave Buddy Lewis said, "Mantle ought to be the greatest player who ever lived."[27]

Mantle arrived at spring training completely healthy for the first time in his career. He was determined to cut down on his strikeouts and hit the ball where it was pitched. Relaxed and confident, he looked like he had finally matured. In his first nine exhibition games, he slammed five home runs, none of which traveled less than 400 feet, two triples, and three doubles. He batted .484. On Opening Day 1956, he created a buzz when he slammed two blasts over Griffith Stadium's deep center field fence. The first traveled an estimated 460 feet, the other 480 feet. Afterward, Ted Williams said, "I see no reason why Mantle can't hit .340 and 40 home runs this year."[28]

Mantle started hot and stayed hot. He slugged 11 homers in his first 21 games and generated speculation that he could break Ruth's record of 60 homers. In a Memorial Day doubleheader against the Senators, he powered a home run in each game. In the nightcap, he almost became the first player to hit a fair ball out of Yankee Stadium. His clout hit the top facade of the right field stands. Two feet higher, and it would have been out of the stadium.

Mickey concluded the doubleheader hitting .425 with 20 homers in 41 games. He belted 16 four-baggers in May, drove in 35 runs, and batted .414. He was 11 games ahead of Ruth's record pace. It looked like he had an excellent chance to bat .400 and knock 60 homers.

He terrorized American League pitchers, and no one wanted to pitch to him. He dominated media coverage and water-cooler conversations. Fans flocked to see him. On June 20, he had 27 home runs after 60 games. He was 18 games ahead of Ruth's pace.

Mantle injured his right knee in the first game of a doubleheader against Boston on July 4. The Yankees sent him back to New York for x-rays, which revealed a strained ligament. Doctors told him to wear a brace on his right knee and rest. He missed four games.

By mid-July, pitchers had stopped pitching to him. They were willing to walk him. Pitchers issued him 14 free passes in the final 10 games of July. Although he was swinging at bad pitches and letting his anger get the best of him, he was batting .371 with 89 RBI and 34 homers.

Mantle clubbed his 46th home run on August 29, putting him four games ahead of Ruth. Stengel observed, "It will be a miracle if Mickey beats Babe. They won't give him anything good to hit if they can help it. And, he goes after the bad pitch they want him to fish for."[29]

The Yankee slugger entered September needing 13 four-baggers to tie Ruth's mark of 60. The Babe clouted a record 17 homers in September, making it difficult for any challenger to overtake him. Mantle didn't clear the fence the final month of the season until September 13, virtually squashing his chance of setting the record. He slammed three more round-trippers that month.

He disappointingly fell short of Babe's record. "When I missed four games before the All-Star break, I didn't think I could beat Ruth's record," he said. "My September drought wasn't because of the Ruth pressure. I was more focused on the Triple Crown."[30]

Mantle captured the 1956 Triple Crown, batting .353, slugging 52 homers, and driving in 130 runs. He edged Ted Williams for the batting title by three points, becoming the first switch-hitter to earn a batting crown. He clipped Al Kaline for the RBI title by three runs. He easily outdistanced Vic Wertz (52 to 32) for the home run crown. He became only the fourth American Leaguer and the second Yankee to earn the Triple Crown. Lou Gehrig accomplished it in 1934. Mickey also led the majors in WAR with an 11.2.

He had come of age at 24 and silenced his critics. He had displayed his spectacular gifts, proving he wasn't overrated. Casey Stengel said, "Mickey Mantle could become the greatest Yankee of all time."[31]

Behind Mantle, the Yankees rolled to 97 wins and another American League pennant. In the 1956 World Series against the Brooklyn Dodgers, he collected six hits in 24 at-bats, including three home runs and six walks. His most memorable moment came in Game 5 when he saved Don Larsen's perfect game with a spectacular catch.

Gil Hodges came to the plate with one out in the top of the fifth. Mantle backed up a few steps and moved over a bit to left field. Hodges, a right-handed hitter, ripped a fastball on a line to left center. "I just put my head down and took off as fast as I could," he said. "I caught up with the ball as it was dropping, more than 400 feet from home plate. I had to reach across my body to make the catch, and luckily the ball just plopped into my glove. If I had stopped a split second later or been a step slower, or if I hadn't shaded over on Hodges, the ball would have dropped for at least a double. It was the best catch I ever made."[32]

The Yankees beat the Dodgers in seven games, and Mantle was voted the unanimous American League Most Valuable Player about a month later. Talk soon began about the possibility of Mantle repeating his Triple Crown feat. No one had ever accomplished it, but many thought the Yankee slugger could. Yogi Berra felt that way, and Joe DiMaggio agreed. "The kid is nowhere near his peak," offered Joe D.[33]

Winning the Triple Crown hadn't decreased the pressure on Mantle. In fact, it probably increased it. Now, he had to prove he could continue to play at a high level. Expectations were higher than ever. Besides being a Triple Crown threat, he was the most likely candidate to break Ruth's home run record. Realistically, however, Mantle said it would be a miracle if he won back-to-back Triple Crowns. "You have to be lucky to win three titles in a season," he said.[34]

Despite a swollen knee, shin splints, a sprained thumb, and a torn ligament in his left ankle suffered during spring training, Mantle got off to a strong start in 1957. From May 15-30, he went 20-for-51, raising his average to .365. In his first 50 games, he reached base 114 times in 221 plate appearances on 61 hits and 53 walks. On June 23, he led the American League with a .392 average. He also had 21 homers and 51 RBI.

In mid-July, he was on pace to break Babe Ruth's record of 170 walks in a season. He was too dangerous to pitch to. The switch-hitter clouted his 200th career four-bagger on July 26, 1957. He reached that milestone at age 25, three years younger than Ruth.

Entering September, Mantle had an outside chance to earn the Triple Crown. But painful shin splints, which occur when the muscular tissue separates from the bone, forced him to the bench and into the hospital. He was used mainly as a pinch-hitter from August 31 until September 6, when he entered Lenox Hill Hospital for five days.

When he returned to the lineup on September 13, he was not 100 percent. He failed to homer in September and drove in just three runs. Washington's Roy Sievers, who finished with a league-best 42 homers and 114 RBI, clubbed eight round-trippers and drove in 22 runs in the final month.

Mantle finished with 34 homers, 94 RBI, and batted .365. Ted Williams won the batting title with a .388 mark at age 39. Although the Yankee outfielder didn't lead in any Triple Crown category, he led the league in walks with 146 and runs scored with 121. His 11.3 WAR led the majors. He also decreased his strikeouts from 99 to 75.

At the end of the season, Casey Stengel said, "Mickey Mantle played on one leg and proved he is one of the greatest players who ever lived despite the handicap."[35]

When the 1957 World Series opened, Mantle's left leg still bothered him, and his right shoulder was sore from a tumble at second base. The Yankee star batted .263 (5-for-19) with one home run as the Milwaukee Braves captured the series in seven games.

Controversy accompanied the results of the American League Most Valuable Player voting when they were announced in mid-November. Mantle edged Ted Williams 233 to 209. Roy Sievers finished third with 205 points. Mickey earned six first-place votes, while Williams garnered five. The crucial difference was Williams received one ninth-place and one 10th-place vote from the 24 sportswriters who voted. While many fans felt Williams was robbed, the Boston slugger said it didn't make any difference to him.

Mantle thought Williams would easily win the MVP award and was surprised but appreciative of the honor. He became just the fourth player to win the MVP award back-to-back. The others were Yogi Berra (1954 and 1955), Hal Newhouser (1944 and 1945), and Jimmie Foxx (1932 and 1933).

With two extraordinary seasons back-to-back, Mantle established himself as a gold-standard superstar at age 25.

He played 11 more seasons, won two more home run titles, earned another MVP award, and played in six more World Series. He chased Ruth's record again in 1961 but fell short when injuries hampered him late in the season. Mantle finished with 54 homers, while teammate Roger Maris broke Ruth's mark with 61. Mickey continued to battle injuries throughout his career. The pressure, expectations, and boos never subsided. No matter what he accomplished, some thought he should have accomplished more.

CHAPTER 3

OUTFIELD

YANKEES

TOM TRESH

TOM TRESH
THE FIRST NEXT MICKEY MANTLE

Tom will be the next Yankee superstar. When he learns to pull the ball, and he undoubtedly will, he'll be in the 40s and maybe even 50s for one or two seasons in the homer column.
—New York Yankee official

At age 24, Tom Tresh of the New York Yankees was the 1962 American League Rookie of the Year, an All-Star, and a World Series hero. A switch-hitting shortstop, who moved to left field for the final two months, he was being compared to Mickey Mantle. As one sports columnist wrote, he had the world in the palm of his hand. Yet, Tresh would only play eight games after turning 31.

Predicted to become one of the game's brightest stars, Tresh's performance went downhill after 1964 when the Yankees started losing.

Surrounded by less talented teammates and subject to higher expectations, Tresh struggled. A severe knee injury in 1967 hastened the end of his career.

The son of a former major leaguer, Tom excelled in athletics at Allen Park High School in Allen Park, Mich. He earned nine letters in baseball, football, and basketball. His father, Mike, played 12 seasons as a catcher for the White Sox and Indians. He taught Tom to switch hit at an early age. Tom, however, didn't embrace the move until he played semi-pro ball after graduating from high school.

Tom, 6-1 and 180 pounds, played shortstop for Central Michigan University as a freshman. Although he was recruited out of high school, he told scouts he planned to attend college. Some scouts backed off, but Pat Patterson of the Yankees persisted. He visited the Tresh family at Christmas and made a new offer—$30,000 to sign. It was an offer Tom couldn't refuse.

In 1958, at age 19, he made a good first impression. He played for Class D St. Petersburg and Class AA New Orleans and batted .305. He played in Greensboro, Binghamton, and Amarillo for the next two seasons. He attracted the most attention in 1961 when he played for Class-AAA Richmond. His slick fielding at shortstop and his potent bat earned him the International League Rookie of the Year honor. He was voted the best-hitting prospect in the league. His .315 average, the second-highest in the league, was 69 points higher than the previous year. The Yankees called him up in September 1961.

Tresh received a big break in 1962 when the Yankees' starting shortstop job opened up. The Army Reserves activated 25-year-old Tony Kubek at the end of the 1961 season because of the Berlin crisis. The Yankees infield of Kubek at shortstop, Bobby Richardson, 25, at second base, and Clete Boyer, 24, at third base had once looked impenetrable to a rookie.

The competition at shortstop between Tresh and 23-year-old Phil Linz was the biggest story of spring training. The two were good friends, competing against each other in the Yankees minor league system. Tresh beat Linz out for the starting shortstop job on two occasions. Linz lacked Tresh's power, had a weaker arm, and wasn't as flashy. Manager Ralph Houk expected an even battle for the starter's job.

When the Yankees opened the 1962 season, Tresh was at shortstop and batting second. It would be 34 years before another Yankee rookie would be the Opening Day shortstop (Derek Jeter in 1996).

Looking for their third consecutive pennant, the Yankees got off to a quick start in April. Tresh transitioned smoothly to the big leagues. In mid-May, former Yankees second baseman Jerry Coleman said, "Tresh is going to be a big star. Tom is a rarity among shortstops these days. He can field and also hit for distance. You don't find many of them anymore."[1]

Tresh provided the Yankees with much of their run production early in the season while his idol, Mantle, nursed injuries. Manager Ralph Houk named Tresh to the American League All-Star team as a reserve. He didn't play in the first game on July 10 but went 1-for-2 in the second game on July 30. The New Yorkers heated up in July as the trio of Mantle, Maris and Tresh punished opposing pitchers. They combined for 66 RBI—Mantle (25), Maris (24), and Tresh (17). Tresh put together a 16-game hit streak from July 8 through July 26. Pleased with his rookie, Houk said, "Tresh is a good hitter. He's a big-league hitter. You have to find a spot for a kid with a bat like that."[2]

At the beginning of August, the Army discharged Tony Kubek, and he rejoined the Yankees. The big question was: Where would he play? Would he get his old job back? And if so, where would Tresh play? Would manager Ralph Houk move Kubek to the outfield? The consensus was Kubek had more range than Tresh, was better at turning the double play, and had more experience. "Tom is a fine shortstop, but Tony is better," offered Houk.[3] Kubek, who had played all three outfield positions, was stationed in left field his first six games back. Even though Tresh hadn't played the outfield since junior high school, Houk moved him to left field and returned Kubek to shortstop. The decision was partly a show of loyalty to a veteran player.

"In a way, it's like starting all over again," said Tom. "I played the best I could. But I realize Kubek is more experienced, and I never said I was a better shortstop. I consider myself fortunate to have been some help to the club while filling in for him. I'm ready to try left field if that's what they want me to do. I'm going to do the best I know how."[4] Instead of being bitter about the move, Tresh was positive and confident. Houk, Kubek, Roger Maris, Yogi Berra, and others believed he would make a smooth transition.

Left field had been a long-time merry-go-round position for the Yankees. Berra, Johnny Blanchard, and Hector Lopez played left field in 1962. Houk hoped Tresh could stabilize the position.

Tom accepted the challenge. To the surprise of many, he looked like he was born to play left field. "Having been a shortstop my entire life, I developed a lot of the tools that are necessary to be a good outfielder. A shortstop has to be able to back on a ball well and has to have a strong throwing arm. You also have to be able to run. I think I had the tools to do it," he said, explaining his smooth transition.[5]

Despite learning a new position, his offensive productivity didn't dip. Houk proclaimed the Yankee outfield of Mantle, Maris, and Tresh as the best in baseball. It featured power, speed, intelligence, youth, and a pair of switch-hitters. "It's a home run outfield, yet it can move and throw you out," he pointed out.[6] The Yankees finished the season in first place with a 96-66 record. Tresh played 111 games at shortstop and 43 in leftfield. He batted .286 with 20 homers, 93 RBI, and 94 runs scored. Maris led the team with 33 homers and 100 RBI, while Mantle added 30 homers and 89 RBI.

Tresh's hitting, particularly his power, surprised Houk. He said, "Not only has Tresh done a wonderful job at shortstop and left field, I'll go further than that. I predict he's going to become one of the top stars in the game in the next few years. He can't miss."[7] The New York skipper believed Tresh would be another Al Kaline. Other observers thought he would be another Mantle. Houk didn't tout Tresh's potential power as much as others. He said, "No one thought he would hit 20 homers (he only hit eight homers the year before in Richmond) or that he would develop that kind of power from both sides."[8] The Yankees faced the San Francisco Giants in the 1962 World Series. The 103-62 Giants featured sluggers Willie Mays (49 homers, 141 RBI), Orlando Cepeda (35 homers, 114 RBI), and Felipe Alou (25 homers and 98 RBI), along with a pitching staff of Jack Sanford (24-7), Juan Marichal (18-11), Billy O'Dell (19-14) and Billy Pierce (16-6).

One of the key World Series questions was, "How would Tom Tresh fare in left field?"

Besides the intense pressure, playing left field in Yankee Stadium in October presented several challenges. The fall shadows, tricky air currents, haze, and glare of the sun could handcuff the best of outfielders. Having heard about the pitfalls, Tom was apprehensive but not scared. Centerfielder Mickey Mantle expressed confidence in him. "I've played alongside of plenty of left fielders, and Tom rates as the best one," he declared.[9]

Tresh stepped into the World Series spotlight in pivotal Game 5 at Yankee Stadium, with the series tied at two games apiece. The game featured the second matchup between right-handers Jack Sanford (24-7) of the Giants and Ralph Terry (23-12) of the Yankees. Sanford blanked the New Yorkers, 2-0, in Game 2. With the game knotted, 2-2, Terry struck out to lead off the bottom of the eighth inning. Then Tony Kubek and Bobby Richardson singled, bringing Tresh to the plate. Tom doubled off Sanford in the fourth inning. The crowd of 63,165 cheered the rookie as he stepped into the batter's box. The left-handed swinger blasted Sanford's second pitch into right field, about ten rows beyond the 344-foot sign. The three-run homer unleashed a deafening roar from the partisan crowd. The Yankees survived Chuck Hiller's solo homer in the ninth inning to secure a 5-3 victory.

In the Yankees locker room, Tresh explained his at-bat to a horde of media members. "I choked up on the bat, and I was trying to get a hit—any kind of a hit. I hadn't seen any good pitches all day from Sanford, and I wasn't expecting any. But when the fastball came over the middle of the plate, I took a fuller swing than I intended, and that was it. It certainly was the biggest hit I ever made in my life and my biggest baseball thrill."[10] To sweeten the moment, his parents were in the stands.

The Giants bounced back to win Game 6 in San Francisco. The crucial seventh game featured Sanford vs. Terry for the third time in the series. The Yankees opened the bottom of the fifth inning as Bill Skowron, and Clete Boyer singled, and Terry walked to load the bases. Kubek grounded into a shortstop-to-second-to-first double play, pushing home the game's first run. Richardson fouled out to end the inning.

The New Yorkers clung to the 1-0 lead in the seventh inning. With one out, Giants star Willie Mays smashed a curling, wind-blown drive deep into the left field corner. Tresh, running as hard as he could, made a sensational back-handed catch of the ball. Willie McCovey followed with a triple but was stranded when Terry fanned Orlando Cepeda.

The Giants threatened in the top of the ninth when Matty Alou singled. Felipe Alou and Chuck Hiller struck out before Mays clubbed a double. Matty Alou, however, was forced to hold at third base. With first base open, the Yankees opted to pitch to the always-dangerous left-handed McCovey. The game ended suddenly when the 6-foot-4 McCovey blistered a line drive to Bobby Richardson at second base. Tresh had saved the game, and the series, with the catch in the web of his glove in the bottom of the seventh inning.

"I was running so fast that I grabbed the ball (which was in his glove) with my (bare) left hand because I knew I was going to hit the wall real hard," said Tresh afterward. "I didn't want to drop it."[11] Relatively unknown seven months ago, the rookie had made a difference in the World Series with his bat and his glove. With two victories and 16 strikeouts, Yankees pitcher Ralph Terry was voted Most Valuable Player of the World Series. Tresh, who led the Yankees with a .321 average, nine hits, and five runs scored, also received consideration.

After the World Series, Tom returned home to Allen Park and resumed classes at Central Michigan University (he had promised his parents he would earn his college degree). He was named the American League Rookie of the Year in early December, collecting 13 of the 20 first-place votes. Other vote-getters were Bob Rodgers, Dean Chance, Bernie Allen, and Dick Radatz.

After a hectic off-season, Tresh reported early to the Yankees' spring training camp. He told reporters he had plenty to learn, wanted to be more than an adequate outfielder, and didn't believe in the sophomore jinx.

The Yankees were ready to anoint him heir apparent to the fading, injury-plagued Mantle, whether the expectations were realistic or not. The cover of one of the pre-season baseball magazines asked the question on many fans' minds: "Is Tom Tresh a One-Year Wonder or

Another Mantle?" The pressure to improve on his rookie performance was palpable.

A Yankee official predicted, "Tom will be the next Yankee superstar. When he learns to pull the ball, and he undoubtedly will, he'll be in the 40s and maybe even 50s for one or two years in the homer column."[12]

Tresh cautioned against such high expectations, saying he wasn't a home run hitter. "Every once in a while, I find myself trying to hit a homer, and the result is usually a pop-up. I can't pull outside pitches. I have to hit with the pitch and let the homers come when they will."[13]

The 1963 Yankees battled injuries throughout the year. A big blow came in early June when Mantle broke a bone in his left foot. His spikes got caught in Memorial Stadium's wire fence when he leaped for a Brooks Robinson home run. Mantle was out of the lineup until early August. He was relegated to pinch-hitting duties before returning full-time in September. Tresh took over center field duties while Mantle was sidelined.

Injuries caused manager Ralph Houk to juggle his lineups. At the beginning of August, Mantle and Maris had played together in the outfield for only eight games. On September 24, Mantle, Maris, and Tresh were in the Yankees' outfield for the first time since June 5. Maris was limited to 90 games, while Mantle saw action in 65 games. Despite all the improvising, the New Yorkers posted a 104-57 record and coasted to the pennant.

Tresh continued to contribute on offense and defense. In 145 games, he batted .269 with 25 homers and 71 RBI and was named to the All-Star team. Tom considered his sophomore season better than his rookie year. "I proved I could do the job as a full-time left fielder," he said. "I know I dropped some points in my batting average, but I know why that happened. I made the mistake of swinging too hard."[14]

Although the Yankees appeared Herculean during the 1963 season, the 99-63 Los Angeles Dodgers turned them into weaklings during the World Series. Dodger hurlers Sandy Koufax, Don Drysdale, and Johnny Podres shackled Yankee hitters, holding them to a .171 team batting average in a stunning four-game sweep.

Tresh entered the 1964 season thinking he could hit 30 homers. "I was batting fifth, and I believed it was my function to go for the long ball," he said.[15] That type of thinking belied the hitter he was and resulted in a frustrating season. The switch-hitter's home run total dropped from 25 to 16, his batting average dipped more than 20 points, and he struck out a career-high 110 times.

The Yankees (99-63) won their fifth consecutive pennant, but it wasn't easy. They finished one game ahead of the Chicago White Sox. Mantle and Maris avoided injuries, playing in 143 and 141 games, respectively. Mantle, 32, turned in his final outstanding season with 35 homers, 111 RBI, and a .303 average. Maris contributed 26 homers, while Joe Pepitone clouted 28 homers and drove in 100 RBI. Jim Bouton, Whitey Ford, and Al Downing anchored the pitching staff. Rookie pitcher Mel Stottlemyre sparked a late-season drive, going 9-3 after being called up in mid-August.

The Yankees faced the 93-69 St. Louis Cardinals in the 1964 World Series. Bill White (21 homers and 102 RBI) and Ken Boyer (24 homers and 119 RBI) supplied the big bats, while Lou Brock (.348) and Curt Flood (.311) added speed. Pitchers Bob Gibson (19-12), Ray Sadecki (20-11), and Curt Simmons (18-7) were tough on opposing hitters.

In the series opener in St. Louis, Tresh slugged a 2-run homer off Ray Sadecki in the second inning. It wasn't enough as the Yankees lost, 9-5. In Game 5, with the series tied at two games apiece, Tresh delivered in a pressure situation. The Cardinals held a 2-0 lead going into the bottom of the ninth with dominating right-hander Bob Gibson on the mound. Mantle reached first on an error, setting the stage for Tresh. Gibson's first pitch was a fastball down the middle of the plate. Tom deposited it into the right field bleachers, 340 feet away. The dramatic homer snapped the Yankees' 17.1-inning scoreless streak. Cardinals catcher Tim McCarver settled the issue in the top of the 10th with a three-run homer. The Yankees bounced back to win Game 6, but the Cardinals captured Game 7 to win the World Series.

In his first three full seasons, Tom played in three World Series, batting .277 with 18 hits, four homers, and 13 RBI. It was clear, however, the Yankees were aging, their talent was on the decline, and they lacked the power from the past.

Tresh entered the 1965 season vowing to swing his natural way and not to exert extra pressure on himself as he had the previous year. Trying to hit home runs had created some problems. He said, "I was never the type of hitter to swing from his heels. As a result, it threw my batting style way off. I started lunging at the ball and falling all over the batter's box."[16]

The Yankees got off to a slow start and never spent a day in first place. Tresh was the club's most consistent hitter and carried the offense for much of the season. He recorded a career highlight on June 6 in the second game of a doubleheader against the Chicago White Sox at Yankee Stadium. He bashed a homer from the right side in the first inning off lefty Juan Pizarro. Then he added round-trippers from the left side in the third and fifth innings off right-hander Bruce Howard. He singled in the seventh off Greg Bollo. He led off the top of the ninth with a chance for his fourth home run. Normally, Tresh wouldn't have tried for a homer. But the Yankees held a 12-0 lead, and he had a rare opportunity. Facing knuckleball pitcher Ted Wills, he had his sights set on the fence but fouled out. It marked the third time he homered from both sides of the plate.

Heading into the All-Star break, Tom led the American League in extra-base hits with 23 doubles, six triples, and 12 home runs. He credited his offensive performance to a shorter swing and a better sense of the strike zone.

Accustomed to winning, the Yankees nosedived in 1965, finishing in sixth place. Tresh won a Gold Glove in left field and led the club in runs (94), hits (168), homers (26), RBI (74), and batting average (.279).

New York fans didn't have much to cheer about in 1966. No one was hitting, and the pitching was abysmal early in the season. Manager Johnny Keane, hired to replace Yogi Berra in 1965, was fired in mid-May. Ralph Houk moved from the general manager's office to take over the managerial reins. Keane had moved Tresh from left field to third base and switched Clete Boyer from the hot corner to shortstop. The move didn't please either player, nor did it help the Yankees. Houk moved Tresh back to left field and Boyer to third base.

The Yankees failed to respond to Houk and finished in 10th place. It marked the first time since 1912 the New Yorkers finished in last place. Tresh felt more pressure and struggled at the plate without a strong supporting cast. Although he clouted 27 homers, including 19 in the second half, he batted just .233. He was at a turning point in his career."I figured if I could hit 19 homers in the second half of the season, I could hit 38 in a season (which would have put him fourth in the American League in 1966). So, I was looking at the point where I just might be coming into my own and be able to hit 35 to 40 homers a year."[17]

Tom was positive going into the 1967 training camp. That feeling didn't last long, as he injured his right knee in the second game. He fielded a grounder, threw across his body, and heard a popping sound as his knee gave way. He fell to the ground in intense pain. The initial diagnosis was strained ligaments, but it turned out to be much more serious. It was a case of loose cartilage. He missed 21 games, returned to the lineup, and reinjured his knee in Houston. Still, he started Opening Day wearing a knee brace, which he quickly ditched.

Instead of undergoing surgery, the team ordered him to play through the injury. He played the entire year on a bad knee. Discussing the decision later, he said, "It was a bad decision, but it wasn't mine to make. It would have been much wiser had they taken me in for surgery right away before I had a chance to really destroy the knee. Because over the course of the season, my knee gave out five more times."[18]

The injury affected his running, fielding, throwing, and hitting. He had to avoid sharp turns and couldn't run full force. He had to take different routes to balls hit to the outfield.

He couldn't throw normally, and that led to shoulder pain. At bat, he had to alter his left-handed swing. Besides the physical effects, the injury affected his mental attitude.

He played because he thought he could help the team. But it turned out he didn't help the club and acquired many bad habits. "In a situation like that, you realize what you're doing wrong, but in trying to correct it, you do something else wrong. First thing you know, you're all fouled up, not hitting at all, and you lose confidence. When that happens, you're really in trouble," said Tresh years later.[19]

Tresh's .219 batting average and his decline in home runs from 27 to 14 reflected his troubles. "This has been the most frustrating year of my life," he said late in the season.[20] He underwent surgery during the off-season to remove the outside cartilage in his right knee.

Although he was eager to report to spring training to prove himself, he was at a critical point in his career. At 28, he was a player in decline. He was on a poor team without a Mantle, Maris, or Elston Howard to give him protection in the lineup. And he generated little or no interest in the trade market.

"Last year was a nightmare from any angle," he said. "I started the year knowing my leg couldn't get any better, and I could never play up to my ability. I never had a chance for a decent year."[21]

His numbers continued to decline in 1968. He batted .195 with just 11 home runs. He was a prime target of the Yankee boobirds, adding to his mental stress and moodiness.

Determined to rebound in 1969, Tresh was in the Opening Day lineup at shortstop (Houk had moved him back to shortstop in the 1968 season) and batting sixth. He never got untracked. He was hitting .183 at the end of April. His swing was totally messed up, but it was more than that. "I was a physical wreck," he said. "I'd gotten hurt, I had gotten phlebitis, and I had strep throat."[22] He requested a trade to the Detroit Tigers to be closer to his family and reunited with former Yankees batting coach Wally Moses.

The Yankees traded Tresh to the Tigers on June 14 for outfielder Ron Woods. Tresh hoped Moses could resurrect his career. Tigers manager Mayo Smith figured it was worth a gamble. Moses worked with Tom at Richmond during his rookie year and in 1966. Tresh had confidence in Moses, saying he could catch little things and stop them before they become bad habits. "If playing in the Detroit park and getting back with Wally doesn't help, I guess I'm beyond help," he said bluntly.[23]

Moses worked to eliminate some of Tresh's flaws at the plate. He moved him back farther in the batter's box, encouraged him to wait on pitches longer, and tried to keep him from lunging at the ball. There were glimpses of the old Tresh. On July 1 and July 2 at Detroit, he went 7-for-7 with three home runs, a double, and seven RBIs. He slammed six home runs in July and 13 overall with the Tigers, but his average hovered in the low .200s.

His future looked like that of a utility player. While hunting in the winter with a companion, he fell and landed hard on his right leg. He needed another operation on his right knee. With plenty of competition in the Tigers training camp in 1970, Tom failed to make the 25-man roster. Detroit offered him an opportunity to go to Class-AAA Toledo, rehab his knee and make the same salary. After nine seasons in the big leagues, it wasn't the deal that interested him. Feeling he hadn't gotten a fair chance to prove himself, he requested his release. The Tigers granted it on April 14. Tresh was 31 years old.

After his baseball days, Tresh owned and operated a Kentucky Fried Chicken franchise. He also joined the Central Michigan University faculty as an administrator in the business school's alumni and placement offices (he had earned his college degree as he had promised his parents). He served as the college's assistant baseball coach for 14 years.

Reflecting on his baseball career, he said, "There's a lot of pressure when somebody says you're supposed to be the next Mickey Mantle. The Yankees were pretty lucky when Mickey Mantle became the next Joe DiMaggio. They just assumed it was that easy to find somebody who could do that kind of job."[24]

Tom Tresh died on October 14, 2008, from a heart attack at 70. In his obituary, the *New York Daily News* wrote, "The switch-hitting Tresh, who drew unfair comparisons to Mantle that he could not live up to after his standout first season, was nevertheless a Yankee fixture in the waning years of their five-decade dynasty."[25]

Teammate Bobby Richardson added, "I always felt badly for him that he was always being compared to Mickey, just because he was a switch-hitting shortstop who moved to the outfield."[26]

CHAPTER 4

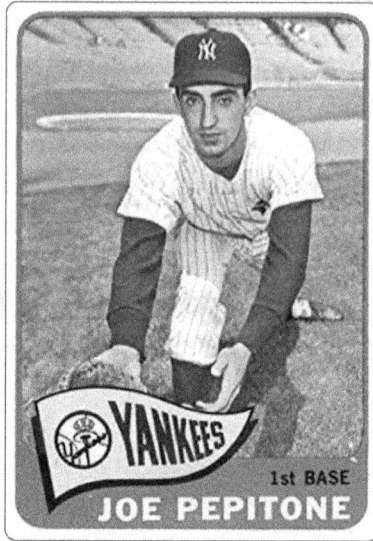

1st BASE
JOE PEPITONE

JOE PEPITONE
THE PLAYER WHO WAS HIS OWN WORST ENEMY

*Joe should hit 40 homers and drive in 100 runs every year
from now on, maybe not every year, but most years.
It's all up to him wanting to do it.*
—MICKEY MANTLE

In late August 1969, *Detroit Free Press* sportswriter Joe Falls wrote, "All I hear about (Joe) Pepitone is his potential. Potential, potential, potential. How long do we have to wait? Even Joe says he should hit 40 homers a year."[1]

By this time, the 28-year-old Brooklyn native had played eight years for the New York Yankees. Despite his natural ability and potential for greatness being touted by baseball immortals such as Joe DiMaggio and

Mickey Mantle, Yankee officials, and a long list of sportswriters, Pepitone had been a major disappointment. He hadn't hit more than 31 homers, driven in more than 100 runs, or batted higher than .271.

The 6-foot-2, 195-pound left-handed hitting first baseman/outfielder frustrated the Yankees with his lack of hustle, determination, and commitment. Baseball wasn't the main priority for the colorful and flamboyant Pepitone. He preferred fast cars, beautiful women, and nights on the town that didn't end until dawn. He seemed to want to be the next Warren Beatty or Frank Sinatra rather than the next Mickey Mantle. His off-the-field behavior led to marital problems, divorces, overwhelming debt, shady relationships with mobsters, and a lack of concentration on the field.

Pepitone was such a habitual slacker that when he promised to give 100 percent and hustle (which he did almost every spring or whenever he signed a new contract), it merited headlines. He never kept his promise for long. It's doubtful if any Yankee wasted as much talent as he did.

Pepitone was a problem for the Yankees almost from the day they signed him (He was fined before he ever played a minor-league game for the Yankees). He grew up in a dysfunctional family with an abusive father. He captained the Manual Training School baseball team. His natural ability attracted more than a dozen major league scouts. In early March 1958, a classmate accidentally shot Joe in the stomach with a .38 revolver. He was rushed to the hospital, where he underwent a 9-hour surgery. He was on the critical care list for 12 days. "Doctors told me if the bullet had been an inch or two left or right, I would be dead," he said.[2]

A week before Joe was shot, his father, Willie, 39, suffered a major heart attack. He was at home recovering when Joe was discharged from the hospital. After the two got into a heated argument, Joe told his mother, "I wish he would die." The next day, his father died. The traumatic event haunted Joe for the rest of his life.

Joe was back on the baseball field playing for the Nathan Famous team on Coney Island within a month. Interest from major league scouts significantly decreased. Instead of 14 teams, only the Philadelphia Phillies, New York Yankees, and Los Angeles Dodgers were interested.

That summer, Yankee scout Ray Garland signed the 17-year-old for $25,000.

The teenager spent his bonus money in record time. He purchased a Thunderbird, a 14-foot boat, a pizzeria for his mother, some expensive suits, and picked up countless tabs at bars and restaurants. One writer observed that Pepitone treated money like confetti. Sadly, it was the way he handled money throughout his career.

The Yankees assigned him to Auburn in the Class D New York Penn League, where he played 16 games. The first night he joined the club, he sprayed manager Tommy Gott with a fire extinguisher in a prank gone wrong. The fine and damages to the hotel cost him $250, almost three weeks of pay. He played for Fargo-Morehead in the Class C Northern League the following year. He clouted 14 homers, drove in 87 runs, and batted .283. In 1960, at age 19, he played for Binghamton in the Class-A Eastern League. His bad attitude and declining batting average raised red flags to the Yankees' front office. The club sent former player Jerry Coleman and scout Bill Skiff to Binghamton to sternly remind the youngster of his potential and responsibility to the club.

While many Yankee officials thought Joe was underperforming at Binghamton (he hit 13 homers and batted .260), Steve Souchock, who instructed rookies in spring training, forecasted big things for him in 1960. "What a sweet ballplayer he will be. Joe will be in Yankee Stadium by 1962 for sure," he predicted.[3]

The Yankee prospect blossomed in 1961 with Amarillo in the Class-AA Texas League. He batted .316, third in the league, slammed 21 homers, and tallied 87 RBI, despite missing 20 games because of injuries. His increased production was partly due to learning to hit left-handed pitching.

The Yankees invited Joe to spring training in 1962, and his presence created a buzz. Joe DiMaggio observed, "Pepitone has good wrists, a good-looking hitter. A nice swing and good power. He's got a knack for going back on the ball in the outfield. That's instinct; you can't teach that to a boy."[4]

Ralph Houk, Yankees manager, said, "I don't think Joe can miss with the tools he has. It's all up to him."[5]

The 21-year-old made New York's Opening Day roster. He didn't expect to start in a talent-laden lineup defending its World Series title. But, he wanted to show the Yankee brass he could play first base or the outfield when needed. He made his major league debut on Opening Day, April 10, 1962, at Yankee Stadium. He pinch-hit for Whitey Ford and grounded into a double play.

He spelled veteran Bill "Moose" Skowron at first base, played the outfield, and pinch-hit. On May 23, the rookie showed he was special, stroking a solo homer and a three-run shot in the 8th inning off Kansas City hurlers Dan Pfister and John Wyatt. He became the 10th player to hit two home runs in an inning and the first rookie since Joe DiMaggio did it on June 24, 1936.

Joe batted .244 and played solid defense in the first four months. The Yankees, however, optioned him back to AAA Richmond on July 30 to get more playing time. He was recalled on September 3. His 63-game tryout had the Yankees front office envisioning him in the 1963 starting lineup.

In December, the Yankees traded 31-year-old first baseman Bill Skowron to the Los Angeles Dodgers, opening up the position for Pepitone. Skowron, an eight-time All-Star, had averaged 25 homers and 97 RBI over the past three years. The club was confident that Joe could match Skowron's offensive production and improve his limited range at first base.

Pepitone fueled the Yankees' optimism. He led the team in home runs and RBI in spring training. Wally Moses, the roving hitting instructor, said, "Joe will hit more home runs this year than Moose ever hit. He has that sweet, smooth swing that reminds people of Joe D."[6]

General manager Roy Hamey was asked who would replace Mickey Mantle when he retired. He replied, "Joe Pepitone, if his head stays the same size."[7] Hamey knew the potential pitfalls of his promising star.

Joe's ego received a boost on Opening Day, April 9, 1963, when he blasted a pair of home runs against Kansas City hurlers Diego Segui and Bill Fischer. Maybe the Yankees had found Mantle's successor.

The first baseman reached his peak batting average of .314 on June 13. Then he nosedived in a month-long slump, dropping his average to .275. Joe explained his slump. He said, "I got impatient and started changing my stance at the plate. I bent lower in a crouch. When I went back to my natural stance, my rhythm was all fouled up."[8]

He came out of the slump when Wally Moses told him he was trying too hard. He advised Joe to hit the ball up the middle. As a result, he hit his first home run in weeks. Pepitone's performance didn't go unnoticed, as he was named to the American League All-Star team.

The Yankees marveled at his defense, as well as his offense. Manager Ralph Houk touted the club's infield of Pepitone at first, Bobby Richardson at second, Tony Kubek at shortstop, and Clete Boyer at third as the best in recent club history. With his tremendous range at first base (he played a deeper first base than almost anyone in the majors), Pepitone significantly improved the defense. Houk explained with Joe at first, second baseman Richardson could shade closer to second base, robbing potential hits up the middle. That freed Kubek to be less concerned about the middle of the diamond.

Pepitone tried to hit the long ball more often as the Yankees came down the stretch. The result was just the opposite. From August 8 through September 1, he failed to clear the fence. Although no Yankee hit 30 homers, batted .300, or drove in 100 runs, the strong pitching, led by Whitey Ford's 24-7 record, propelled the New Yorkers to first place.

Joe batted .271 with 27 homers and 89 RBI. He led the Yankees in RBI and was second to Elston Howard in home runs and batting average. Howard was named the American League's Most Valuable Player.

Joe took full advantage of being a young, handsome New York Yankee and celebrity. He went on the town every night, hung out at nightclubs, bedded a bevy of women, gambled, and spent more money than he made. His exorbitant debts triggered occasional threatening visits from mobsters telling him to pay up or else.

The Yankees faced the Los Angeles Dodgers in the 1963 World Series. Houk believed the Yankees had a better all-round club than the 99-63 pitching-rich Dodgers. Sandy Koufax (25-5) and Don Drysdale (19-17), and reliever Ron Perranoski (16-3) led the National League club. Houk predicted the Yankees would win the World Series.

The Dodgers turned the Series into a lop-sided affair, sweeping four straight. Pepitone was involved in a critical play in the bottom of the seventh inning of the fourth game. The game was tied 1-1 when Junior

Gilliam of the Dodgers grounded to the third baseman, Clete Boyer, who threw to first. Pepitone, however, lost the ball in the sea of white shirts behind third base. The ball hit Joe on his wrist and bounded to the stands along the right field line. Gilliam advanced to third on the error and scored on Willie Davis' sacrifice fly, breaking the 1-1 tie. Joe's error cost the Yankees Game 4.

Joe, who batted .154 in the Series, took full responsibility for the error. "I just blew it," he admitted. "I was the goat of the game, and I guess they (the fans) will never let me forget it."[9] He received lots of hate mail, but he never tried to duck questions about the error when it came up at banquets or personal appearances.

Pepitone reported to spring training in 1964, full of optimism. "I don't want to be a good player; I want to be a great player," he crowed to reporters.[10] His goals were to bat between .290 and .300, slug 35 homers, and drive in 100 runs.

Mickey Mantle touted Joe as a potential superstar. "Joe should hit 40 homers and drive in 100 runs every year from now on, maybe not every year, but most years. It's all up to him wanting to do it." He added, "Joe's got everything. He's cocky, but he's a great attitude toward the game. He's got the best wrists in the American League. Aaron is the only better wrist hitter. He's got a great arm and range at first base. The only thing he has to do is bear down."[11]

Joe received a substantial raise of $5,000, bumping his salary to $15,000. He was limited in spring training as a deep bone bruise to his left hand caused him to miss two weeks. When the 1964 season opened, his hand still bothered him, and he started slowly. To compound matters, Jim Kaat of the Twins hit him on his left hand on April 22. On May 9, he was hitting .186. By the end of the month, however, his batting average was .290. He was named an All-Star Game reserve.

The Yankees battled the Chicago White Sox and Baltimore Orioles in a tight race for the 1964 pennant. The New Yorkers needed a strong September to clinch the title. The club went 22-5. Rookie right-hander Mel Stottlemyre compiled a 5-2 record after going 4-1 in August. Pepitone, along with a healthy Mantle and Maris, carried the offense. The 99-63 Yankees edged the White Sox by one game.

Playing in 160 games, Pepitone delivered 28 homers, drove in 100 runs, and batted .251. He was second to Mantle in homers (35 to 28) and RBI (111 to 100). In his first two full seasons, the Brooklyn star clouted 55 homers and drove in 189 runs. The spotlight fueled his late-night adventures and irresponsible behavior. Despite his improved offensive production, he slipped defensively. He committed 18 errors compared to 8 in 1963. He was the constant target of Yankee boobirds.

The Yankees faced the 93-69 St. Louis Cardinals in the 1964 World Series. The Cardinals were offensively well-balanced, with third baseman Ken Boyer and first baseman Bill White each driving in more than 100 runs. Ray Sadecki (20-11), Bob Gibson (19-12), and Curt Simmons (18-9) anchored the pitching staff.

Pepitone's World Series highlight came in Game 6 on October 14, with the Yankees trailing three games to two. In the top of the eighth inning, the Yankees held a 3-1 lead. New York scored a run and loaded the bases with Pepitone on deck. The Cards removed right-hander Barney Schultz and replaced him with southpaw Gordie Richardson. Joe greeted him with a blast to deep right field, scoring Mantle, Howard, and Tresh. He became the 10th player and the sixth Yankee to wallop a grand slam in the World Series.

In Game 7, with ace Bob Gibson on the mound, the Cardinals jumped out to a 6-0 lead after five innings and never trailed en route to a World Series-clinching 7-5 victory. It was the second consecutive disappointing Fall for the Yankees. Once again, Pepitone floundered, batting .154 (4 for 26).

After the World Series, the Yankees fired Yogi Berra and replaced him with Johnny Keane, who had just guided the Cardinals to the World Championship. Pepitone and Keane clashed from the beginning. To compound matters, Joe's wife, Barbara, kicked him out of the house and asked for a divorce. Joe was upset because his wife was moving to California, and he would not be able to see his children. His wild spending resulted in $40,000 in debt, much of it to people who didn't like to be owed money. With everything on his mind, it was no wonder he started the 1965 season in an 0-for-22 slump.

"For me, the 1965 season was one long agonized scream," Joe wrote in his autobiography. "I tried to muffle it with endless partying and rebelling against authority, and before the season was over, I was in Lenox Hill Hospital feeling my mind might snap, crackle, and pop."[12]

In mid-July, Joe, who had moved to right field to fill in for the injured Roger Maris, was in the midst of a 4-for-34 slump. He failed to deliver in the clutch, time and time again. He batted .177 with runners in scoring position and two outs during the 1965 season. The crowd relentlessly let him know how upset they were with his failures. Frustrated, he lashed out at the fans, calling them "bush." That only intensified the fans' animosity. It also put him in hot water with the Yankees' front office.

A couple of days later, Keane fined Pepitone and benched him indefinitely after he was 90 minutes late to the ballpark. Joe responded: "I'm going to quit after this year. Baseball isn't fun anymore. The fans can go and take a big jump somewhere. What are they booing me for?"[13] In truth, Joe knew he was out of shape, lacked concentration and failed to hustle as the result of his carousing, lack of sleep and outside financial pressures.

With four games remaining in Boston in the regular season, Joe said, "I was literally disassembling before my very eyes. I could barely face myself in the mirror, and I didn't know what I was going to do. But I felt it was going to be something destructive, something crazed."[14]

He missed the plane to Boston, and general manager Ralph Houk called him to ask what was happening. Joe said he needed help. Houk advised him to check into Lenox Hill Hospital. His image as a happy-go-lucky, devil-may-care 25-year-old was a facade. "I had so much ability, and the Yankees needed me straightened out if that was possible," he recalled years later.[15]

The once-mighty Yankees finished in sixth place, 25 games out of first. Despite being named as a reserve on the All-Star team, Pepitone was a shadow of himself. He smacked 10 fewer home runs (28 to 18) and drove in 38 fewer runs (100 to 62) than in 1964.

Houk called Joe into his office in the fall of 1965. He delivered his ultimatum: "Change your ways, or you aren't going to be a Yankee for long." Joe asked if he was going to be traded. Houk said the club couldn't get much for him at this point. Houk continued, "It makes me sick the way you're throwing your life away. It's a shame. My God, what a future you have; you could almost be a DiMaggio. You can do it all; there's no telling how far you can go."[16]

On the winter banquet tour, Pepitone confessed, "I didn't give 100 percent last year. I not only hurt myself, I hurt people who had confidence in me. I should be hitting 35-40 homers a year. Instead, I'm up at bat, wondering where my next dollar is coming from. I know what a fool I've been."[17]

A number of his teammates resented him for his lackadaisical ways and flaunting of the rules. He was funny in the clubhouse, kept everyone loose, and was a media magnet. His coiffured hair, gold jewelry, mod outfits, portable hair dryer, and outlandish behavior were the subjects of many news stories. But the Yankees weren't paying him to be a comedian, fashion model, or celebrity. They were paying him to be a productive baseball player, and he wasn't.

Joe announced he planned to get married, and all of his problems were behind him. "They've been telling me to get serious for eight years. Well, now I am. And I'm all through with the playboy stuff."[18]

Yankee fans didn't have much to cheer about in 1966. The club finished in 10th place, 26.5 games out of first. The newly married Pepitone had a strong bounce-back season. Playing first base and center field, he led the New Yorkers in home runs (with a career-high 31) and RBI (83) while batting .255.

He had a chance at 40 homers but failed to clear the fence in the season's final month. A broken left index finger, the result of punching the dugout wall after striking out, and a sore wrist, which he injured sliding, hampered him at the plate. There was still hope the 25-year-old would realize his potential.

The Yankees rewarded his effort with a hefty $14,000 raise. Joe revealed the club had hired someone to help him manage his money and pay off his debts. He, his wife, and his five-month-old daughter lived on a $100-a-week allowance.

Pepitone reported to 1967 spring training happy and enthusiastic. He was convinced this was going to be his year. His goals were 40 homers, 100 RBI, and a .275 batting average. Plans were for him to move to center field while the aging Mantle took over first base. Joe was more comfortable as an outfielder. He thought playing the outfield would help him hit better because there would be less defensive pressure. He had won two Gold Gloves at first base, and his goal was to win one in the outfield.

Despite his good intentions, Joe slipped back into bad habits. This was compounded by several minor injuries, including a sprained left wrist, a sore left elbow, and a sprained back muscle. All of his numbers fell. His home runs dropped from 31 to 13, while his RBI dipped from 83 to 64.

After the disappointing season, he admitted, "I took it too easy, got on the field too late, and didn't loosen up enough before games."[19] He also revealed he was overweight all season.

Once again, Joe promised to work hard in 1968 and smash 40 home runs. By this time, few people had taken him seriously. In spring training, Joe DiMaggio observed, "Joe has the ability, but he has no concentration."[20] Pepitone agreed with him.

Many people felt 1968 was a make-or-break year for the Yankee slugger. In mid-April, Joe suffered a hairline fracture in his left elbow and went on the 21-day disabled list. When he returned, he batted .295 with five home runs and 19 RBI in the first 20 games. On June 5, he clouted a grand slam and a two-run triple. Later that month, he was sidelined when he pulled a ribcage muscle while bashing a home run. Injuries limited him to 40 of the team's first 80 games.

Manager Ralph Houk said, "Joe should be a great hitter. With those quick wrists, he should be one of the best hitters in the game. I don't know why he isn't, but I wish I did. Maybe one day he will do all the things he has the ability to do."[21]

The Yankees' faith in Pepitone was waning. It was evident on August 3 when Houk pinch-hit for him with Baltimore southpaw Pete Richert on the mound, bases loaded, and one out. The Yankee skipper replaced Pepitone with right-handed slugger Rocky Colavito. It was the first time Pepitone had been removed for a pinch-hitter, and it was a strong message to the veteran. Houk platooned Joe in the outfield for the season's final two months.

It was the second disappointing season in a row. Joe, limited to 108 games, tallied 15 homers and 56 RBI while batting .245. The Yankees were tired of waiting for the troubled 28-year-old to realize his potential.

After the 1968 season, Mickey Mantle retired. Pepitone was slated to move back to first base. Houk professed he hadn't given up on Joe. But he was only counting on him as a part-time player, particularly since he had trouble hitting southpaws the past two seasons. The veteran told reporters he had matured, and 1969 was going to be the first year he wasn't going to get lazy; in fact, he was going to work hard every day. "After all, you can't be 17 all your life," he proclaimed.[22]

Joe found his power stroke in the first half of 1969, clouting 17 homers. He hit just eight homers in the second half of the season. Things started to fall apart in August. Pleading severe personal problems, he failed to show up for two games against Minnesota. He joined the club in Chicago. He didn't play in the next two games because of a sore back and shoulder. After being told he had been suspended indefinitely and fined $500, Joe left the bench mid-game, got dressed, and departed the stadium without permission. He became the first Yankee suspended since Buddy Rosar in 1942.

According to the *New York Daily News*, Joe had been knee-deep in financial and female trouble for the past three years. His first wife was suing him for $20,000 in back alimony, and his second wife had left him. Joe denied he was behind in alimony payments or involved with loan sharks, as the New York newspapers reported. He acknowledged he was wrong for leaving the team. He apologized to manager Ralph Houk and his teammates and rejoined the club. The straw that broke the camel's back was walking out on the club.

On December 4, 1969, the Yankees traded Pepitone to the Houston Astros for 26-year-old outfielder Curt Blefary, a malcontent the Astros wanted to unload. It commented on how low Pepitone's value had dropped over the years.

After eight seasons, the Yankees could no longer wait for the 29-year-old to mature or realize his potential. They had put up with a lot because they thought he could help them win. Arthur Daley of *The New York Times* wrote, "Joe has wasted his talent prodigiously."[23]

Astros manager Harry Walker didn't anticipate any problems with Pepitone. "I've heard of a lot of players who were supposed to be problems, but when they come over to me, we have no problem at all."[24] Walker hadn't met Pepitone.

Predictably, Joe promised to work hard, obey the rules and be productive. He said playing for the Astros was going to be fun. Neither management nor the fans expected him to be a superstar. Unlike in New York, he didn't feel overwhelming pressure.

Joe opened the 1970 season in right field. He got off to a solid start. He walloped eight home runs, three triples, and seven doubles and tallied 14 RBI in the first 29 games. He moved from the outfield to first base when rookie John Mayberry failed to produce.

On July 9, he was sidelined when hit on the left elbow with a pitch. At the All-Star break, he traveled to New York to take care of some business. The Astros told him his absence wouldn't be excused. He was fined $250 when he missed a workout the day after the All-Star game. He protested, saying he was injured and couldn't have participated in the workout. General Manager Spec Richardson suspected him of malingering. He suggested Joe be hospitalized until he was well, but Joe refused. "When you're hurt and told practically to your face that you're lying, it makes it hard to want to stay," he said.[25]

He filed a grievance with the Players Association and urged Richardson to ask for waivers on him. Joe was assigned a roommate on the next road trip. He hadn't had a roommate for seven years. He said he was promised he wouldn't have a roommate. "They're just going to be watching me the rest of the year, looking for things to fine me on," he complained. "I know I won't be able to take it. It'll be like being in prison."[26]

He and Richardson talked but came to no solution. Joe left the field before a game while the other players were practicing. He undressed in the clubhouse, exited the stadium, and did not show up for the next game. The Astros suspended him indefinitely without pay.

The Chicago Cubs purchased Pepitone for the $20,000 waiver price on July 29. The Cubs were four games behind the Pittsburgh Pirates in the National League East. "It's a helluva good deal for us," offered Cubs manager Leo Durocher. "He's a fine player."[27]

Astros manager Harry Walker countered: "Joe can be a good player when he wants to be. I expect he'll come into Chicago and hustle. He hustled for us in spring training and the first month or two of the season, then he got tired and started to come up with a lot of excuses."[28]

Joe livened up the Cubs' clubhouse. He was a media darling with humor, toupees, hair dryer, and stylish clothes. This time, however, he also produced. He drove in 31 runs in his first 31 games. In 56 games, he knocked 12 homers and drove in 44 runs as the Cubs finished in second place.

Recharged for the 1971 season, the newest Cubs hero played some of the best baseball of his career. He fashioned a 19-game hitting streak and batted .429 from June 3 through June 20. He raised his average to .348, the third highest in the National League.

At age 30 and with nine years of major league experience, a happy Pepitone said he was starting to learn what the game was all about. "The last four years, I didn't give a damn. They knew it, and I knew it. I also knew I could play ball if I was happy. Now, I'm happy."[29]

In mid-May, he hurt his elbow, making a throw from the outfield. He was placed on the 15-day disabled list. He played with periodic rest when he returned. Floating bone chips in his left elbow hindered his performance at the plate. He had 13 homers and 45 RBI at the midway point and finished with just 16 homers and 62 RBI in 115 games. He was virtually sidelined during the season's final three weeks because of his elbow. He underwent surgery to remove bone chips at the end of the season.

Although Joe finished with a career-high .307 batting average, he fell out of favor with the Cubs' front office late in the season. He and Ron Santo got into a shouting match with manager Leo Durocher about his persistent criticism, particularly of pitcher Milt Pappas. Vice president John Holland denied Pepitone was on the trading block.

Joe swung the bat well in 1972 spring training. Baseball's first strike occurred from April 1 through April 13. When the season started, he had lost his timing and couldn't buy a hit. His 1971 season looked like a mirage. He was hitting .120 and relegated to the bench when the club traveled to New York to play the Mets on April 23. He wondered why he had been singled out. He wasn't the only Cub not hitting. He felt like a scapegoat.

When the Cubs traveled to Houston, he was back in the lineup. But Joe's stomach was so upset he couldn't play that game or the next. The benching stirred up a lot of negative emotions. Joe visited the team physician when the club returned to Chicago. He was diagnosed with gastritis, an inflammation of the stomach lining. He called out sick on April 30 and finally reported to the team on May 2.

When Pepitone arrived at the ballpark, he was told Cubs vice president John Holland wanted to see him. As he walked into Holland's office, he announced he was quitting baseball. He drafted a letter to National League president Chub Feeney, requesting to be placed on the voluntary retired list. He wrote, "I am no longer interested in playing professional baseball."[30]

Holland informed Joe that once he went on the retired list, he couldn't be reactivated for 60 days. He said if Joe changed his mind, he would be welcomed back.

Joe told reporters, "I just lost my interest in baseball. It wasn't a question of whether I was on the bench or playing. It was no longer fun playing baseball, and it hasn't been. Actually, this has been on my mind for about six years."[31]

He decided to return to the Cubs within a month. His reactivation date was June 30. Pepitone irked many of his teammates when he walked out on the team. He was going to have to win them over, as well as earn playing time.

"Quitting the Cubs had been the stupidest thing I had ever done," wrote Joe in his autobiography. "Simply because I was benched for a game. I'd acted like a spoiled kid because that's exactly what I was and had always been. When something went wrong, it was always easier to run from it than confront it."[32]

Pepitone lost one-third of his $60,000 salary as the Cubs went 16-7 during his absence. He was reinserted into the lineup at first base on June 30. He had a productive July. He slammed six of his eight home runs, but his bat was quiet afterward. He strained an Achilles tendon and missed the season's final three weeks.

Joe rejected an offer to play baseball in Japan and signed a one-year contract with the Cubs. At age 32, he was at the crossroads of his career. His future looked bright when he led Chicago in batting average and RBI in spring training. Manager Whitey Lockman, who had replaced Leo Durocher halfway through the 1972 season, played Joe at first base and batted him cleanup on Opening Day 1973.

Joe was shocked when the Cubs informed him on May 19 that he had been traded to the Atlanta Braves for Andre Thornton, a promising 23-year-old minor league first baseman. He was bitter about working hard in spring training, and the club traded him.

He arrived in Atlanta with just as many personal problems as he had in Chicago. He was deeply in debt, battling his ex-wives (he had married for the third time), and dealing with emotional problems. After three games with the Braves, he left the team, despite manager Eddie Mathews trying to talk him into staying. The Braves engineered a trade of Pepitone to the Yakult Atoms in the Japanese Central League.

Shortly after joining the Atoms in late June, the club granted him a two-week leave to return to the United States to iron out his marital problems. He returned to Japan, played a few games, jumped the team (the fifth club he had walked out on), and returned to the United States. Although he counted on the money from playing baseball in Japan to solve some of his financial problems, he greatly underestimated the adjustments needed to adapt to the culture.

After two years out of the game and a series of unsuccessful ventures, Joe, 35, tried a comeback in 1976. He attended spring training with the San Diego Padres. When he didn't make the team, he joined the Hawaiian Islanders, an independent team. He crushed the first home run in Aloha Stadium on Opening Night, April 17. He pulled a hamstring early in the season. After playing 13 games, he was released on May 13. He batted .222 with three RBI.

Years later, Phil Pepe of the *New York Daily News* wrote that Joe Pepitone "was an exceptional talent gone to waste. He had a quick bat, beautiful swing, and a stroke tailor-made for Yankee Stadium's right-field fence. He had no peer defensively at first base and played center field better than any player since Joe DiMaggio. He also had flair and charisma, which made him popular with Yankee fans. With his talent, he should have been a star for years and an all-time Yankee."[33]

A pair of Yankee hurlers marveled at his wasted talent. Tom Metcalf, who pitched briefly for the 1963 club, observed, "Joe's a guy who could have been in the Hall of Fame. He had some of the greatest tools I've ever seen."[34]

Bill Monbouquette, who hurled for the New Yorkers in 1967 and 1968, said, "Pepitone had as much ability as any player I've ever seen play."[35]

In the end, Joe admitted he squandered his fabulous talent. In his autobiography, he wrote, "In 12 years in the majors, I hit 219 home runs. I should have hit closer to 400. My batting average was .258. It should have been .298. Much closer. All I had to do was to take care of myself a little better, have a minuscule regard for my body, and concentrate about 90 percent of the time instead of 50 percent of the time. I spent most of my time letting my talent alone carry me along, making so little effort myself that now all I was left with was guilt."[36]

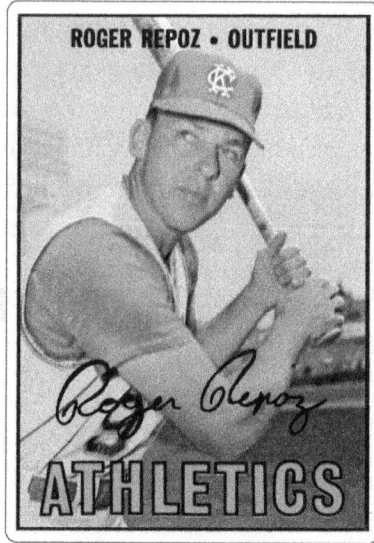

CHAPTER 5

ROGER REPOZ • OUTFIELD

ATHLETICS

ROGER REPOZ
THE QUICK STARTER

Roger Repoz is rated the nearest thing to Mickey Mantle and Roger Maris that the Yankees own in the minor leagues.
—JOSEPH DURSO OF *THE NEW YORK TIMES*

In 1965, Yankee great Mickey Mantle told an out-of-town sportswriter, "Roger Repoz is quite a prospect. He can do it all, run, hit, field and throw. He could be the next great player on the Yankees."[1]

Talk about pressure. It's tough enough when people expect you to be "the next Mickey Mantle," but it's even tougher when Mantle practically anoints you. Repoz, a 6-foot-3, 190-pound, left-handed hitting outfielder, had the tools to be a superstar. But, he displayed flashes of brilliance for only several brief periods during his 8-year major league career. His failure to become an everyday player hindered his career.

Repoz, a Bellingham (Washington) High School graduate, attracted attention from scouts when he pitched and played first base for Western Washington State. In 1959, he posted an 11-2 won-lost record and a 0.90 ERA. He won two games in the NAIA (National Association of International Athletics) national tournament and was voted the tournament's MVP.

The Baltimore Orioles offered him a contract for $6,000. He turned it down, figuring his value would increase with another year of college experience. At the end of the 1960 season, however, the Orioles were no longer interested, but the New York Yankees were. Yankee scout Eddie Taylor refused to match the Orioles' previous offer and succeeded in signing the collegian for $4,000.

Repoz didn't attract much notice during his first three years in the minors, spending time in St. Petersburg, Modesto, and Augusta. In 1963, the 22-year-old exhibited power as he slugged 20 homers for Modesto in the Double-A California League. While his home run total was encouraging, it was accompanied by a .221 average and an alarming 166 strikeouts in 489 at-bats (one strikeout every 2.9 at-bats). The following season, Repoz showed his power was real. He smashed 23 homers for Class-AA Columbus (Ga.) in the Southern League. He still struggled to make contact, fanning 120 times while batting .234.

The New York Yankees called up Repoz in September 1964. The club used him mainly as a late-inning defensive replacement for Mickey Mantle. Although the Yankees made their fifth consecutive World Series appearance in 1964, the team was aging, and their best years looked like they were in the past.

Repoz, 24, was not high on the Yankees' watch list in 1965 because of his concerning strikeout rate and low batting average. He blossomed, however, when he was promoted to Triple-A Toledo in the International League. He thrived under the tutelage of manager Frank Verdi and batting instructor Wally Moses. A new batting stance sparked his improvement. Roger experimented with several stances while in the minors. Verdi and Moses got him to shorten his stride, hold his hands at his waist, and position the bat up straight and cocked over his left shoulder rather than behind his ear.

"I've struggled with a lot of different stances in six years of pro ball," he said. "This is the first year I feel relaxed and comfortable."[2] Moses advised him to hold his bat and place his feet where he felt most comfortable.

The results were encouraging. Repoz maintained his power, significantly increased his batting average, and decreased his strikeout rate. Everything started to come together. "There's a lot to hitting, and it's simply taken me a long time to learn," he explained.[3]

In the first 57 games with Toledo, he led the club in batting, hits, homers, and RBI. His 12 homers also led the league. Toledo manager Frank Verdi believed Roger was the best player in the league. *New York Times* sportswriter Joseph Durso wrote, "Roger Repoz is rated the nearest thing to Mickey Mantle and Roger Maris that the Yankees own in the minor leagues."[4]

The Yankees watched Repoz closely. They hadn't planned to call him up until the 1966 season, but the club was in trouble in the summer of 1965. Mickey Mantle and Roger Maris were hurt, and the club lacked outfielders. Plus, they craved another source of power.

Johnny Johnson, director of the Yankee farm system, said, "The next Yankee star is Roger Repoz. There is no question about it."[5]

Roger joined the Yankees on a 12-game road trip at the end of June. In his first game, he walked as a pinch-hitter. The following game, he notched his first major league hit, a two-run homer in the ninth inning, off the Orioles' hard-throwing southpaw Steve Barber. It started an impressive streak.

He again homered the next day against Boston's Dave Morehead in Fenway Park. His third round-tripper came off Detroit's Joe Sparma in the second game of a July 5 doubleheader. Minnesota's Dave Boswell was the victim of his fourth homer on July 9. Looking like the Yankees' star of the future, the center fielder continued his hot streak. He went 4-for-5, including an inside-the-park homer, against the Twins' Mudcat Grant in the second game of a July 10 doubleheader. In 10 days, he collected 16 hits in 43 at-bats for a .372 average, hammered five homers, and drove in 10 runs.

The sizzling Yankee was the talk of the American League. Teammate Clete Boyer observed, "Roger really has quick wrists, the quickest I've seen. When he finds out what he can do with it, watch out. He doesn't have real good control of the bat yet."[6]

When announcer Merle Harmon interviewed Repoz before the *NBC Game of the Week*, his first question was, "How does it feel to be the next Mickey Mantle?" Caught off guard, he replied, "Uh, I don't know."[7]

After five years in the minors, Roger never thought he would make the majors. "I always felt like I was a normal guy," he said, refusing to buy into the hype. "I wasn't going to be the next Mickey Mantle."[8]

When the Yankees returned home after the 1965 All-Star Game, the cruel Baseball Gods laughed at Roger's hot streak. The rookie spiraled into a depressing 0-for-29 streak. Reality replaced dreams as his average dropped below .200. He looked like a major league want-to-be instead of a star.

"I was still tearing the cover off the ball," he recalled years later. "But, all of a sudden, I was hitting it right at somebody. The pitchers found out pretty quickly they could throw me off-speed stuff, and I would swing at anything."[9]

The Yankees were in sixth place in September, and manager Johnny Keane looked to the next season. "Everyone has to be interested in the long ball potential of a young outfielder with Repoz's equipment," he said.[10] Keane considered platooning Roger since he had trouble against southpaws. The plan was to move him into the lineup against left-handed pitching gradually.

In 79 games in 1965, Repoz hit .228 with 12 homers. Although he was more confident, he still had trouble making contact, fanning once every 3.8 at-bats. The Yankees had to decide if he was a future superstar, an average everyday player, or a platoon player.

The Yankees had a lot of questions going into the 1966 season. Mantle returned from surgery on his right shoulder; Maris returned after having played just 48 games because of an injured hand; shortstop Tony Kubek retired, and the team batted .235, the second-lowest in the American League.

Tom Tresh, Mickey Mantle, and Roger Maris were expected to be the starting outfield. Repoz, Roy White, and Lou Clinton were counted on to provide the necessary depth. General manager Ralph Houk announced plans to platoon Mantle and Repoz in spring training. Injuries limited Mantle, and Repoz had trouble hitting left-handed pitching. "It makes sense," said Houk. "I believe it will help both men and give us more steady hitting."[11]

New York sputtered early in the 1966 season. Repoz was limited to a late-inning defensive replacement for Mantle. When Maris got injured, he played regularly for a couple of weeks. He was hitting a healthy .349 in 43 at-bats when the Yankees traded him to the Kansas City Athletics. The Yankees were playing sub-.500 baseball and mired in seventh place.

Houk was desperate to acquire a starting pitcher to replace Whitey Ford, who hurt his arm and was on the disabled list. The trade involved Repoz, 25, and pitchers Gil Blanco and Bill Stafford for the Athletics right-handed pitcher Fred Talbot, 24, and catcher Billy Bryan.

Athletics manager Alvin Dark figured Repoz's power and defense would help his lackluster club. Under Dark, Roger played every day. In 101 games, he clouted 11 homers to pace the punchless Athletics, who managed just 70 round-trippers, far behind Detroit's American League best of 179. Roger batted .216, splitting his time between center field and first base.

Two young, bright prospects from Arizona State University pushed Roger out of Kansas City. Rick Monday was the number one pick in the 1965 amateur draft. The outfielder signed with the Athletics for $105,000 and made his debut on September 3, 1966. Reggie Jackson, the second selection in the 1966 amateur draft, inked a $95,000 contract with Kansas City. The muscular outfielder broke into the majors on June 9, 1967. A week later, the Athletics traded Repoz to the California Angels for 38-year-old pitcher Jack Sanford.

Angels manager Bill Rigney said, "Getting Repoz is one of the better deals we ever made."[12] An unnamed baseball executive called the trade highway robbery. At first, Repoz was surprised by the trade. But he quickly saw the opportunity of playing every day for a pennant contender that featured several power hitters.

Repoz was serving his two-week military reserve duty when the trade was made. He was out of shape when he joined the Angels, and it took several weeks for him to be ready to start. Roger filled in for center fielder Jose Cardenal when he was injured late in the season.

Repoz was in the Angels' 1968 Opening Day lineup, playing center field and batting sixth. He blistered opposing pitchers the first couple weeks, hitting safely in 11 of 13 games and smashing four homers.

The Angel outfielder appeared on the verge of fulfilling his potential after hearing and reading the phrase "the next Mickey Mantle" after his name for years. He was realistic about his talent, despite his encouraging early statistics. "I've tried not to pay attention to the comparisons to Mickey Mantle," he said. "I tried not to let it affect me. It was an honor, and it made me feel good. When I was asked about Mickey Mantle (who was in his final season), there's only one answer: No one will ever do what he's done. You could only hope to play the position as well as he did; that's about it."[13]

Roger considered 1968 his make-or-break season. Angels' hitting instructor Joe Gordon agreed. "I believe this is the year Roger will find himself," he said. "He has enormous potential."[14]

Repoz credited part of his early success to Exer-Genie, an exercise machine developed by the Aero Space Center for use by astronauts. The machine worked on a combination of isometrics and weightlifting. There were 10 to 12 exercises for baseball players. Employing isometrics, Roger pulled against a weight for 10 seconds, rested for eight seconds, and then repeated the process.

Roger enjoyed his most productive day in the major leagues on May 4, 1968. He slammed a pair of three-run homers in Detroit. He victimized the Tigers' Earl Wilson and Jon Warden. His seventh and eighth of the season gave him the major league lead. He also led the American League in RBI with 19.

Playing regularly was the key to his swift start. "I have a better attitude. Bad days don't bother me. I forget about them. It used to be I would have a bad day and fall into a week-long slump," he said.[15]

His power deserted him from mid-May until the end of the season. He failed to hit a home run from May 14 through July 18, a span of 45 games. He clubbed two in July, one in August, and one in September. The season, which looked so encouraging after he slugged six homers in April, ended in disappointment. In 133 games, he batted .240 with 13 home runs and 54 RBI. He was one of the reasons the Angels slumped and finished eighth.

The Angels improved slightly in 1969, finishing third in the American League West. Repoz had little to do with it. He started poorly and floundered the rest of the season. He lost playing time in the outfield to 23-year-old Jay Johnstone and at first base to 21-year-old Jim Spencer. He was called on frequently to pinch-hit. Playing in 103 games, he was limited to 219 at-bats, his lowest since his rookie season. He batted an embarrassing .165, a drop of 76 points from the previous year. The drop was the steepest in the American League.

There was talk of trading him. The Detroit Tigers considered him a platoon player and a pinch-hitter with some power. They thought he could take advantage of Tiger Stadium's short right-field fence. The deal, however, was never made.

Lefty Phillips took the managerial reins from Bill Rigney on May 27, 1969. He was a Repoz booster. He told general manager Dick Walsh not to cut Repoz's pay because there wasn't a better hustler on the team. "I wanted to show Roger we hadn't lost faith in him."[16] Phillips voiced support for him in spring training when he told reporters, "I wouldn't be surprised if Roger was my cleanup hitter this season."[17]

Roger earned a spot in the 1970 Opening Day lineup, batting sixth and playing center field. He started strong, batting over .300 in the first six weeks. He credited manager Lefty Phillips for restoring his self-respect.

"Playing regularly is the key," he said. "You can work on your problems when you're in the lineup every day. When you play once in a while, you can't find those little mistakes and get rid of them."[18]

Repoz, 30, finished strong, clouting seven homers in September to give him a career-high 18. He batted .238 and added 47 RBI as the Angels finished third in the American League West.

The Angels acquired centerfielder Ken Berry from the White Sox. He was expected to play between Alex Johnson in left field and Tony Conigliaro in right field. When Angels general manager Dick Walsh announced the club's set lineup before spring training, Repoz's name was absent.

Roger was surprised and frustrated. He was coming off one of his most productive seasons, yet he had little chance of a steady job. Although he could play all three outfield positions and back up Jim Spencer at first base, he wasn't interested in being the team's insurance player. He preferred to play every day.

The frustrated Angel said, "Mr. Walsh will argue that he can't pay me what I want because I won't be a regular. Well, he's going to have to pay me what I would make as a regular, or he can trade me." He added: "I'd like just once for a club to tell me I will play every day for a year. If it never happens, I will never know how good of a ballplayer I might have been."[19]

Seeing action as the Angels' fourth outfielder, Repoz never got into a groove. He batted .199 with 13 homers and 42 RBI.

He spent most of the early season in 1972 with Salt Lake City, the Angels' Triple-A Pacific Coast League team. He had just three at-bats with the major league club before he was traded to the Baltimore Orioles for infielder Jerry DaVanon. The Orioles, already loaded in the outfield with Don Buford, Paul Blair, Don Baylor, and Merv Rettenmund, assigned him to Rochester, their Triple-A International League club. At Rochester, he suffered through a 4-for-45 slump. Still, he managed to hit .251.

In 1973, he accepted a $30,000-a-year contract offer from the Taihelyo club in Japan. He signed with the Yakult Swallows the following season and enjoyed the most success of his career. He launched 122 homers in four full seasons, including a career-high 36 in 1976. He retired in 1977 at age 36.

Repoz credited Ted Williams' book, *The Science of Hitting*, for his late success in Japan. Williams advocated patience and waiting for your pitch. "I had always been an aggressive hitter, and I had no patience," he said. "I learned it about 10 or 12 years too late."[20]

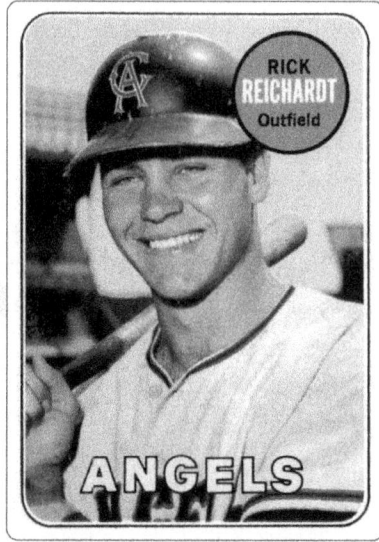

CHAPTER 6

RICK REICHARDT
THE $200,000 BONUS BABY

*His hitting display was impressive. The only other time I have been
so impressed by a youngster was when Willie Mays joined
the New York Giants in 1951.*
—LOS ANGELES ANGELS MANAGER BILL RIGNEY

University of Wisconsin's Rick Reichardt attracted baseball scouts like an
ice cream truck attracts kids. On Sunday, May 17, 1964, the stands were
packed with more than a dozen scouts to watch the 6-foot-3, 215-pound
junior outfielder in the Big Ten conference playoffs.

Although he went hitless the day before, snapping his 17-game hitting streak, he treated the scouts to an extraordinary show in a doubleheader against Illinois. The right-handed slugger bashed three home

runs, rapped two singles, and barely missed a fourth homer. As if that wasn't enough, he stole home. Scouts left the ballpark in a dream-like trance.

Jack White, director of scouting for the New York Yankees, raved, "Rick is the best prospect I've seen in 25 years. He can run as fast as any player in the majors. He has the fastest bat I've ever seen."[1] Los Angeles Angels scout Nick Kamzic marveled, "Rick is the most amazing and explosive player I've seen in 18 years. The boy exudes power."[2]

The 21-year-old Reichardt had tape-measure power, tremendous speed, and the ability to hit for a high average. In 1964, he led the Big 10 conference in home runs (10), batting average (.443, the second highest in the nation), and stolen bases (9). Having batted .429 the previous season, he became the first Big Ten player to earn back-to-back batting titles. He was named first-team All-Big Ten, first-team All-American, and 1964 National Player of the Year by *The Sporting News*.

Reichardt's athleticism was off the charts. He earned 12 varsity letters at P.J. Jacobs High School in Stevens Point, Wis. He was All-State in football and captured the state long jump title. He didn't play baseball until his senior year. Because of the short Wisconsin baseball season, his father, an orthopedic surgeon, advised him to devote his time to track in the spring. He wanted Rick to focus on developing his speed. He ran the 100 and 200 and competed in the long jump. In college, he was timed in 9.9 seconds for the 100.

When Rick accepted a football scholarship to the University of Wisconsin, baseball was an afterthought. He played defensive back, running back, and flanker. As a sophomore, he played in the 1963 Rose Bowl against the University of Southern California. The following season, he paced the Big Ten in receiving.

The only reason Rick went out for baseball in his sophomore season was to avoid spring football practice. He never anticipated being the most sought-after amateur baseball player in the country in two years.

National Football League teams also were tracking him. Observers believed he would be an All-American if he played football his senior year. Two NFL teams said they would draft him in the first round of the 1965 draft.

Rick was in an enviable position and determined to leverage it as much as possible. Eighteen of the 20 major league teams were reportedly pursuing him. He, his father, and their attorney visited virtually every club to evaluate their interest and offers. Teams projected Rick as the next Mickey Mantle, a game-changer and a gate attraction.

The Reichardts' approach transcended money. They looked at what teams Rick could help the most, where he would be happiest, and how management treated him. Rick preferred museums, art galleries, and symphonies to nightclubs and bars. He wanted a suitable environment to pursue his interests. Los Angeles Angels co-owners Bob Reynolds and Gene Autry, the singing cowboy of films and an astute businessman, impressed him.

Roland Hemond, farm director for the Angels, encouraged the owners to pursue Reichardt. "I've never seen a young prospect I have ever wanted more for my club," he said.[3]

The Angels were scheduled to break ground on Anaheim Stadium in the summer of 1964. Reichardt offered the promise of a bright future, increased attendance, and an opportunity to overshadow the attention fans and the media paid the Los Angeles Dodgers. The Angels played their home games in Dodger Stadium, also known as Chavez Ravine.

Reynolds and Autry rounded up a record $200,000 in bonus money, equal to $1.7 million today. The specific amount, however, was not released. At the time, it was estimated to be between $100,000 to $175,000. It was not, however, the highest offer. The New York Yankees dreamed of Reichardt wearing pinstripes and being heir to Mickey Mantle. They offered $250,000.

Colorful Kansas City Athletics owner Charlie Finley figured the youthful slugger was just what his cellar-dwelling team needed. Years later, Reichardt recalled a meeting he and his father had with Finley. "Charlie had taken us to dinner at The Fish Shop in Stevens Point. He offered me $300,000 to sign, then upped it to $350,000. I was so excited, I excused myself, went to the restroom, and threw up."[4]

Rick came within a minute of signing with the Yankees. He was set to call Ralph Houk, Yankees general manager, and tell him he had decided to sign with the club. But before he could make the call, Bob Reynolds of the Angels phoned and dissuaded him from contacting Houk. Rick decided to sign with the Angels for less money.

Reichardt signed his contract on June 24, 1964, before a large contingent of press and television cameras in the penthouse suite of Gene Autry's Hotel Continental on the Sunset Strip in Hollywood. When asked why he signed with the Angels, he replied, "I felt like I would have a better opportunity with the Angels because the organization is young, and I could advance more rapidly. Also, Bob Reynolds, club president, and Gene Autry, chairman, are both outstanding men."[5] He seriously considered signing with only three teams—the Angels, Cardinals, and Yankees.

Upset with Reichardt's record-setting $200,000 bonus, baseball owners established the baseball draft in 1965 to restore competitive balance, eliminate the bidding among teams and suppress exorbitant bonuses. Teams drafted in inverse order of their finish. In 1965, the Kansas City Athletics drafted Arizona State University outfielder Rick Monday. His signing bonus was $100,000, half of Reichardt's. A drafted player did not match Rick's bonus until 1979 when first baseman Todd Demeter signed with the New York Mets for a $208,000 bonus.

After Rick signed the contract, the Angels whisked him away to Dodger Stadium, where he took batting practice. The muscular outfielder put on an attention-getting hitting display. He slugged four or five balls into the seats and a couple off the outfield walls. Angels manager Bill Rigney said, "His hitting display was impressive. The only other time I have been so impressed by a youngster was when Willie Mays joined the New York Giants in 1951."[6]

Reichardt traveled with the Angels to New York and Baltimore before joining Quad Cities in the Class-A Midwest League, where he played for manager Chuck Tanner. The manager was impressed. He said, "Rick has a quicker bat than 50 percent of the players in the big leagues."[7]

Tanner related an incident where Reichardt scored from first base after a teammate blooped a hit over first base that rolled into short right field. "I've never seen a faster man in a baseball uniform," he said.[8] Besides his speed on the bases, Rick played center field and caught everything. Tanner said when asked about his power, "He has more power than General Electric."[9]

Rick played 34 games for Quad Cities before being shipped to the Hawaii Islanders in the Class-AAA Pacific Coast League. He played 23 games under manager Bob Lemon.

He made his major league debut on September 1, 1964, after just 57 games in the minor leagues. The Angels faced the Yankees at Dodger Stadium. Mickey Mantle, his favorite player, batted cleanup and lefty Al Downing was on the mound for New York. He went hitless in a 4-1 loss. Afterward, he admitted to being more nervous than he had ever been. He played 10 more games and compiled a .162 batting average without a home run or an RBI.

Rick warned reporters he was no miracle man. But no one listened. They expected him to join Mickey Mantle and Harmon Killebrew as the top power hitters in the American League.

Reichardt played for Seattle in the Class-AAA Pacific Coast League in 1965. Manager Bob Lemon and his staff worked with him on hitting techniques, fielding, and improving his arm strength. Rick's throwing arm was one of his liabilities. Stan Musial deemed it not good enough for a major league center fielder but more than adequate for a left fielder. Rick thought he potentially had a major league center fielder's arm. His arm strength was not fully developed because he played so little baseball.

Lemon said, "It's too early to tell how good he'll be. He has all the natural ability in the world, including power. He needs to make contact more often, and that comes with experience."[10] Lemon believed Rick would be ready for the major leagues after a full season at Triple-A.

When Rick got off to a slow start in Seattle, the Angels brass decided he needed to change his stance. The club had him stand straight with the bat up high like Tony Conigliaro of the Boston Red Sox. His average, however, continued to plummet. Finally, he returned to his natural stance, slightly open with his weight on his back foot so he could wait on the breaking ball. His average began to climb.

He played 135 games and batted .280 with 13 homers and 63 RBI. Even though he swung at too many bad pitches, it was an encouraging season. He joined the Angels in early September and started every game for the remainder of the season. His 20-game totals were a .267 average, one homer, and six RBI.

Many observers predicted 1966 would be his breakout season. Angels manager Bill Rigney said outbidding the Yankees for Rick was the best thing the Angels had ever done. "Rick has everything it takes to succeed Mickey Mantle as the big star in the American League."[11]

The Angels opened the 1966 season as the newly dubbed California Angels. Rick was eager to erase the memory of the end of the 1965 season when he said he was "overmatched, inadequate, and ineffectual."[12]

He started in left field and batted fifth. The bonus boy walloped the first home run in Anaheim Stadium, a 420-foot blast, on April 19. He clouted a pair of home runs in the eighth inning at Fenway Park as the Angels romped 16-9 less than two weeks later. He became the 11th player since 1900 to achieve the feat. His performance gave him six home runs, the best in the American League. Despite the expectations, pressure, and scrutiny, Rick delivered dividends on the Angels' hefty investment.

"The first time I saw Rick Reichardt, I thought he fell off a Wheaties box," offered baseball announcer and former St. Louis Cardinal Joe Garagiola.[13]

Sixteen-year veteran Angels first baseman Joe Adcock observed, "Rick has unlimited ability. He's quick with the bat, and he has great power."[14]

Manager Bill Rigney said Reichardt had the intangibles like Mays, Mantle, and Al Kaline. He was convinced Rick could dominate, particularly if the Angels could get him to be more aggressive at the plate.

Rick attributed his productive start to a new batting stance. He typically had problems with breaking stuff away and fastballs inside. Rigney moved him on top of the plate, a la Frank Robinson. The new stance made his bat quicker, allowed him to see the ball better, hit more frequently to the opposite field, and be more confident. Although pitchers tried to brush him off the plate, he refused to move. As a result, he was hit more often (13 times) than any other batter in the league.

Rick blasted his 14th home run and registered his first four-hit game on July 2. He lifted his average to .295. Shortly after, he complained of severe headaches, dizziness, and high blood pressure. The Angels announced he suffered from a congenital blockage of the kidney. The club sent their star, leading the Angels in average, home runs, and RBI, to the Mayo Clinic for examination and tests.

Surgeons had to remove his right kidney. Reichardt had hoped for a type of plastic surgery that would improve circulation to his kidneys. After a six-week recovery, he rejoined the team. On the season's final day, manager Rigney called on him to pinch hit in the bottom half of the eighth inning. Although he popped up to shortstop, he received a standing ovation from the home crowd of 13,280. He said, "That was my greatest thrill in sports."[15] In 89 games, the 23-year-old batted .288 with 16 homers and 44 RBI.

Reichardt was eager to report to spring training in 1967. The doctors said he might need rest periods during the season to help him recuperate from the surgery. Rick got off to a rocky start in spring training and never got untracked. The question loomed of whether or not he could achieve his potential.

Rigney talked up his budding star. "Rick has come along at a time when the American League needs a next hero in the mold of Mickey Mantle. I will be sincerely surprised if he does not become that hero and the league's superstar."[16]

When the comment was relayed to Rick, he replied, "A second Mantle? I'm just happy to be the first Rick Reichardt."[17]

Seemingly reinforcing Rigney's praise, *The Sporting News* featured Reichardt on the cover of its May 20th issue. Rigney, however, turned more critical of Rick as his erratic, lackadaisical fielding and lack of concentration at the plate cost the team runs. His poor fielding angered Angels pitchers and irked Rigney. One of the Angels pitchers said, "The only time I pray is when a ball is hit to Reichardt."[18] When cornered by the pitcher, who was the victim of one of his costly errors, Rick replied, "It's only a game."[19]

Rigney believed Rick was distracted by managing his investments and other off-the-field business activities. He admonished the bonus baby. "Rick hasn't approached the game with the dedication it demands."[20]

Rick sometimes lacked total concentration, but he was still confident in his abilities. "I believe I have the potential to be a superstar," he insisted.[21]

Having misjudged countless fly balls and amid a month-long slump, Rick went for an eye examination. The results revealed blurred vision in his left eye, and he was fitted for glasses. He wore them for the first time for a July 7 doubleheader at Anaheim Stadium. In the first game, he rapped three hits, including a homer, and drove in three runs. In the nightcap, he went 1-for-4 and drove in a pair of runs. Unfortunately, it didn't last. Rick, who said he suffered from night blindness, hit nearly 40 points higher in day games than in night games (.286 to .247) during his career.

In mid-August, Reichardt was still mired in a batting slump. He was confused at the plate because he frequently altered his stance at the behest of the Angels staff. Finally, general manager Fred Haney told him, "Forget everything you have ever known and do things naturally."[22] More comfortable at the plate and outfield, he caught fire the final six weeks of the season, hitting .350.

In his first full season, the 24-year-old played 146 games, batted .265, slugged 17 homers, and drove in 69 runs. His 90 strikeouts, failure to wait on pitches, and poor pitch selection were major concerns. Many observers rated his season as disappointing.

Rick entered the 1968 spring training camp more optimistic than ever. He was 100 percent healthy for the first time. He no longer experienced headaches. The Mayo Clinic had given him a clean bill of health.

"Only lack of ability can keep me from having a great year," he said. "I have never felt stronger. I've hit balls harder in batting practice this spring than I ever did last year. This season, I don't have any excuses."[23]

The Angels hoped this would be his breakout season. Reichardt, now 25, was more mature and had a full season under his belt. He entered the season with two goals: Play 150 games and hit in the same position in the lineup for the entire season. He believed everything else would fall in order if he could do those things. "I don't know what my ultimate potential is, but I do believe I will eventually hit a lot of home runs," he said.[24]

He had a lot of people in his corner, even though he hadn't realized his potential. Rigney felt the Angels' $200,000 investment was still a wise one.

Angel teammate Don Mincher said, "Rick is the key to the Angels. I definitely believe he is going to be a superstar. The question is it going to be this year or next?"[25]

Baltimore Orioles manager Hank Bauer considered Reichardt a potential Mantle. "A body like Mantle, he has a chance if he ever puts it all together."[26]

Rick started 1968 in an unspectacular fashion. He went into a month-long slump in July, batting .194. The boobirds were relentless. Every time he struck out or popped up with men on base, boos filled the stadium.

Angels manager Bill Rigney said, "Right now, Rick doesn't have a good swing. He has tremendous anxiety at the plate. I think he thinks he has to show everyone what he can do every time he goes to the plate. He commits himself too soon. He can't wait. He's going to be a good player, but he's going to make it hard for himself. Sometimes I wish he would just go out there and play the game and not think so much."[27]

A *Sporting News* article headlined "Reichardt, Ex-Mr. Wonderful Goes on Angels Trade Block" appeared in late September. The Angels needed help, and Rick was their best bargaining chip. Although he improved his home run total each of the past three seasons, he failed to meet the team's sky-high expectations. Frequently compared to Mickey Mantle, the 25-year-old was but a shadow of the superstar. Mantle won the Triple Crown at age 24 and batted .365 at age 25. Would Reichardt be a late bloomer, or had he already reached his potential?

Rick achieved his pre-season goals: He played 150 games (151) and batted third, fourth, or fifth 90 percent of the time. The results were a .255 average, 21 homers, and 73 RBI. His 118 strikeouts were the fifth-highest in the league, far behind Reggie Jackson's 171.

Determined to improve, he went to the Arizona Instructional League for six weeks. There, he worked with instructors Chuck Tanner and Al Monchak. Rick was still constantly changing his approach at the plate. His goal was to settle on one swing and stance and stay with them.

He played little baseball in high school and college. Then he was rushed through the Angels' farm system, failing to learn some baseball fundamentals. He believed he would have greatly benefited from the Arizona Instructional League three or four years earlier. It was like going back to sixth grade, in a baseball sense.

Approaching 26, he said, "I think I'm at the crossroads. Perhaps I've reached a plateau, or perhaps I go on to be the type of player who warrants a great deal of attention. I'm enthused about the future."[28]

As the Angels floundered in the first two months of the 1969 season, manager Bill Rigney's patience with Reichardt ran out. "I'm getting awfully tired of seeing Rick use half of his talent," he said. "I think he should be hitting 40 homers a season. He should be a superstar."[29]

Rigney was frustrated that Reichardt wasn't waiting on pitches, swung at too many bad pitches, hadn't developed a power swing, and often failed to deliver in the clutch.

"Rick is wasting his talent and hurting the team," said Rigney. "He has everything Killebrew has, plus blazing speed."[30] Yet, the Angels feared Reichardt, batting cleanup, had become a singles hitter. The club needed power and timely hitting. Rick wasn't supplying either.

Describing Reichardt, reporter Ross Newhan wrote, "He is an amalgamation of theories, and now he is a jigsaw puzzle without all the pieces. Perhaps, they never should have tampered with his swing."[31]

The Angels fired Rigney on May 27, and Lefty Phillips took over as manager. His patience with Reichardt was far less than Rigney's. One of his charges was to tap Rick's potential.

At the end of June, the Angels had the majors' lowest batting average, fewest homers, and fewest runs scored. The club was troubled that Rick had only 14 extra-base hits. All the pressure and expectations had taken their toll. They had handicapped his development. "I believe I'm a good, solid player," he said. "But, with this club, at this time, I don't believe I am to be a superstar."[32]

He continued to struggle in the clutch. He went 45 plate appearances without driving in a run from the end of July to mid-August. He drew one walk and didn't register an extra-base hit during the 11-game dry spell. Of his 80 hits, 62 were singles. The boos increased, and trade talks heated up.

"Rick's a mixed-up kid right now," said Phillips. "It's not that he doesn't want advice. In fact, I think he looks for advice too often."[33] Phillips denied any riff between him and Reichardt or that he was a difficult player to handle.

Baltimore Sun reporter Ken Nigro watched Reichardt play in late August and wrote, "He's never been the same since the kidney operation. He doesn't look like he's swinging right, and when he does get hold of one, it doesn't have enough oomph to get out of the park."[34]

Rick's 1969 stats were disappointing—.254 batting average, 13 homers, and 68 RBI.

In parts of six seasons, including three full seasons (1967-69), the one-time bonus baby produced 68 homers and 260 RBI in 554 games. The Angels had been patient but believed they had been significantly short-changed.

It was clear Rick's future was not with the California Angels. He requested to be traded.

On April 27, the Angels traded Reichardt, 27, and third baseman Aurelio Rodriguez, 22, to the Washington Senators for third baseman Ken McMullen, 27. Senators manager Ted Williams was convinced he could straighten him out at the plate. "He's got a lot of potential, and he's going to play," he declared.[35]

Williams saw Reichardt as another reclamation project. The Hall of Famer had great success with Senator hitters in 1969. Players who improved their batting averages included Eddie Brinkman (79 points), Del Unser (56 points), Mike Epstein (44 points), Ken McMullen (24 points), and Frank Howard (22 points). Williams likened Reichardt to Howard. Before becoming a star, the 6-foot-7 outfielder needed a couple of seasons in the minors and part-time duty with the Dodgers.

Rick was happy to get out of Southern California and away from manager Lefty Phillips. "Ever since I came up to the big leagues, I've been getting advice on how to hit. Nothing has worked the way I would have liked. Ted Williams is my last hope."[36]

Rick was convinced he was coming into his prime. He refused to believe he was a utility player. "Being traded to the Senators is the best thing that has happened in years," he said. "It's a blessing. I've always wanted to work with Ted Williams."[37]

Leaving the Angels lessened the pressure and expectations he had dealt with since 1964. The signing bonus was an albatross, and he wanted to shed the superstar expectations.

He didn't play as much as he wanted in 1970. He never started more than six games in a row. The Senators had a crowded outfield, and Williams, for the most part, platooned him. Rick hated the idea, but he kept quiet because he didn't think Williams would change his mind. The platoon numbers, however, didn't work out. The right-handed Reichardt batted eight points higher against right-handers than left-handers (.258 to .250). In his part-time role, he swatted 15 homers, drove in 46 runs, and batted .253 in 277 at-bats. Williams failed to work his magic, as Rick's batting average was the lowest of his career.

He had 12 homers at the All-Star break but had only 109 plate appearances after July 31. The Senators faltered down the stretch, going 7-22 in September, including a 14-game losing streak. Frank Howard had a monster season—44 homers, 126 RBI, and 132 walks. But the Senators didn't get enough offensive help from the rest of the lineup. Much of the blame fell on Reichardt's shoulders.

He reflected on his season under Williams, "I enjoyed playing for him. He surprised me in that he didn't try to change my stance or mechanics. He stressed the mental and psychological sides of hitting. He emphasized studying pitchers, knowing what they throw, and concentrating on the possibilities. He said to wait on your pitch, and look for your pitch, middle in. He stressed you can't make a living hitting the outside pitch."[38]

Rick was unhappy with his part-time status, and the Senators wanted to cut his salary by 20 percent. He requested a trade. On February 9, 1971, the Senators traded Reichardt to the Chicago White Sox for pitcher Jerry Janeski, a 24-year-old right-handed pitcher who won 10 games in 1970, his rookie season.

Paul Corcoran of the Copley News Service wrote, "Reichardt, 27, highly touted in the past, is no more than a journeyman, traded to Chicago for a relatively unknown rookie pitcher. Reasons he hasn't reached his potential include kidney surgery and a basic handicap; he couldn't throw and was an average fielder. He lacks confidence and has a basic flaw in his swing. So far, he has been unteachable in an effort to correct it."[39]

Roland Hemond, director of player personnel for the Chicago White Sox, predicted success for Reichardt. "I believe Rick is a late bloomer. At age 28, he is about the same spot where a kid of 23 or 24 would be if he signed out of high school."[40]

Hemond believed the pressure of being a bonus boy hurt Reichardt. With less pressure, more experience, and an opportunity to play for

Chuck Tanner, his first minor league manager, Hemond expected Rick to become a good, solid ballplayer.

Rick, however, had to win a starting job in spring training. He had to prove he was more than a platoon player. He earned a spot in the 1971 Opening Day lineup, playing left field. His batting average reached a high of .330 on June 21. Manager Chuck Tanner thought he should have made the All-Star team. He considered him one of the best outfielders in the American League.

Reichardt benefited from a batting tip Ted Williams passed along to Tanner while playing in the majors. Tanner, in turn, passed it along to Rick. Williams told Tanner to cock his leg and sort of bend it at the knee when the pitcher delivered the ball. As a result, said Williams, you wait longer on the ball, see it better and hit it more solidly and consistently.

Don Merry, a staff writer for the *Independent Press-Telegram*, wrote, "In Chicago, Reichardt has appeared to come of age. He is no longer at war with himself, no longer seeking to become the superstar that is not his destiny."[41]

Reichardt said, "I'm happy and relaxed. There is no pressure here; that was always part of my life in California. I think I've finally found my niche."[42]

In California, he worried more about what people thought he was supposed to do than what he could do. He admitted he was an immature bonus baby. He had an inflated opinion of himself and was quick to get down on himself.

His kidney operation in 1966 affected him physically and mentally. While he had recovered physically, he hadn't mentally. After the operation, he became too cautious and fearful of permanently damaging himself. He no longer played with abandonment.

Reichardt faltered down the stretch. He batted .278 with 19 homers and 62 RBI. He said he would have had more homers and RBI if he played in a more hitter-friendly park than Comiskey Park. His performance against the Washington Senators, however, was personally satisfying. He went 22-for-50 (.440) with 5 homers and 12 RBI. (Take that, Ted Williams). "This has been my most satisfying season," he said. "I've played my best all-around baseball."[43]

Manager Chuck Tanner platooned Rick in center field with Jay Johnstone in 1972. Reichardt's power was almost non-existent. He didn't hit his first homer until June 18. He suffered a groin injury in mid-August, which hampered him for the rest of the season. He was limited to 101 games and 291 at-bats. He clouted eight homers and drove in 43 RBI while batting .251.

Rick and teammates Mike Andrews and Stan Bahnsen started the 1973 season without signed contracts. General manager Stu Holcomb had cut Rick's salary by 20 percent. The trio was playing under "renewal contracts" offered to the players at the beginning of the season. They denied they planned to sue baseball next fall in another challenge to the reserve clause. "This game has been too good to me for me to slap it in the face," said Rick.[44]

Playing without a signed contract didn't bother Reichardt. Filling in for the injured Carlos May in left field, Rick got off to his best start. He was hitting .360 in mid-May. Manager Chuck Tanner said, "What has pleased me the most about our reserves is the way Rick Reichardt is filling in. I believe he is one of the most underrated players in the majors. He does a good job defensively, is hitting .300, and has a knack for driving in the big run."[45]

The fans, the media, and radio announcer Harry Caray heavily criticized Rick for his contract holdout. The contract dispute reached a critical level when Holcomb resigned pitcher Stan Bahnsen. Holcomb said Bahnsen was an important part of the organization. Reichardt and Andrews took it to mean they weren't. Reichardt walked out on the team during a June 26 game. His teammates felt he had selfishly let them down. Two days later, the White Sox gave Rick his unconditional release. He later signed as a free agent with the Kansas City Royals. Royals manager Jack McKeon used him mainly as a designated hitter and pinch hitter. It was another frustrating season. Rick, limited to 87 games and 280 at-bats, batted .250 with three homers and 33 RBI.

The 32-year-old Reichardt was optimistic about the 1974 season. In high spirits, he reported two weeks early to spring training to work with hitting guru Charlie Lau. He delivered a single in a pinch-hitting appearance in the third game of the season. Two days later, Rick, the team's player representative, was given his unconditional release, despite having a two-year, no-cut contract. "I was a sacrificial lamb to the owners because of my involvement with fighting the reserve clause," he said years later.[46] No team picked him up. "There's no question I could have played longer," he said. "I was only 32 and in good shape."[47]

Reflecting on his career, he said, "It was very tough to try to live up to be the next Mickey Mantle. It was very tough for a young player like me."[48] He believes, however, that he made the most of the talent he possessed. "I thought I had good physical skills, maybe not as good as others thought, and I was a good player. My only regret is that I didn't play enough in the minor leagues."[49]

Angels manager Bill Rigney said if the media and fans had been more patient, Reichardt might have accomplished more. "Everyone wants an instant fix, and everybody thought Rick was going to lead the Angels to the promised land. There was too much pressure on him too soon. I always liked Rick because he never backed off of that pressure. Considering all the high expectations and the kidney surgery, I think Rick did as well as he could have. I don't think it's fair for anyone to say Rick didn't pan out because he played just as hard as he could."[50]

Bobby Murcer | OUTFIELD

BOBBY MURCER
THE OTHER OKLAHOMA KID

Bobby has been a hitter ever since I first knew him. He has a smooth stroke, hits to all fields, and has more power than we thought he had. You have to see him to realize how much he can do. He has a chance to be a great one.
—Yankees manager Ralph Houk

It was inevitable that Bobby Murcer would be compared to Mickey Mantle. He grew up in Oklahoma City, about 200 miles southwest of Commerce, where Mantle spent his youth. Scout Tom Greenwade signed both for relatively small bonuses. Murcer made his debut with the New York Yankees when he was 19; the same age Mantle was when he first put on pinstripes. He played shortstop like Mantle and earned a reputation in the minor leagues as an outstanding hitter.

The comparisons were unfair to Murcer. *Washington Post* sportswriter Shirley Povich observed, "Murcer is admittedly not another Mickey Mantle. He isn't as strong as Mantle, doesn't hit the ball as far, can't bunt well or run as fast."[1]

Murcer, a 5-11, 175-pound left-handed hitter, never believed he was the "next Mickey Mantle." But the Yankees and the media beat the drum loudly and consistently, and fans, desperate for a hero, wanted to believe it. The pressure to meet expectations never subsided.

Although Murcer enjoyed a 17-year career and was a 5-time All-Star, he never obtained superstar status. He was a star who, for a couple of seasons, was perhaps the best player in the American League. Though he wasn't another Mantle, he most likely maximized his talent.

Bobby was ten years old when Mickey won the American League Triple Crown in 1956 with 52 homers, 130 RBI, and a .353 batting average. Practically every Oklahoma boy who swung a bat idolized Mantle, and Murcer was no exception. He rooted for the New York Yankees in baseball and the Oklahoma Sooners in football.

At Southeast High in Oklahoma City, Murcer was All-State in football and baseball. He was All-City in basketball and one of the state's top scorers. Eight colleges, including the University of Oklahoma, offered him football scholarships. Baseball, however, was his first love, and Bobby figured his future was on the diamond, not the gridiron. The Los Angeles Dodgers expressed the most interest in signing him. The club offered a $20,000 signing bonus and a college education. The Yankees offered just $10,000 and to pay for college.

The night after Bobby graduated from high school, Yankees scout Tom Greenwade promised he would take him to Kansas City to watch the Yankees and introduce him to the players. They traveled to Kansas City a couple of days later. He met Yogi Berra and Mickey Mantle and took batting practice in a Yankees uniform. He signed a contract with the Yankees the next week. Signing for less money didn't bother Bobby. He figured to cash a string of World Series checks to offset the difference.

The Yankees assigned 18-year-old Bobby to Johnson City, Tenn., in the Appalachian Rookie League. He made a quick impression. He batted .365 in 32 games before being sent to the Florida East Coast

Instructional League. His 34 errors at shortstop, however, caused concern. The following season he was promoted to Class-A Greensboro in the Carolina League. Bobby delivered an all-round performance at the plate with 16 homers, 90 RBI, and a .322 average. But he was weak in the field, committing 55 errors. He finished third in the Carolina League batting race and was voted the team MVP and Topps Player of the Year in the Carolina League.

He made his major league debut on September 8, 1965. He registered his first major league hit, a two-run homer off Jim Duckworth of the Washington Senators, six days later. The 19-year-old experienced the biggest thrill of his career on September 18, when he was in the starting lineup with Mickey Mantle on "Mickey Mantle Day."

Mantle recalled the first time he met Murcer. "I got to the ballpark late one day, and Whitey Ford ran over to me and said, 'There's a guy out there at shortstop who's supposed to be the next you.'"[2]

Bobby battled 30-year-old veteran Ruben Amaro for the starting shortstop position in 1966. He was confident in his hitting but shaky about his fielding. He had a strong but erratic arm.

Yankees general manager Ralph Houk described Murcer as "one of the finest young players I've seen."[3]

New York manager Johnny Keane said, "Kids like this don't come along very often. He's a hitter. He has a history as a hitter. He has played two years in the minors, and his record is exceptional."[4]

Bobby played well during spring training and appeared to have the edge as the starting shortstop. When manager Johnny Keane told him he had made the club, his play declined. "I was overawed when it looked like I was going to make the club," he said. "I started thinking about all those great players I would play with, and it overwhelmed me. When I started making those errors, I could have cried."[5]

Amaro was at shortstop, and Murcer was on the bench when the season opened. In mid-April, Amaro collided with outfielder Tom Tresh, tearing up his knee and sidelining him for most of the season. Murcer filled in for seven games, including a 3-error game against the Orioles, before the team shipped him to Class-AAA Toledo, where he could play daily.

The Yankees' front office watched him closely. They perked up on June 26 when the left-handed slugger smashed four consecutive homers in a twin bill. He went 6-for-8, homering in the last two at-bats in Game 1 and the first two at-bats in Game 2. It was the kind of power they coveted.

On the flip side, Murcer endured a 3-for-62 slump resulting from being overeager and chasing bad pitches, mainly curve balls. His average fell from .315 to .250, but he finished at .266. At shortstop, he continued to make too many errors. The Yankees called him up in September 1966. He batted just .174 in 21 games.

Eager to prove himself, Murcer, 21, reported to the Yankees' 1967 spring training camp. Unfortunately, he received his draft notice from the Army the same day. He reported to basic training at Fort Bliss, Texas, and was assigned to the radio corps in Fort Huachuca, Ariz. He played no baseball for two years.

Discharged at the end of 1968, Murcer played winter baseball in Puerto Rico. He grew an inch and gained 10-15 pounds, mostly muscle, during his stint in the Army. More importantly, he matured. "I went in a kid; I believe I came out a man," he said.[6]

When Bobby reported to the Yankees' spring training camp in 1969, Mickey Mantle had retired, and the club was without a star. With an eye on increasing attendance and fan interest, the Yankees looked to Murcer. He created a sense of excitement, the ball jumped off his bat, and he had a colorful Midwest personality.

Murcer excelled offensively but struggled defensively. The Yankees moved him to third base, but he wasn't comfortable there.

The Yankees considered Murcer a special player and a key to their future. It was evident when longtime clubhouse attendant Pete Sheehy asked Mantle who he thought should inherit his locker at Yankee Stadium. When Sheehy suggested Murcer, Mantle replied, "Yes, that's who I was thinking of." Murcer thanked Mantle, saying, "I hope I can do one-quarter as well as you."[7] The prospect also wore Bobby Richardson's number one. When the second baseman retired in 1967, he asked Sheehy to put his uniform in storage until Murcer returned from the Army.

Bobby collected multiple hits in five of the first six games in 1969. He was batting .393 when the Yankees arrived at Yankee Stadium for

Opening Day. He slammed a homer, a double, and a single and drove in four runs against the Washington Senators.

As the season progressed, manager Ralph Houk grew concerned that Murcer's defensive woes would affect his hitting. Shortly after Bobby made four errors in two games, Houk switched the budding star to right field, lifting some of the pressure. Houk believed Murcer's speed and strong arm would help him make the necessary adjustments without any problems.

By the end of May, the 23-year-old led the American League in home runs (11) and RBI (43) while batting .320, fifth in the league. His performance fueled the Mickey Mantle comparisons. "It's an honor, but I only accept myself as Bobby Murcer," he said. "That kind of talk doesn't bother me or put pressure on me."[8]

Manager Ralph Houk was concerned Murcer would change his style in quest of the long ball. The short right field fence in Yankee Stadium beckoned him. Houk said pitchers could usually handle hitters who tried to pull everything.

He praised Murcer: "He's been a hitter ever since I first knew him. He has a smooth stroke, hits to all fields, and has more power than we thought he had. I can't compare him to anyone. You have to see him to realize how much he can do. He has a chance to be a great one."[9] Bobby jammed his heel, sliding into second base on May 30. The injury forced him to the bench for more than a week. Discouraged after he lost his groove and momentum, he tried to yank every pitch out of the ballpark. The results were disastrous. In June, he failed to homer, drove in just five runs, and batted .202.

He didn't get untracked until August. He slugged 13 home runs in the final two months of the season. Some observers attributed his mid-season slump to the pressure from increased publicity. Others said he was swinging at too many bad pitches.

He finished with 26 homers, 82 RBI, and a .259 batting average. He was second on the team in homers, one behind Joe Pepitone's 27, and the leader in RBI. Since Murcer had exceeded 90 at-bats before 1969, he wasn't eligible for the Rookie of the Year Award. Lou Piniella of the Kansas City Royals earned that honor.

Murcer had his own private coach—Mickey Mantle—during 1970 spring training. Mantle's job was to teach his heir apparent the fundamentals of playing center field. Murcer's progress encouraged Mantle. "I think Bobby Murcer will be one of the best players in the American League in a couple years," he claimed.[10]

Murcer opened the season in center field. He started slowly and got hot in June, batting .340. In a June 24 doubleheader against the Cleveland Indians, the left-hander launched four consecutive home runs. He cleared the fence off Sam McDowell in the ninth inning of the first game and followed with a pair of four-baggers off Mike Paul and one off Fred Lasher. He became the 11th player and the fourth Yankee to achieve the feat.

Although the Yankees won 93 games, they finished 15 behind the Baltimore Orioles. Murcer, who raised fans' hopes in 1969, was a disappointment. His home runs fell from 26 to 23, his RBI dropped from 82 to 78, and his batting average dipped from .259 to .251.

The Sporting News observed, "Murcer, who was expected to rise in the star class, has been ordinary and must be listed as another disappointment. He's going to continue to be a disappointment until he realizes pitchers aren't dummies. If he concedes pitchers are dedicated to getting him out, not letting him hit, he could become a good player."[11]

Manager Ralph Houk expected more of the potential star in 1971. But he was realistic. He didn't buy the romantic notion that Murcer was Mickey Mantle incarnate. "I look at Bobby Murcer this way," he explained. "Everyone expects too much of him. He's just not that good. He doesn't have to be. He's not going to hit 50 home runs, but he's a damn good ballplayer."[12]

Murcer decided he was a .300 hitter, not a home run slugger. He was happy with his average of 25 homers in his first two seasons but not his batting average in the .250s. He reported to spring training determined to improve his bunting, hit the ball where it's pitched, and forget about the fences.

"I decided to stop trying to pull everything," said Bobby, who had grown tired of the pop-ups and soft grounders due to trying to pull outside pitches. "This is the year I'm going to try and hit with my head instead of just swing a bat."[13] His strategy was to look for a pitch in his power zone until he got one strike. After that, he would go with the pitch.

His new approach paid quick dividends. He sprayed hits to all fields and was batting .377 at the end of May. In addition to being more selective at the plate, he started to bunt more. Mantle harped on Murcer about bunting more, or at least faking a bunt. He said Bobby cheated himself out of 20 to 30 hits a season by not using the bunt as a weapon.

A notorious streak hitter, Murcer found consistency. He put together 9, 10, and 14-game hitting streaks in the first half of the season. "I'm a streak hitter, but I no longer worry if I have a hitless day. I tell myself I'll get one tomorrow."[14]

The Yankees' center fielder was selected to the 1971 American League All-Star team. He started the game with Carl Yastrzemski in left field and Frank Robinson in right field. He went 1-for-3 as the ALers won 6-4.

Batting .341 at the All-Star break, Murcer expounded on his success. "I got momentum early this season, and success brings confidence. I've been able to discipline myself, and I'm not helping the pitchers."[15]

He remained consistent all season and finished with a .331 batting average, second to Tony Oliva's .337. His batting average was 80 points higher than the previous season. He supplemented it with 94 RBI, 94 runs, and 25 homers. The center fielder paced the Yankees in seven offensive categories. He finished seventh in the Most Valuable Player voting.

His performance created a buzz, convincing some fans he was the next Mickey Mantle. Once again, Murcer dispelled that notion. "I don't consider myself another Mickey Mantle. Mickey was one of the greatest. I can never do the things he did, but I think I can do enough to be a star. Mantle was a superstar."[16]

Would the Yankees and their fans be content with a star instead of a superstar? Discussions arose as to what Murcer needed to do to be a superstar. Mantle said, "Two or three years like 1971, and he would have to hit 40-50 homers."[17]

Houk didn't believe Murcer could hit 40-50 homers, but he thought he could bat .350 if he fared well against left-handed pitching. "Bobby needs to take more advantage of his speed," he added. "He needs to steal more bases in crucial situations. Plus, he needs to play in a World Series and receive national publicity."[18]

The 1972 season didn't start until mid-April because of the baseball strike. Murcer started the season out of shape and overweight. The result was a sluggish start. But, as the weather heated up, so did Murcer. He batted .367 in June and stayed hot the rest of the summer. He made his second consecutive All-Star appearance.

The Yankee star put together his second impressive year in a row. He closed with a .292 average, a league-leading 102 runs, 96 RBI, and 33 home runs, second in the league to Dick Allen's 37. He led the league in total bases with 314 and earned a Gold Glove in center field.

Murcer earned $65,000 in 1972 and figured he was due a hefty raise. *The Daily News* noted the Yankees had spent a lot of money and spilled a great quantity of ink trying to convey the impression Murcer was a superstar. Now, they had to prove it by meeting his salary demands—$100,000 a year. At 26 years and ten months, Murcer became the second youngest player to earn $100,000 when he signed a new contract in March 1973. Only Johnny Bench of the Cincinnati Reds was younger.

Whether Murcer was a bona fide superstar or not, the $100,000 contract declared he was. He joined Joe DiMaggio and Mickey Mantle as the only Yankees to earn six figures in a season.

When a reporter asked Murcer if he was another Mantle, he replied, "There will never be another Mick."[19]

Of course, the Yankees weren't paying him to be a cheap imitation of Mantle. And the $100,000 contract raised the fans' expectations considerably. He continued to deny he felt pressure to be the next Mickey Mantle. But no one who had ever been in his position had escaped it.

George Steinbrenner purchased the Yankees in January. The new boss made it clear he wanted a winning team. Many writers favored the Yankees to win the American League East in 1973, increasing the expectations and pressure.

Murcer matched Mantle's salary but had a long way to go to match his achievements. By the time Mantle was 27, he had won a Triple Crown, led the league in runs scored four times, home runs three times, RBI once, won a batting title and earned two Most Valuable Player Awards. Murcer led the league in runs scored once and total bases once.

The Yankees led the AL East from June 20 through August 4, 1973. By September 13, however, they had fallen 14 games behind the league-leading Baltimore Orioles. The collapse was a team effort. The starting pitchers struggled, the bats went silent, the bench failed to deliver, and the defense was porous. Murcer, the cleanup hitter, clouted three home runs in a game on July 13 and didn't homer again until August 19. In a disappointing season for the Yankees, he batted .304 and drove in 95 runs. His home runs fell from 33 to 22.

Bobby expected another raise when he arrived in Fort Lauderdale the following spring. He signed for $120,000, making him the highest-paid Yankee of all time.

Murcer dealt with significant changes in 1974. Yankees manager Ralph Houk, a Murcer fan and friend, resigned to take the Detroit Tigers job. Bill Virdon, a former center fielder, replaced Houk. Virdon was very different than Houk. He was aloof, exacting, and not open to players' opinions.

A major renovation of Yankee Stadium, which opened in 1923, necessitated the Yankees to play in 1974 and 1975 in Shea Stadium, home of the New York Mets. Shea Stadium was expected to challenge Murcer. Instead of Yankee Stadium's friendly 296 feet down the right field and 344 feet to straightaway right (the areas where he hit most of his homers), Shea Stadium measured 338 feet down the right field line and 371 feet to the right field power alley.

Murcer quickly grew disenchanted with Shea Stadium. In mid-May, he said, "The Mets can have it. It'll be like playing on the road for two years for me."[20] While Bobby hit well for average at Shea, his power was non-existent.

On May 28, the Yankees were mired in last place, losing 13 of their last 16 games. Murcer was batting .250 and hadn't homered in 150 at-bats. Without warning, Virdon moved Murcer from center to right field and put Elliott Maddox in center. It seemed like a small move, but it had a tremendous impact on Bobby. It hurt his pride. After all, wasn't he the Yankees' superstar center fielder? Upset, he complained to Virdon to no avail. Virdon explained the move to the media: "Bobby is a good center fielder, but Maddox is better. The move is good for the team."[21]

In an exciting 1974 AL East race, the Yankees moved into first place on September 4 and led until September 23, 1974. The hard-charging

Baltimore Orioles proved unstoppable as they won 14 of the final 15 games. The Yankees went 5-1 the final week but finished two games out of first. Murcer bashed his first homers of the season at Shea Stadium on September 21 and 22, the 153rd and 154th games of the season. In the final 10 games, he drove in 13 runs and delivered three game-winning hits. He ended up with just 10 homers, two at Shea Stadium, 88 RBI, and a .274 average. Many observers wondered if his power outage hadn't cost the Yankees the pennant.

Phil Pepe of *The Daily News* wrote that Murcer, a four-time All-Star, hadn't earned his $120,000 in 1974. "Fans knew it, his teammates knew it, and Murcer knew it."[22]

The Yankees made a bombshell deal on October 22, 1974, when they traded Murcer to the San Francisco Giants for outfielder Bobby Bonds. The trade blindsided Murcer. "I felt devastated, stunned, and betrayed," said the 28-year-old.[23] He said George Steinbrenner assured him that as long as he owned the Yankees, he would be part of the team.

It was one of the biggest one-for-one trades in baseball history and the first time $100,000 players had been swapped for each other. Bonds was a power-hitting, right-handed outfielder the Yankees sought. He had more power and speed than Murcer. Many felt he was the best player in baseball. Yankee outfield Ron Blomberg said, "The trade was outstanding for the Yankees. Bonds is a super, super superstar. Murcer is a star, but I don't think he's a superstar."[24]

Neither Murcer nor Bonds had gotten along with their managers. Perhaps, a change of scenery was the answer to restoring them to their potential.

Giants manager Wes Westrum was excited about adding Murcer. "Bobby is a very aggressive hitter. He has a good arm and above-average speed. He's a bulldog competitor," he said.[25]

Although Bobby tried to be positive, he quickly soured on San Francisco and the Giants. The Giants finished fifth in the NL West in 1974, drew the fewest fans in the National League, and played in one of the worst stadiums in baseball. To make matters worse, there were rumors the club would be sold and moved to Toronto or some other locale.

Murcer made headlines more often in 1975 for his constant complaining about cold and windy Candlestick Park than his on-field performance. In July, he complained, "This is the worst place I've ever seen. It's summer everywhere in the United States, but here. I wouldn't come to a game here if they were playing in the World Series. I'm just glad I don't have to pay to get in."[26]

Murcer played well enough to make the All-Star team for the fifth consecutive year. He had predicted hitting 25-30 home runs, but he hammered just 11. He was, however, productive. He led the team with 91 RBI while batting .298 as the Giants finished third. The club rewarded him with a lucrative $175,000 contract. He became the highest-paid player in Giants' history.

Murcer and the Giants got off to slow starts in 1976. Fans and the media quickly let the Oklahoma outfielder know they didn't think he was earning his money. By Memorial Day, the Giants had settled in the NL West basement. Murcer, a constant target of criticism, informed the media he would no longer answer baseball-related questions. Still bitter about the trade from the Yankees and unhappy in San Francisco, he wanted to be somewhere else.

He was criticized for his poor play and failure to play up to his potential. The media took him to task for his puny batting average and occasional home run power. One San Francisco sports columnist wrote that Murcer was the most hated player to wear a Giants uniform.

At the end of July, Murcer was hitting .257 with 14 homers, and the Giants were mired in last place. First-year San Francisco manager Bill Rigney said, "Murcer hasn't had the type of season at bat or in the field that we expected."[27] The outfielder made it clear he wanted to be traded.

Even though Murcer led the club in homers (23) and RBI (91), it was a joyless season.

"This has been the most miserable year I've spent in baseball," he said. "There have been only a few bright spots, but everything else is a downer."[28]

The Giants granted Murcer's wish, trading him to the Chicago Cubs on February 11, 1977. It was a five-player transaction that boiled down to the 31-year-old Murcer for 26-year-old third baseman Bill Madlock, a two-time batting champ. After batting .354 and .339, Madlock sought a substantial raise and a multi-year contract. Although the Cubs refused to meet his demands, they awarded Murcer a 5-year, $1.1 million contract. He became the highest-paid player in Cubs' history.

The veteran slugger assured Cub fans they wouldn't miss Madlock. "I'll hit more home runs, out run him on the bases, and play better in the field," he said.[29] Murcer's adrenalin started pumping when he thought of the wind blowing out at the cozy confines of Wrigley Field. Fans expected him to slam 30-40 homers.

The Cubs were baseball's surprise team in the first half of the 1977 season. They parlayed good, all-round play with solid pitching to stake an 8.5-game lead at the end of June. Relief pitcher Bruce Sutter protected many late-inning leads, tallying 20 saves. The club faltered in the final two months, going 20-40 down the stretch. In September, outfielder Jerry Morales and Murcer went 19 and 23 days, respectively, without an RBI. Morales suffered from a wrenched back, while Murcer battled a bruised heel. The Cubs finished 20 games out of first. Murcer led the club in home runs (27) and RBI (89) and batted .265.

The Cubs acquired powerful right-handed Dave Kingman during the off-season. The move was expected to bolster the offense and benefit the left-handed swinging Murcer. Kingman would afford him protection in the lineup, making it harder for hurlers to pitch around him.

The slugger's presence in 1978 didn't help Murcer, who struggled all year. He launched just three homers at Wrigley Field and nine overall. He was lackadaisical in the field and disinterested at bat. Manager Herman Franks reportedly lectured him in a clubhouse meeting about not hustling. "You embarrassed me," complained Murcer afterward. "What do you think you have been doing to me?" bellowed Franks.[30]

Murcer was labeled a "$340,000 white elephant."[31] His repeated failures with men on base with less than two outs outraged Cubs fans. Critics said his RBI total (64) was a disgrace for any player batting in the middle of the order. Murcer was at the center of another disappointing season.

A dark cloud hung over the Cubs outfielder when he reported to spring training in 1979. Pre-season scouting reports cast him in a bad light. One scout said, "Murcer appears to have lost interest in the game." Another wrote, "The Cubs tried like hell to trade him (he nixed a trade to Texas), but a guy with a $320,000 contract coming off that kind of season is a leper. He's only 32, but there's no pop left in his bat."[32]

Fans booed Bobby, the constant target of their wrath on sports talk radio during the winter. They thought he was an overpaid underachiever.

The 1979 season was only a few weeks old before manager Herman Franks criticized his highest-paid player. "Murcer is lackadaisical, but that's not his trouble. His greatest problem is that he doesn't realize he's taking a lackadaisical approach to the game."[33] With the team going nowhere, Bobby was at odds with his manager, the fans, and the media.

Young right fielders Scott Thompson, 23, and Mike Vail, 27, pushed Murcer for playing time. It was clear they were the future of the Cubs. "I can still play this game; I don't care what anyone says," he insisted.[34]

The Cubs traded Murcer to the New York Yankees on June 26, 1979, for minor league pitcher Paul Semall. "We gave Murcer a good shot this summer, but I wasn't satisfied with his production from the number five or number six spots in the lineup," said general manager Bob Kennedy.[35]

The trade was one of the happiest days in Murcer's life. "I feel like a new man," he said. "I've never been happier in my life. New York is where I belong. It's like coming home again."[36]

Murcer lacked the drive in San Francisco and Chicago he had in New York. He developed some bad habits and didn't care if he corrected them or not. He claimed he hadn't lost any power; it was just a matter of mechanics that needed to be fixed.

Some writers thought he was a shadow of himself. They wrote that if he wasn't washed up, he was close to it. After joining the Yankees, he had 5 RBI in his first 30 games and just one hit in the last 15. But, he turned in one of his most memorable games on August 6, 1979. Earlier that day, he had eulogized 30-year-old Yankee catcher Thurman Munson, who had died when a private plane he was piloting crashed en route to his home in Canton, Ohio. Munson was one of Bobby's best friends. Despite the emotional toll of the funeral, Murcer requested to play that night in a nationally televised game against the first-place Baltimore Orioles at Yankee Stadium. He slammed a three-run homer in the seventh inning and drilled a dramatic two-run game-winning single in the ninth to account for all the runs in a 5-4 victory.

Although the Yankees finished fourth in 1979, they had enjoyed success in Murcer's absence. They won two pennants (1976 and 1977) and a World Series (1977).

Murcer faced the prospect of platooning for the first time in his career. The Yankees were laden with outfielders. They included Reggie Jackson,

Ruppert Jones, Oscar Gamble, Lou Piniella, Joe Lefebvre, Bobby Brown, and Paul Blair. Of the eight, Murcer probably ranked seventh.

Manager Dick Howser used Murcer sparingly in the first six weeks of the 1980 season. Murcer complained to owner George Steinbrenner and the media. He couldn't figure out why he wasn't playing, and he resented it. He stressed he needed to play regularly to maintain his stroke. He received more playing time when Oscar Gamble broke his foot, Ruppert Jones had stomach surgery, and Reggie Jackson nursed a series of minor injuries. Limited to 297 at-bats, Bobby delivered 13 homers and 10 game-winning hits.

Although Murcer long denied feeling pressured to be touted as the next Mickey Mantle, he was more honest near the end of his career. "It's nice to say it didn't bother me, but that's not the truth. I was deeply hurt, hurt to the point where I didn't know who I should talk to. It was all pretty tough to handle."[37]

The Yankees captured the 1980 AL East pennant with 103 wins. The New Yorkers faced the Kansas City Royals in the American League Championship Series. After the Yankees lost the series opener, Murcer started Game 2. He faltered in two crucial situations. Trailing 3-0 in the top of the fifth, Graig Nettles smacked an inside-the-park home run. Bucky Dent grounded out, and Bobby Brown walked. Willie Randolph doubled Brown home, making it 3-2. Murcer struck out, stranding the potential tying run on third base. In the top of the eighth inning, Willie Randolph singled with one out. Murcer struck out again. Bob Watson followed with a double, but Randolph was thrown out at the plate.

Bobby cried in the clubhouse when he blamed himself for the 3-2 defeat. "It seems I was never destined to be on a winning team," he told reporters.[38] The Royals won Game 3 and swept the series.

It was a disappointing end to the season. "They shunted me aside," lamented Murcer. "They were telling me I was done in certain areas. I was telling them I wasn't. I tried to fight it, probably as hard as anybody. I tried my best to open their eyes. When that didn't happen, I figured I was beat."[39]

The Yankees had an abundance of talent in 1981. The veteran, whose main value was as a left-handed pinch-hitter and designated hitter, was nearly cut in the spring. The major league strike interrupted the season from June 12 to August 9. The strike necessitated a split-season format. The Yankees, winners of the first half, faced the Milwaukee Brewers, winners of the second half, in the American League Divisional Series (ALDS). Murcer, limited to 50 games in the regular season, saw little action in the post-season. New York defeated Milwaukee, 3 games to 2, in the ALDS and then swept the Oakland A's in three games in the American League Championship Series.

The Yankees faced the Los Angeles Dodgers in the 1981 World Series. New York lost in six games, and Murcer had two disappointing pinch-hitting appearances. In Game 3, the Yankees trailed 5-4 when he pinch-hit for pitcher Rudy May with runners on first and second and one out. He popped up a bunt to the third baseman, who completed a double play to kill a potential rally. In the final game, he pinch-hit for starter Tommy John in the fourth inning with runners on first and second, two outs, and the score tied 1-1. He flied out.

Murcer, 35, became a free agent at the end of the season. His future was tenuous. The Yankees invited him to spring training after no other team signed him. Owner George Steinbrenner called him the consummate Yankee and the best pinch-hitter in the American League. Bobby was one of three left-handed designated hitters at the club's disposal. Could the Yankees afford to keep him? A hot streak at the end of spring training earned him a spot on the Yankees roster.

Used almost strictly against right-handed pitching, Murcer saw action in 65 games in 1982 as a pinch-hitter or designated hitter. He displayed some power with 7 homers in 141 at-bats.

He made the roster in 1983, but he was seldom used. He was on the verge of being cut almost daily. The Yankees placed him on waivers on June 20 to give him his unconditional release. The club needed the roster spot to bring up rookie Don Mattingly to replace injured Ken Griffey Sr. at first base.

Murcer exchanged his baseball uniform for a spot in the WPIX broadcasting booth. He enjoyed a long broadcasting career and witnessed the Yankees win four World Series titles from 1996-2000. The 17-year veteran was disappointed that he never won a World Series in 13 seasons with the Yankees.

He was diagnosed with a brain tumor on Christmas Eve, 2006. He had surgery that week and doctors later discovered the tumor was malignant. The beloved Yankee died on July 12, 2008, at age 62.

Upon his death, Phil Pepe of the New York *Daily News* wrote, "Had Murcer come along at another time, it might have been different. Had he been surrounded by better teammates, had he come along five years after Mantle retired, had he not had to suffer under the inevitable comparisons, Bobby Murcer might have never left the Yankees in the first place. He might have stayed here for his entire career, and the numbers he could have achieved in New York might even have qualified him for the Hall of Fame."[40]

CHAPTER 8

STEVE WHITAKER
THE HOT-TEMPERED SLUGGER

Steve Whitaker could be the next big hitter for the Yankees.
He has one of those beautiful Yankee Stadium swings. We expect
big things from him.
—New York Yankees manager Ralph Houk

The first time Hall of Famer Joe DiMaggio saw Steve Whitaker, the Tacoma, Washington, left-handed hitter, was 18 years old and attending a Yankees camp. He watched the youngster take batting practice for a while before turning to manager Ralph Houk and saying, "That kid can't miss."[1]

"When Joe D first saw Steve, he thought he was the best-looking hitter he had ever seen," recalled Houk. "He didn't know his stats, but he was terribly impressed with his style."[2]

With high praise like that, how could a player's major league career consist of parts of five seasons, three with the Yankees, and only one season as a starter?

That praise, however, was often countered with labels like "hot head," "his own worst enemy," and "get him mad, and he'll get himself out." As talented as Steve Whitaker was, his uncontrollable temper proved his downfall.

Whitaker grew up in a poor family on the wrong side of the tracks. Times were tough, and he was often left on his own. "We didn't have any money," he said. "I lived in a house that had plaster falling from the ceiling."[3] Sports helped keep him out of trouble. At Lincoln High in Tacoma, he was the school's starting quarterback and star baseball player. Ben Chaney, a lumber tycoon who sponsored local baseball teams, is credited with discovering Steve. The Tacoma athlete played on Chaney-sponsored teams from age 9 through high school.

According to Steve, there wasn't much negotiation when Yankees scout Eddie Taylor approached the family about signing the Tacoma teen to a contract. Whatever amount Taylor offered, the family would accept. Anything looks good when you have nothing.

The Yankees signed the 6-foot, 180-pound Whitaker for $5,500, a cheap amount. While the club thought it was getting a bargain, it was unknowingly getting damaged goods. "I'd hurt my arm, and I had been hiding it," said Steve. "I'd go to tryouts and hit well, and they'd want me to take infield. I didn't listen. I acted like I hadn't heard them. I'd go change into my civilian clothes. When I came out, they'd say, 'We wanted to see you throw.' Oh, I'd say I didn't know that. I faked the hell out of it."[4]

In 1962, the Yankees sent Whitaker, 19, to the Rookie League with strict instructions to the coaching staff not to mess with his swing. It was smooth, powerful, and ideally suited for Yankee Stadium. He attracted more attention in 1963, when he clouted 14 home runs in a little more than 100 games, splitting his time with three teams.

His breakout year came in 1964, at age 21, with Greensboro in the Class-A Carolina League. He sat out the season's first six weeks with a broken hand. He told club officials he tripped over some bats, but the truth was he injured his hand in a fight at the Valhalla Bar in Hollywood, Fla. When he returned to action, he slugged 27 homers, drove in 100 runs, and batted .303 in 113 games. That got the attention of the Yankees' brass.

Unfortunately, Steve earned a reputation as a hothead. He argued with umpires, threw helmets, smashed water coolers, and admonished fans. His temper, not opposing pitchers, was his biggest enemy. He was always mad at somebody, including himself. He didn't like to lose, and he didn't like to make an out.

"I really beat myself up," he said. "There was no room for failure in my game. I expected too much from myself in every at-bat. If I went two-for-four, I beat myself up over the two outs. I used to beat myself up terribly."[5]

Steve, 22, started the 1965 season with Columbus (Georgia) in the Class-AA Southern League. He got off to a terrific start, hitting .375 in the first six weeks. Then he experienced a horrendous 0-for-41 slump, and his average plummeted to the .220s. As his average plunged, his temper rose, and his detrimental antics increased. He stopped running out grounders and hustling. Manager Loren Babe warned him to straighten out, but he didn't seem to be able to control himself.

"I was going crazy," he said. "I didn't know what to do or how to end the slump. I had been in slumps before, but nothing like this."[6]

The breaking point came when Whitaker hit a lazy fly ball to center field; he threw his helmet down and ran directly into the dugout. As he stepped into the dugout, the outfielder dropped the ball and threw the embarrassed Whitaker out at first base. The next day he was demoted to Class-A Fort Lauderdale in the Florida State League. Before he departed, Babe told him, "You're never going to be what you should be unless you control your temper. You're hurting yourself and your ball club."[7]

The demotion was a rude shock. It could have been the end of the line for the potential star. Fortunately, Fort Lauderdale manager Jack Reed had a knack for working with young players and instilling confidence in them. He was patient and understanding. He was willing to forget about Steve's bad behavior. Reed asked him to help the team win the Florida State League title. And that's what he did. Reed served as a calming influence and helped him control his emotions on the field. At the end of the season, the Yankees informed Steve that he would be invited to spring training camp in 1966.

The demotion was a turning point in Whitaker's career. Whitaker said about Reed, "He changed my viewpoint of this game. He made me realize that nobody gets a hit every at-bat."[8] Steve also did some deep thinking about his future.

Years later, Reed was asked who was the best player he ever managed, and he replied, without hesitation, "Steve Whitaker." He added: "Steve could have been a superstar if he had his head on right. He was an All-American kid off the field, but on the field, he was a Jekyll and Hyde. If he got a hit the first time up, he'd be super the rest of the game. If he popped up, there's no telling what he might do. He might throw his helmet, break his bat, or not run the ball out. He couldn't control his emotions on the field."[9]

In 1966, Whitaker attended the Yankees' spring training camp, where he gained some valuable experience and a boost of confidence. The invitation was the Yankees' way of letting him know they thought he could be a major leaguer. After spring training, he was assigned to the Columbus team. He was reunited with manager Jack Reed, who had been promoted from Fort Lauderdale.

Steve started the season displaying all the traits the Yankees were convinced he possessed. By mid-May, he was among the Southern League leaders in homers, average, and RBI. He blasted 5 homers during a 7-game road trip. He credited his surge to laying off bad pitches and not getting mad at himself. He admitted the inability to control his temper was his downfall in 1965.

On May 11, the left-handed slugger became the first player to hit two balls out of Evansville, Indiana's Bosse Field, one of the largest parks in the league. Right field was 339 feet and featured a 12-foot brick wall. In the first inning, with a man on, Whitaker walloped a ball over the right-field wall. It traveled an estimated 380 feet. He duplicated the feat in the ninth inning with two men on. This time the ball traveled an estimated 440 feet and landed in the street behind the wall. He added a two-run single for three hits, two homers, and 7 RBI.

Steve was promoted to Class Triple-A Toledo in the International League after spending two-thirds of the season at Columbus. In a total of 122 games, he compiled 25 homers, 87 RBI, and a .300 average. The Yankees called him up on August 22. New York manager Ralph Houk announced that Whitaker, 23, would play against lefties and righties for the remainder of the season.

"Steve Whitaker could be the next big hitter for the Yankees," enthused Houk. "He has one of those beautiful Yankee Stadium swings. We expect big things from him."[10] Walking into the Yankees' clubhouse and stepping onto the field at Yankee Stadium was a surreal experience for Whitaker. He idolized Mickey Mantle since he was nine years old. Now, he was going to be in the same lineup and outfield with him. He wondered what he would say to Mantle, how he would address him and how he should act. The day he reported, however, Mantle broke the ice almost immediately. He came over to Steve in the clubhouse and said, "What took you so long? I thought you would be here a year or so ago. Anything you need, let me know."[11]

Whitaker made his major league debut on August 23, 1966, at Yankee Stadium against California Angels right-handed starter Dean Chance. He was so nervous in his first at-bat that he tripped over the dugout steps going to the plate. He swung at everything the former Cy Young winner threw. After striking out, he returned to the dugout dejected. Houk asked him if he was nervous. "To tell you the truth, Skip, I don't remember seeing a single pitch," he replied.[12]

He registered his first major league hit off Chance in his third at-bat. It was the start of a tremendous debut week. The Yankees opened a three-game series against Detroit on August 26. Whitaker tripled and homered against Earl Wilson in the opener. The following game, he whacked a pair of doubles and an inside-the-park homer. He touched southpaw Mickey Lolich for a grand slam in the series' final game. He went 7-for-12 (.583) with three homers, 7 RBIs, a pair of doubles, and a triple. He was named American League Player of the Week.

Steve credited his success to being relaxed. He didn't feel any pressure because he didn't feel like he should have been in the big leagues. True to his word, Houk started Whitaker every game, except one, down the stretch. The Yankees, mired in last place, had nothing to lose.

Pitchers quickly made adjustments and exploited Whitaker's weaknesses. The Yankee rookie tried to pull everything down the short right-field line. Pitchers countered with a steady diet of soft slop on the outside corner. The result was a truckload of ground balls and weak fly balls. As Steve began to press, his emotions dominated. Once he got mad, pitchers could get him out with pitches right down the middle of the plate.

"I think I could have been a hell of a lot better player if I had analyzed the game to see what good players do on a daily basis—how they prepare and how they adjust," he said years later. "In the big leagues, it's all about adjustment. When the pitchers started adjusting, I didn't make the same adjustments back to them."[13]

Steve was hitting .290 on September 6 when his average started to dip. He finished with a .246 batting average, 7 home runs, and 15 RBI. His late-season performance, however, was a cause of optimism.

Yankee President Mike Burke touted Whitaker, a major part of the youth movement, as the future of the heralded franchise, which had fallen on hard times. "Steve has all the equipment to succeed," offered Burke. "He has the chemistry that could give him star quality. A lot of virility, full of fire, and an attractive personality."[14]

Whitaker, the heir apparent to Roger Maris in right field and Mickey Mantle in the power department, signed a contract for $9,000 during spring training. When he was issued Maris's old locker and his number 9 uniform, it represented more overwhelming pressure for him. It wasn't what he needed.

In 1967, Steve was expected to platoon in right field with Bill Robinson, another up-and-comer with the potential to be a superstar. Whitaker became the everyday right fielder when center fielder Joe Pepitone injured his ankle, and Robinson replaced him.

Steve exerted more pressure on himself as he failed to generate the expected power. As a result, his temper exploded more frequently. There were run-ins with umpires, broken bats, and smashed helmets. When he struggled, the veteran Mantle invited him to dinner at his apartment. They talked for hours. Mantle shared his similar experiences and tried to lift Steve's spirits.

Steve's hottest streak of 1967 came from July 20 to August 1. He put together a 10-game hitting streak, including five consecutive multi-hit games. He collected 17 hits and lifted his average 30 points to .260. He faded late in the season, and his power became almost non-existent. He slugged just one home run in the season's final two months. In 122 games, he batted .243 with 11 home runs and 50 RBI. He had expected to hit 35 home runs. Steve, who never felt relaxed or in a groove, and the Yankees were disappointed.

Whatever confidence and optimism Steve gained in 1967 dissipated quickly in 1968. He had a sore arm for most of spring training and his playing time was limited. He started the first five games of 1968 but went 1-for-17 (.058). He quickly earned a place on the bench. Manager Ralph Houk relegated him to pinch-hitting and an occasional start against right-handed pitching. He exhibited no power, and his average never approached the .200 mark. Steve was frustrated by not playing every day.

Steve was batting only .121 at the beginning of July when he reported to Fort Drummond to serve his two-week stint in the Army Reserve. The Yankees' outfield solidified with Roy White in right, Joe Pepitone in center, and Andy Kosco in left while he was gone. He received a telegram at Fort Drummond from the Yankees telling him to report to Triple-A Syracuse in the International League. The club hoped he would regain his batting eye. It was a shock, and it hurt. When he left Fort Drummond, he headed for Atlantic City instead of Syracuse. He was AWOL for about ten days, much to the displeasure of the Yankees. He played 11 games for Syracuse before being shipped to Triple-A Hawaii in the Pacific Coast League. The Yankees called him up at the end of September, and he got into two games.

"The whole year was like a nightmare," said Whitaker. "I didn't play much in spring training or early in the season. I'm a streak hitter, and I can carry a club. But I can't do it if I'm not playing regularly." [15]He figured his days in New York were limited. Left unprotected by the Yankees in the expansion draft that fall, the Kansas City Royals selected the 26-year-old outfielder. His outstanding potential appealed to them. The Royals were well aware of his temper and his tendency to get down on himself, but they hoped they could change that.

Yankees manager Ralph Houk praised Whitaker. "Steve can be a star, not only a big leaguer but a real star. He is a good kid, and I hope he makes it in Kansas City."[16] Not everyone, however, was so optimistic. Yankee scout Steve Souchouk bet Royals manager Joe Gordon that the hot-tempered Whitaker wouldn't make it through one season with the club.

Whitaker got into hot water with the Royals before reporting to spring training. Moe Drabowsky, the Royals player rep, called him and told him not to report to spring training. The players union called for a boycott to protest an unresolved point in the first collective bargaining agreement between the owners and the players. Steve decided not to report. He didn't know; however, he would be one of just three or four Royals players not to report. When he finally reported to camp, general manager Cedric Tallis met him and demanded to know why he hadn't reported earlier.

Souchouk collected his bet from Joe Gordon when the Royals traded Whitaker and pitcher John Gelnar to the Seattle Pilots for Lou Piniella on April 1. Piniella, a rookie, also hadn't reported to training camp. It seemed the two clubs were trading headaches. When Whitaker arrived at the Pilots' training camp, general manager Marvin Milkes delivered a straightforward message to him: "If you try any of that crap here, you're gone. You won't even get a uniform to think about putting on."[17]

The Royals got the best of the deal as Piniella was named 1969 American League Rookie of the Year, while Whitaker was shipped to Triple-A Vancouver after 69 games with the Pilots. When the Pilots told him to report to Vancouver, Whitaker again went AWOL. This time for about two weeks. Steve compiled a .250 average and 6 homers with Seattle. The stat sheet didn't reflect the number of headaches he gave the Pilots' manager, Joe Schultz, and the front office.

The Milwaukee Brewers (formerly the Seattle Pilots) traded Whitaker and Dick Simpson to the San Francisco Giants for Bob Bolin on December 12, 1969. The Giants used Steve mainly as a pinch hitter. The club sent Whitaker to Triple-A Phoenix in early May. He found his groove, smashing 16 home runs and driving in 53 runs. But, his time in Phoenix wasn't trouble-free. He had a run-in with manager Hank Sauer, and they almost came to blows. Whitaker once again assured himself of a one-way ticket out of town. He played in 1971 and 1972 with Hawaii in the Pacific Coast League with no major league teams interested in him. Approaching age 30, he retired in 1973.

Years later, he professed he had no bitterness about his major league career. He acknowledged, however, the extraordinary expectations others had of him. "It really hurts a player to be billed as the next Mickey Mantle," he said. "Instead of being his own man, a player comes up trying to fill someone else's shoes."[18]

Few players hated to make an out more than Steve Whitaker. And he was never able to accept failure. "You have to take this game seriously, but I took it too seriously," he admitted.[19]

CHAPTER 9

BILL ROBINSON
THE BLACK MICKEY MANTLE

God's here.

—What many fans thought after Bill Robinson
homered on Opening Day 1967

When 23-year-old Bill Robinson stepped into the batter's box on Opening Day, April 10, 1967, the hopes of Yankee fans and the front office weighed on his shoulders. The Yankees hit rock bottom the previous year, finishing in last place for the first time since 1912. Fans and executives looked for hope, a hero who could lead the way back to the glory days.

"There was never a player who looked more like a star than Bill Robinson—tall, lean and graceful," observed Charles Dexter, a New York sportswriter.[1] Besides his good looks, the 6-foot-3, 190-pounder could hit, field, run and throw. He hit .333 in spring training and was voted the James P. Dawson Award as the outstanding Yankee rookie in spring training.

Robinson strolled to the plate in the top of the first inning before 44,000-plus fans at RFK Stadium in Washington, D.C. The right fielder batted second, behind Tom Tresh and ahead of Mickey Mantle. He grounded out to the shortstop. He no longer had the Opening Day jitters when he came up in the top of the third inning. After Tresh doubled, Robinson slammed a 380-foot home run over the left-center field fence and into the bullpen. It ignited a seven-run inning en route to an 8-0 win over the Senators.

Despite the elation that day, the home run may have been the worst thing to happen to Robinson. He had been labeled not just "the next Mickey Mantle" but the "Black Mickey Mantle." The Yankees had been slowly integrating, adding their first Black player, Elston Howard, in 1955. Howard, voted the American League's Most Valuable Player in 1963, was popular with fans. But he was 37 and approaching the end of his career. Other Black Yankee prospects included Horace Clarke, Jerry Kenney, and Roy White. Robinson faced unbearable pressure—he was expected to replace a hero, save a franchise, and lift up the Black race.

When the home run landed in the bullpen, Robinson said many fans thought, "God's here."[2] Years later, Yankee manager Ralph Houk admitted he thought he had the next superstar in Bill Robinson. Even before spring training, however, Robinson cautioned the media that "it's too early to compare me to Mickey Mantle."[3] That didn't stop them.

After the Opening Day home run, Robinson spiraled into a depressing, three-year slump that almost ended his major league career. Unrealistic expectations made it difficult for the heralded rookie to succeed. "I was supposed to be the next Mickey Mantle when I was traded from Atlanta to New York," he said. "That's something I would never, ever do in life, to say this guy reminds me of that guy."[4]

Platooning with rookie Steve Whitaker in right field, Robinson struggled after Opening Day. In early June, he was batting .101 (8-for-79). Yankee beat writer Jim Ogle wrote, "The fewer the hits, the harder he tries. He's as tight as a drum at the plate and completely off stride."[5]

Bill said, "After a while, I started to feel the pressure. Because I knew the club expected a lot from me, and I couldn't help. And, the harder I tried, the worse it got."[6] Mantle tried to alleviate the pressure, telling the rookie, "You can't be me. You have to be yourself."[7]

Trying to shake the slump, Bill studied his stance and noticed he was striding too fast and tying up his hands. As a result, every pitcher was jamming him inside, and he had trouble getting the ball out of the infield. He opened his stance about six inches and cut down his stride. Then he began to hit and regained some of his confidence.

The game started to be fun again, and he felt more comfortable at the plate. Unfortunately, he pulled a hamstring trying to beat out a hit in Kansas City. The Yankees, unwilling to risk a more serious injury, kept him out of the lineup for nearly three weeks. When the disappointing season concluded, Robinson sported a .196 average with seven homers and 29 RBI in 116 games.

Yankees manager Ralph Houk still had faith in his potential star. "Bill battled through a rough couple months, straightened himself out, pulled a hamstring, and was out three weeks," he said. "Then he played the rest of the season on one leg. He'll prove me right."[8]

Based on his minor league performance and scouting reports, Houk and the Yankee front office were convinced Robinson was a much better player than they saw in 1967. He had been an All-State baseball player and a star basketball player growing up in Elizabeth, Pa., near Pittsburgh. The Milwaukee Braves signed the 18-year-old for a $10,000 bonus.

Bill gained attention in his third minor league season when he batted .316 for Waycross, Ga., in the Class-A Georgia-Florida League. His performance was even more impressive because he achieved it while battling discrimination and racism in the Deep South.

In 1964, he batted .348 for the Yakima Braves and won the Northwest League batting title. He was promoted to the Class-AAA Atlanta Crackers in the International League, where he showed he could handle better pitching. In 1966, he played for Class-AAA Richmond, batting .312, bashing 20 homers, and driving in 79 runs. He doubled his home run and RBI totals from the previous season.

He made his major league debut with the Atlanta Braves on September 20, 1966. He appeared in six games and collected three hits, including his first against Al McBean of the Pirates.

Because the Braves had a set outfield of Rico Carty, Mack Jones, and Hank Aaron, Robinson's role was limited. The Yankees, however, sought a right-handed hitting outfielder. Although Robinson only had 11 at-bats in the majors, the Yankees coveted his youth and potential. The Yankees liked him so much that they traded their everyday veteran third baseman Clete Boyer to Atlanta in December 1966 for him.

The Yankees resisted sending Robinson to the minors after his disappointing 1967 rookie season. Instead, they nursed him, encouraged him, and praised him. The club sent him to the Florida Instruction League to work on his swing and gain experience playing third base.

The Yankee outfielder was eager to start the 1968 season. He had a lot to prove to himself and others. He wanted to erase the memories of the past season. He opened the season platooning with Steve Whitaker in right field. When center fielder Joe Pepitone was injured in mid-April, he took over center field duties.

Mired in a deep slump, his bat remained silent. After the All-Star break, he received more playing time and began to look like the highly touted player the Yankees traded for. His confidence soared as he played every day against all kinds of pitching. He batted .282 in the second half of the season. He finished with a .240 average, six homers, and 40 RBI.

He said, "I guess everyone has to learn a lesson. I used to think homers were the most important thing. I finally convinced myself; however, they aren't as important as hits and a good average."[9] He was convinced that if he had gotten off to a better start, he could have finished with a .300 or better batting average.

Reflecting on his nightmarish season-and-a-half slump, he said, "It wasn't big league pitching that stopped me. The pitching is better in the majors than the minors, but not that much better. At first, I thought I was having bad luck, hitting balls right to fielders. Then, as time went by, I became a psychological case. I started to press. I couldn't relax. I couldn't sleep. The slump got to me. My teammates told me I was trying too hard. That didn't help. It was on my mind all the time."[10]

Houk was encouraged. "In the last two months, Bill looked like the player we expected him to be. I think he's found himself, and he's ready to prove he's a real major leaguer. We know he can run, field, and throw. But we were waiting to see if he could hit, and we've seen it."[11]

Robinson looked to capitalize on the momentum of the second half of the 1968 season. That never happened. The Yankee outfielder struggled from the outset, starting 1-for-29. What was expected to be a breakout season for the 28-year-old turned into a disastrous year. Robinson posted a .171 batting average with just three homers.

Bill owned a .207 lifetime batting average after three seasons and 316 games in the major leagues, and a ton of hype. He had been counted on to be an outstanding right-handed hitter with power. Instead, he was one of the Yankees' biggest disappointments.

Yankees general manager Lee MacPhail said, "I know a lot of people wonder why Bill Robinson is still around. He has too much talent to quit at this point. He has changed his hitting style completely and has made good progress. I was very encouraged by what I saw of him. Bill is a fine athlete and still has a chance to be a good player."[12]

Bill had a poor spring training in 1970, and the Yankees shipped him to Class-AAA Syracuse in the International League. Although the move upset Robinson, the Yankees figured it was the only way their potential star could straighten himself out.

Years later, Robinson reflected on his time in New York. "I tried too hard. I couldn't cope with New York City. I think I would have done better if I had gone to a smaller city like Anaheim or Arlington. But I went from Elizabeth, Pa., to New York City when I was just 23."[13]

Robinson once thought he would conquer the Big Apple but discovered it was a sour bite. He pressed too hard, tried to hit a home run every at-bat to impress the fans, and gripped the bat so tightly he couldn't hit. He dreaded going to Yankee Stadium.

"The boos really tore me up when I was with the Yankees," he said. "All ballplayers hear them, and I couldn't take it. I'd be across the George Washington Bridge and heading home to New Jersey before the people even got to the clubhouse. I just couldn't take it anymore."[14]

At Syracuse, Robinson failed to put up any eye-popping numbers. He and two other "next Mickey Mantle" prospects, Ron Blomberg and

Tony Solaita, helped the Chiefs win the International League title. The Yankees parted ways with the 27-year-old in December 1970 when they traded him to the Chicago White Sox for Barry Moore, a pitcher with one winning season in six years.

The White Sox invited Robinson to spring training in 1971 as a non-roster player. Chicago assigned him to its Class-AAA Tucson team in the Pacific Coast League. Upset by the move, Robinson didn't believe he had been given a fair chance to make the White Sox. He told the team he was quitting baseball. The club told him to be patient because a trade was possible.

He decided to play because he had something to prove. His attitude changed that season. "I adopted an I-don't-give a damn attitude," he recalled. "I eliminated the word pressure from my vocabulary. I learned to relax and have fun. I decided to let my God-given talent shine through. I let the Lord come into my life, and he helped me."[15]

A comment by Los Angeles Dodgers outfielder Willie Davis was the catalyst for the change. Davis, discussing his perspective on baseball, said, "It's not my life, and it's not my wife. Why worry? They can't kill you for making an out or an error. If you mess up, there is always your wife to say, 'I love you' when you come home. That's what is important."[16] With a refreshed attitude, Robinson played out the season. On December 13, 1971, the White Sox traded him to the Philadelphia Phillies for minor league catcher Gerardo Rodriguez. When the 1972 season opened, he was still entrenched in the minors, playing for the Phillies' Class-AAA Eugene, Washington, club in the Pacific Coast League. He batted .304 with 20 homers and 66 RBI in 65 games, making it difficult for the Phillies to ignore him. The Phillies called him up on June 23. After 313 minor league games and two and a half seasons, Bill was back in the major leagues.

He started almost half of the Phillies' games playing all three outfield positions. Although he batted .239, he gave a good account of himself at bat and in the field. Now 30, he was determined to make the most of his chance with the Phillies. However, he wasn't in the 1973 Opening Day lineup, as Willie Montanez was in right, Del Unser in center, and Greg Luzinski in left. Even though he batted .350 in the first three weeks of the season, he wasn't a regular.

Bill went 6-for-9 in a doubleheader on May 19. In a span of eight games, he collected five 3-hit games, earning a starting position. He was confident, and each swing was no longer a matter of life and death. He was among the Top 10 hitters in the National League when he suffered a broken finger and missed almost the entire month of June. Danny Ozark moved him to the leadoff spot when he returned. He went on a power surge in mid-August, blasting five homers in six games. "It's just a case of relaxing and making good contact," he explained.[17]

A painful left elbow, resulting from undergoing surgery to remove bone chips in June, slowed him down in September. His elbow hurt like a sore tooth every time he swung the bat. As a result, he slugged just one homer in September. For the season, he batted .288 and walloped 25 homers. He proved he was the player people once thought he was. Eight seasons after his debut, he found himself.

The emotional high of his career-best season didn't last long. On Opening Day 1974, he found himself on the bench as Mike Anderson started in right field. Hadn't he earned a starting job? The snub irritated him and festered. Robinson exploded when Ozark pinch-hit for him in the eighth inning with two outs and bases loaded in the second game of a doubleheader. Ozark hadn't talked to him before he made the move. Ironically, Robinson won the first game with an 11th-inning squeeze bunt.

Robinson told the media he wanted to be traded to get away from manager Danny Ozark, even if it meant going to the minors. He didn't think he was being treated fairly.

"No one knows how hurt I was I didn't make the Opening Day lineup," he said. "It hurt me as bad as anything that's ever happened to me in baseball. I should have started based on what I did last year. I should have started even if I didn't have a hit in spring training."

He continued his tirade. "I could have said nothing, but I've had it. I'm 30, and I think Ozark is hurting my career. He's completely destroyed my confidence, wrecked my mind. Danny has blown my mind, and I can't cope any longer."[18]

From that point on, Robinson was labeled a malcontent. He was in Ozark's doghouse. He played less and less as his name became more

prevalent in trade rumors. In 1974, he was limited to 280 at-bats (compared to 452 the previous season). On April 5, 1975, Robinson's wish
was granted when the Phillies traded him to the Pittsburgh Pirates for
pitcher Wayne Simpson.

Pirates manager Danny Murtaugh planned to use Bill as a pinch-hitter and defensive replacement in the outfield. Bill appreciated Murtaugh's
straight and honest talk. He had a new attitude. "I've learned to take
things in stride, adjust and keep my mouth shut."[19]

Murtaugh used his bench freely, and Robinson became a semi-
regular. He played all three outfield positions and was the club's primary
right-handed pinch-hitter.

Robinson expanded his role as a super sub in 1976. He filled in for
Richie Hebner at third base and outfielders Richie Zisk, Al Oliver, and
Dave Parker. On June 5, he smashed three home runs in a 15-inning
game against the Padres at Three Rivers Stadium. Relaxed and feeling like
he belonged with the Pirates, he was one of the most productive players
on the team. In 122 games, he batted .303 and slammed 21 homers to
tie Richie Zisk for the team high.

He was the Bucs' leading right-handed slugger. He was voted the
team's Most Valuable Player and earned the Roberto Clemente Memorial
Award for community service. He played five different positions and batted .455 as a pinch-hitter. The extra depth he supplied helped the Pirates
to second place in the National League East, six games behind the Phillies.

Being the number one utility man in baseball wasn't enough for
Robinson, approaching age 34. He knew he didn't have many years left in
the majors and wanted to be an everyday starter. Opportunities opened
up for him as the Bucs traded left fielder Richie Zisk to the Chicago
White Sox, and third baseman Richie Hebner signed as a free agent with
the Philadelphia Phillies.

Pirates manager Chuck Tanner said, "A player like Robinson can do
some things that you can't judge his value on paper. He adds versatility
to our team, and he's been around long enough to adjust to situations."[20]

The Pirates upset Robinson, who expected to be the team's starting third baseman when they traded for third baseman Phil Garner in
mid-March. Robinson ended up splitting his time between first base,

replacing aging and injured Willie Stargell, and left field, virtually play-ing every day.

After a quick start in April 1977, he was hampered by a pulled hamstring in May. He recovered quickly and went on a tear in July and August. He batted .333 in July and drove in 24 runs. The right-handed slugger was even hotter in August, knocking in 28 runs and powering 10 homers. He came to the plate 24 times in a six-week span with a runner on third base and less than two outs. He drove in the runner on 22 of the occasions. "It's all too good to be true," he commented. "Playing regularly and batting cleanup on a team that hits like the Pirates.[21]

When asked what the secret was, he replied, "I don't try that hard anymore. I don't give a damn when I go up to the plate. You're con-cerned, sure, but I go up there perfectly relaxed and let my God-given ability follow through."[22]

No longer a super sub, Robinson proved he was a clutch hitter who could ignite an offense. He set career highs in homers (26) and RBI (104) while hitting .304. Despite the Bucs' 96 wins, they finished five games behind the Phillies in the National League East.

The Bucs traded Al Oliver to the Texas Rangers, opening up left field for Bill. His long road to success was symbolized when he was introduced as part of the Pirates' 1978 Opening Day lineup. "It may have been my most exciting day in my life," he said. "For the first time in 11 years, I was in the Opening Day lineup."[23] The last time he was in an Opening Day lineup was in 1967 with the New York Yankees. And that was only because he was a right-handed hitter.

A thumb injury hampered his performance in 1978. He used a plas-tic bandage to protect his thumb, but it messed up his swing. He lost his power, failed to make solid contact consistently, and his production dipped. The failure to produce as the team's cleanup hitter ate at him. He began to press and swing at bad pitches. Despite a strong final month of the season, his offensive production was way below the previous year. His batting average dropped nearly 40 points; he clubbed 12 fewer homers and drove in 24 fewer runs.

The Pirates put it all together in 1979. Robinson played an integral role, platooning in left field with John Milner and filling in at first base for Willie Stargell. He finished third on the team in home runs (24) and RBI (75), playing in a career-high 148 games. The Bucs moved into first place at the end of July and edged the Montreal Expos by two games in the National League East. They went on to defeat the Cincinnati Reds in the NL Championship Series.

In the 1979 World Series against the Baltimore Orioles, Robinson collected five hits in 19 at-bats as the Bucs won in seven games. In Game 7, Robinson singled with one out with the Pirates trailing 1-0 in the top of the sixth inning. That set the stage for Stargell's two-run blast that gave the Pirates a 2-1 lead, which they never relinquished. The Pirates won 4-1.

The Pirates, looking to improve their pitching, offered Robinson as trade bait during the off-season, but they didn't find any takers. He returned in 1980 and platooned with John Milner in left field. He bruised his Achilles heel and was placed on the 15-day disabled list at the end of July. The Pirate veteran batted fewer than 100 times after the All-Star break.

Bucs manager Chuck Tanner considered Robinson the team's security blanket in 1981. He could play left field, right field, and first base. Tanner used him mainly as a pinch-hitter until he underwent surgery on his Achilles heel. The injury and the players' strike kept him out of the lineup until August 10. He was limited to 39 games.

He saw sparse action with the Pirates in 1982 before he was traded to the Phillies on June 15 for outfielder Wayne Nordhagen. Phillies manager Pat Corrales used the 39-year-old veteran as a pinch-hitter and right fielder.

Granted free agency in November 1982, he re-signed as a free agent with the Phillies. He played just 10 games before Philadelphia released him on June 9, 1983. He accepted a coaching position with the Phillies after his release.

Before his retirement as a player, he said, "The good Lord has blessed me with everything I ever wanted in life. And, in baseball, I've achieved all of my goals. I'm happy and contented now, but I've never forgotten where I came from."[24]

In his 16-year career, he played 1,472 games while slugging 166 homers and batting .258.

George Vecsey of *The New York Times* reflected on Robinson's career after he earned a World Series ring as a coach with the Florida Marlins in 2003. "Bill Robinson is an inspiration to athletes or anyone else who ever had a bad day or a bad couple of years," he wrote. "You can always come back. You can go from failure to the World Series."[25]

After his playing days, Bill served as a major league coach and hitting instructor. He died suddenly on July 27, 2009, in Las Vegas while working as a minor league hitting instructor for the Los Angeles Dodgers.

CHAPTER 10

TONY SOLAITA
THE POWERFUL SAMOAN

Tony has as much power as anyone I have ever seen. I believe
he can hit home runs as far as anyone.
—DETROIT TIGERS MANAGER RALPH HOUK

After a monstrous season for High Point-Thomasville (Hi-Tom) in the Class-A Carolina League, Tolia (Tony) Solaita, a 21-year-old Samoan, made his major league debut on September 16, 1968, with the New York Yankees. The muscular 6-foot, 210-pounder replaced legendary Mickey Mantle at first base in the top of the sixth inning against the Detroit Tigers at Yankee Stadium.

Solaita, who was called up to the Yankees a week earlier, recalled his debut. "Manager Ralph Houk said, 'Tony, you're in there.' I was starting to sweat already. I turned to Rocky Colavito and said, 'I'm going in,' he replied, 'Nothing to it. It's like a Hi-Tom game.' Some Hi-Tom game. I went to first base, and my knees were knocking."[1]

The left-handed swinger nervously stepped into the batter's box in the bottom of the eighth. He wasn't there long as Tigers hurler John Hiller struck him out on four pitches. The 28,000 Yankee fans got a glimpse of the young player some had dubbed the "next Mickey Mantle." Little did they realize it would be his only at-bat with the Yankees over the next five years. Although the Yankees were in fifth place, manager Ralph Houk kept Tony on the bench for the final 11 games of the season. Tony couldn't understand why he didn't get an opportunity to play more.

Five days after his debut, Solaita turned many heads in a home run-hitting exhibition before the Red Sox-Yankees game at Yankee Stadium. He was selected to compete against Mickey Mantle, who was less than two weeks away from retiring after an 18-year career, Rocky Colavito, Carl Yastrzemski, Reggie Smith, and Ken Harrelson. Whoever hit the most home runs in 10 swings would win the competition and $250. Tony topped the bona fide power hitters with four homers, and he just missed a fifth. It was one more reason he merited attention.

But instead of becoming the next Mickey Mantle, the mild-mannered and non-confrontational Solaita got buried in the Yankees farm system. Although the Yankees valued him enough to protect him in the 1968 expansion draft, they never gave him another chance at the big league level. He didn't return to the major leagues until age 27, when the Kansas City Royals selected him in the Rule 5 draft in 1973. Players who had been signed at age 18 or younger need to be added to the team's 40-man roster within five years, or they would be eligible for the Rule 5 draft.

Tony was born in Nuuli on the South Pacific island of Tutuila, part of American Samoa. He is the only native of American Samoa to play in the major leagues. He played cricket on the remote island and moved to Hawaii at age 8, where he was introduced to baseball. Three years later, his family moved to San Francisco.

Tony earned four letters in football and four in baseball at Jefferson High School in suburban Dale City. He tossed a no-hitter in high school, but his bat attracted more attention than his arm. He was an unheralded major league prospect, drawing the attention of the Giants, Yankees, and Orioles. Yankees scout Dolph Camilli, a former Brooklyn Dodger, signed him after one tryout. The signing bonus was a modest $1,000. Years later, Tony joked about his signing bonus. "It was almost nothing," he said. "I signed for a steak dinner, and I had to leave the tip."[2]

In 1965, the Yankees sent the 18-year-old to the Florida Rookie League, where he did little to stand out. The following season, he split his time between the Gulf Coast Rookie League, Class-A Greensboro in the Carolina League, and Class-A Binghamton in the New York-Penn League.

Playing for Class-A Fort Lauderdale in the Florida State League in 1967, Tony captured the Yankees' attention with a record-setting 14 homers. Most of the ballparks were not hitter-friendly. Tony's output convinced the Yankees he had real power. He hammered just four homers the year before. His new-found power resulted from a tip from Fort Lauderdale manager Bill Shantz and Steve Souchock, the Yankees' minor league coordinator. They told him to open his stance. Tony discussed the difference: "Last year, I couldn't see the ball when they pitched me inside. With an open stance, I can see the ball."[3]

The Yankees' next move in 1968 was to loan him to Class-A High Point-Thomasville in the Carolina League. The club was a co-op, which was supplied by 14 different major league teams. Meanwhile, Gary Washington, another Yankee first base prospect, was placed with Kinston, the Yankees' Class-A team in the Carolina League. It was a blow to Solaita's pride.

"The lowest of the low," said Tony, who wanted to continue to play with his friends in the Yankee organization. "What hurt most was having to play against Kinston, the Yankees team in the Carolina League. I felt strange playing against guys who were supposed to be my teammates."[4]

After the slight, he decided to show the Yankees they were wrong. He was determined to do something to make the front office notice him. Playing first base for the Hi-Toms, he forged an incredible season—49 homers, .302 average, 122 RBI, 106 runs scored, and 113 walks in 138 games. In the Carolina League playoffs, he added two more homers, including one off Raleigh-Durham's Jon Matlack, one of the Mets' top prospects. According to Tony, the ball cleared the 370-foot fence and a two-story building behind the fence.

His 49 regular-season homers were tops in organized baseball. Solaita had 25 homers midway through the season, and it appeared he had an excellent chance to top the league record of 55 by Leo (Muscles) Shoals for Reidsville in 1949. But he started pressing for more homers, and soon he stopped hitting altogether. When his average dipped below .300, he tried just to meet the ball. Before long, he was slamming home runs again. His 49 homers were the third highest in Carolina League history, behind Shoals and Leon Wagner, who slugged 51 for Danville in 1956.

Hi-Tom manager Jack McKeon said, "This kid (Tony) has been nothing short of outstanding. This is a good league with good pitching, and he has hit everything in sight. He has tremendous power. He's hit some of the longest shots I've ever seen anyone hit in any league."[5]

Tony's season earned him the 1968 Topps Minor League Player of the Year Award. It marked the first time a Class-A player won the award since its inception in 1958. The 21-year-old was clearly one of the Yankees' brightest prospects.

The Yankees invited Tony to their 1969 spring training camp. With the retirement of Mantle, who led the club with 18 homers in 1968, the New Yorkers were looking for more power in their lineup. Some thought Tony might be able to supply that power. Seven-year veteran Joe Pepitone, who had played plenty of first base before being switched to the outfield, was moving back to first base, according to Yankees manager Ralph Houk. Besides Solaita, other competitors at first base included Gary Washington, Frank Tepedino, and Les Boehmer.

"I'm not expecting to set the camp on fire," said Tony. "I'm going to try to forget about the homers and just meet the ball. I want to show them I can hit consistently."[6] But, he failed to impress the brass, going 2-for-16. He had trouble getting around on the ball and looked bad at the plate.

But no one knew, however, he suffered a hairline fracture in his foot while doing pre-camp exercises. Early x-rays didn't reveal the fracture, and he apparently aggravated it in spring training. The injury didn't come to light until the end of spring training. When he was informed he would be headed to the minors, he looked at the move as possibly helping him in the long run.

Solaita opened the 1969 season at Class-AAA Syracuse, where he struggled before being demoted and loaned to Class-AA Columbus (Ga.), an affiliate of the Chicago White Sox. The move agreed with him, as he blasted nine homers in the first 31 games. He joined the Chicago White Sox Class-AAA Tucson team for the latter part of the season. Playing for three teams, he tallied 23 homers in 110 games.

He returned to the Yankees' spring training camp in 1970, but the club used him sparingly. He failed to stand out at the plate, and the club punched his ticket for Class AAA Syracuse.

The 23-year-old put it all together at Syracuse, where he played for manager Frank Verdi. Platooning with Len Boehmer at first base, he batted .308 with team highs in homers (19) and RBI (87). Despite the showing, the Yankees failed to call him up in September.

The following spring, he went 7-for-15 and thought he had a serious chance of making the Yankees. But Danny Cater, who had been obtained in a trade with the Oakland A's, had played 155 games at first base and batted .302 for the Yankees in 1970. Besides Cater, John Ellis, Curt Blefary, and Felipe Alou also could play first.

Still, Tony was surprised when he was among the first group of players cut. He heard that one of the reasons was he couldn't hit the high and inside pitch. Yet, he said he had such a big year in Syracuse because he had learned to lay off that pitch.

He wondered what more he had to do. After all, he felt he had done everything the Yankees had wanted him to do. "The Yankees won 93 games (in 1970) with those guys, and they want to stick with them," he observed. "They probably had their mindset, and I was out of the picture. I never complain. Houk says I'm in their plans, but you don't know."[7] Disappointed, Solaita let his frustrations show in 1971 as he hit .235 with Syracuse, a 73-point drop from the previous year. In 1972, he struggled to hit .205 with Syracuse before being demoted to Class-AA West Haven. After two lackluster seasons, he said, "I was wrong. I should have tried that much harder. Instead, I sulked."[8]

During the off-season, the Yankees traded Solaita to the Pittsburgh Pirates. The Pirates assigned Tony to their Class-AAA Charleston (W.Va.) team. He admitted the change of scenery might provide a lift. "I don't know what I ever did wrong with the Yankees," he said. "But I don't think they ever considered me."[9]

However, the thought of playing another Class-AAA season soon got Tony down. He considered quitting. Then, he received encouraging news when the Kansas City Royals claimed him in the 1973 Rule 5 draft. He would be reunited with manager Jack McKeon, who had managed him at High Point-Thomasville.

McKeon believed the 27-year-old Solaita was worth the modest $25,000 risk. "I thought Tony deserved the chance. How can they say he can't hit major league pitching if he doesn't get the chance? Tony worked his tail off for me in 1968. Last year, Syd Thrift watched him play for Charleston and reported he could help us. We drafted him on Syd's word."[10]

Tony, who admitted he had some hitting flaws in the past, said he was more mature and disciplined at the plate. He was confident he could play every day and hit in the big leagues. McKeon believed Solaita could provide power from the left side as a pinch-hitter or designated hitter while occasionally filling in for slugger John Mayberry at first base. McKeon added that Tony was a good defensive first baseman with soft hands like Mayberry. When McKeon was told during the off-season that Tony had a blind spot (high and inside), he replied, "That's alright. If he just hits the mistakes, he can hit a ton of homers for us."[11]

During the first two months of the 1974 season, Solaita got an occasional start at designated hitter or first base while also pinch-hitting. His opportunity to play every day came in late June when Mayberry pulled a hamstring. From June 24 through July 11, Tony started 17 consecutive games at first base. He went 19-for-62 (.306) and raised his batting average by almost 20 points to .291.

Tony was feeling confident and comfortable at the plate. He observed, "When you're playing every day, there isn't the pressure like when you get up to the plate once a game. Usually, when you pinch-hit, the game is on the line, and you have to do it right then. But I don't care what my job is as long as I can help the team."[12]

"Tony has been an important part of this team," stressed McKeon. "Early in the season, he was pressing. I think he was trying not to let me down. I told him to go up and get his three rips and not to worry."[13]

The Royals rookie got another opportunity later in the season when Mayberry broke his hand. Playing in 15 consecutive games, Tony batted .250 with three home runs. In the two stints filling in for Mayberry, he batted .281 but failed to show much power. He had, however, proven his point. He could play every day and be productive. Solaita appeared in 96 games for the fifth-place Royals while batting .268 with seven homers and 30 RBI.

Tony was expected to fill the same role with the Royals in 1975. On May 14, the designated hitter electrified the crowd at Tiger Stadium with a tape-measure homer off Lerrin LaGrow. His towering right center field homer hit the light tower about 100 feet up and bounced off the roof about 370 feet away. If the ball had been five feet higher, it would have gone over the roof, a feat only eight other players had achieved.

Tigers manager Ralph Houk, who piloted the Yankees when Solaita was in their farm system, said, "He's got as much power as anyone I've ever seen. I believe he can hit home runs as far as anyone."[14]

"I honestly think Tony could play regularly for a number of clubs and hit 20 home runs a year," added Jack McKeon.[15] While Tony's blast was jaw-dropping, McKeon said he didn't think it was his longest. He cited a home run Tony launched against the Yankees' Dick Tidrow at Shea Stadium in 1974. The ball hit the facing on the second level in right field.

Although Solaita's playing time was limited, McKeon was an obvious fan. He said, "Tony rates among the top 2-3 players I've managed when it comes to on and off-the-field considerations."[16]

Playing in the shadows of John Mayberry at first base and an aging 40-year-old Harmon Killebrew as a pinch-hitter and designated hitter, Solaita was impressive when he got an opportunity to play. In late June, he was batting .301 with seven homers. On June 18, he wrestled the spotlight away from Mayberry and Killebrew when he went 3-for-3 against California fireballer Nolan Ryan, including two homers, four RBI, and five runs scored.

It was the impetus for sportswriters and fans to call for more playing time for Solaita, who had been shoved into the background for two seasons. Ken Picking, a sportswriter for the *Fort Myers News-Press,* suggested Solaita take over Killebrew's role. He wrote, "Tony has shown awesome potential with the bat. At 28, he is reaching his baseball prime, and it would be unjust if it was foolishly wasted."

He continued, "Kansas City knows Tony is not the 'play me or trade me' guy, but they seem to be taking advantage of his quiet, patient personality. He deserves so much more because he has proven himself, and supposedly that's what it takes to earn a regular job."[17]

In early September, Tony added to the argument he should be playing every day when he became the first player to wallop three homers in one game at Anaheim Stadium. He touched Dick Lange for a homer in the fourth inning and then slammed a pair of 450-foot round-trippers off southpaw Mickey Scott in the sixth and ninth innings. "It was my biggest day in baseball," said the Samoan afterward.[18]

Tony appeared in 93 games with 231 at-bats during 1975. Yet, he was second on the Royals in homers with 16, behind Mayberry's 34. His home run ratio (1 per 14.4 at-bats) was better than Mayberry's (1 per 16.2 at-bats) and second in the league to Dave Kingman's (1 per 13.9 at-bats).

Whitey Herzog replaced Jack McKeon as the Royals' manager in late July 1975. Tony opened the 1976 season without his biggest booster in the dugout. Herzog used Tony sparingly as a designated hitter and pinch-hitter. In mid-July, the first-place Royals put him on waivers, and the California Angels immediately claimed him. At the time, Tony hadn't hit a home run in 77 at-bats, and he was batting .235.

Angels manager Dick Williams hoped Solaita could deliver power to an anemic lineup. The club was buried in last place and tied with the St. Louis Cardinals for the fewest homers in the majors. In 1975, the Angels launched just 55 homers, the lowest in the majors. Tony was disappointed to leave a first-place team, but he was looking forward to playing more. Ten days after acquiring Solaita, the Angels fired Dick Williams and replaced him with Norm Sherry. In the second half of the season, Tony played first base regularly.

The Angels created a buzz during the off-season when they acquired free agents Joe Rudi, Don Baylor, and Bobby Grich. Solaita, 30, was penciled in as a starter at first base for the first time. But, minor injuries and a slow start limited his playing time. Manager Norm Sherry gave Don Baylor, Ron Jackson, and Willie Mays Aikens playing time at first base. "I just didn't do the job," admitted Tony. "It's easy to fall into bad habits, and it's hard to get out of them. That's what happened to me.[19] The Angels and Solaita both had disappointing seasons. The Angels finished in fifth place, and Tony hit .241 with 14 homers in a career-high 116 games.

Ron Jackson's hot start at first base in 1978 put Solaita and newly acquired veteran Ron Fairly on the bench. Tony was relegated to pinch-hitting and an occasional start as the designated hitter or first baseman. He delivered in the clutch as a pinch-hitter, going 7-for-19 in the season's first three months. "I've always been able to come off the bench and hit," he said. "It's the toughest job in baseball. You know your teammates are counting on you, and it feels good to come through."[20] Limited to 94 at-bats, Tony batted .223 and delivered one home run.

The Montreal Expos purchased Solaita's contract on December 5, 1978. The Expos wanted him to back up the 37-year-old Tony Perez at first base and pinch-hit. On July 30, he was traded to the Toronto Blue Jays. His role was to give first baseman John Mayberry an occasional breather and be the designated hitter. He adequately filled the roles with the Expos and Blue Jays.

The 32-year-old Solaita was granted free agency on November 1, 1979. Finding no interest from any other major league team, Tony signed with the Nippon Ham Fighters in the Japanese League. He unleashed his power, blasting 155 homers in four seasons, including a high of 45 in 1980. That same year, he unloaded four consecutive homers and drove in 10 runs in a game against the Nankai Hawks. Home run king Sadaharu Oh was the only other Japanese League player to swat four homers in a game.

After Tony's playing career in Japan ended in 1984, the San Francisco Giants expressed some interest in signing the 37-year-old, but he opted to retire. He decided to return to American Samoa to start a youth baseball program. In 1990, he was shot and killed, at age 43, in a property dispute.

Tony Solaita never expressed any bitterness about a career that might have been. A victim of his own potential, he missed an opportunity to perhaps start for an expansion team when the Yankees protected him in 1968.

"I never dreamt I would get my time in (4 years for a major league pension)," he said, near the end of his career. "I was 27 and going nowhere. By the time the Yankees traded me, I was ready to quit. I think I've played well, considering my stats and games played."[21]

RON BLOMBERG
RON BLOMBERG
NEW YORK YANKEES   1st BASE

CHAPTER 11

RON BLOMBERG
THE OFTEN-INJURED JEWISH HERO

In time, the House that Ruth Built may be remembered as the House that Blomberg Remodeled.
—DAVE ANDERSON OF *THE NEW YORK TIMES*

Ron Blomberg should be known for much more than being baseball's first designated hitter, a feat that merely required being in the lineup and timing. As the New York Yankees' number one pick in the amateur draft in 1967, the 6-foot-1, 205-pounder, radiated superstar potential. He could hit for power and average, and he had exceptional speed.

Instead of being one of the greatest sluggers in Yankee history, Blomberg clouted just 52 homers, including a high of 14 in 1972, in parts of eight seasons. His production was limited by a series of injuries, which caused him to miss nearly three seasons, and his inability to hit left-handed pitching.

Blomberg was an elite athlete at Druid Hills High in Atlanta, where he lettered in baseball, football, basketball, and track. He was the first high school athlete to be named to *Parade*'s All-America team in baseball, football, and basketball. He received more than 100 college scholarship offers for football and a similar amount for basketball. Ron signed a letter of intent to play basketball for legendary coach John Wooden at UCLA.

Top college baseball programs also targeted him. Scouts from the Dodgers, Braves, Indians, and Yankees attended his high school games. Blomberg batted .472, slugged five homers, and drove in 45 runs during his senior year. He added an exclamation mark to his performance when he swatted a 420-foot home run to straightaway center field while playing in a high-school All-Star game in Atlanta's Fulton County Stadium.

In 1966, the Yankees finished last and were desperately seeking power bats and players with box office appeal. Blomberg, who had grown up following the Yankees and idolizing Mickey Mantle, was on the top of their list. Yankees general manager Lee MacPhail observed, "I can't imagine any high school boy being a better hitter than Ronnie."[1]

Besides being a left-handed hitter with a swing ideal for the short right field in Yankee Stadium, Blomberg was Jewish. He offered an instant connection with the 2.5 million Jews who lived in New York City. It was a potential box office bonanza.

At age 18, Ron signed with the Yankees for $75,000. The first round of the 1967 draft also produced future Hall of Famer Ted Simmons, Jon Matlack, Doug Rader, and Bobby Grich. After the draft, the Yankees flew Blomberg and his parents to New York City, where they saw a Broadway play, dined, and met the New York Yankees. The trip's highlight was when Ron dressed in the Yankees locker room before taking batting practice and met Mickey Mantle.

"The biggest thrill of my life was meeting Mickey Mantle," he said. "He was just as nice as I hoped he would be, and he watched me work out. He told me to take it easy, that it was just a matter of time until I put it all together."[2]

Mantle told Ron he hoped he would break some of his records someday. Blomberg wasn't the only one with stars in his eyes. The Yankees front office was delighted by the prospect of the Atlanta slugger being heir to Mantle.

Ron's first stop was Johnson City, Tennessee, in the Rookie League. In mid-July, he was batting .410 and had blasted a 450-foot home run. He finished with a .297 average and 10 homers.

Cloyd Boyer, roving minor league pitching coach for the Yankees, praised Blomberg. "He's one of the best-looking kids I've ever seen. He swings the bat like a big leaguer, and he has one of the best conceptions of the strike zone I've ever seen in a kid. He gets an awful lot of walks. He doesn't swing at bad pitches."[3]

In 1968, Ron played for Kinston (N.C.) in the Class-A Carolina League. He struggled as the Yankees converted him from a first baseman to a center fielder. That same year, the 19-year-old became eligible for the military draft. The Yankees placed him in a National Guard unit in Atlanta that included professional football and basketball players, doctors, pilots, and a few future politicians. The National Guard required one weekend a month and a two-week stint in the summer for six years. He needed to fly to Atlanta on a Friday night, participate in the reserves on the weekend and fly back to wherever his team was playing on Monday morning. It was a major disruption while he was at Kinston and during his career.

The next season, he was promoted to Manchester in the Class-AA Eastern League. His game started to come together as he smashed 19 homers, batted .284, and was named to the Eastern League All-Star team. He appeared to be destined to be a future New York Yankee.

The Yankees called Blomberg up late in the 1969 season. He made his major league debut on September 10 against the Washington Senators. One month past his 21st birthday, he walked in his appearance as a pinch-hitter against Dick Bosman. Playing in three more games, he delivered three hits in six at-bats, including his first major league hit against Washington's Jim Hannah.

The Yankees invited him to their 1970 spring training camp. Blomberg saw a lot of action, played well, and even received encouragement from

Washington Senators manager Ted Williams, who told him, "You have a great stroke. Keep it up."[4]

A 1969 scouting report on him, published in *Baseball Digest,* said: "Real comer, good speed, good arm and hits with power. When the rough edges are rubbed off, he should be a classy performer."[5]

He arrived in Syracuse in the Class Triple-A International League in 1970, one step from the major leagues. A decision by manager Frank Verdi had a drastic impact on his major league career. Although Blomberg had never been a platoon player, Verdi decided mid-season to play the left-handed hitter mainly against right-handed pitchers, saying he had other outfield prospects he wanted to evaluate. Verdi implemented the change when Ron returned from a two-week National Guard stint. Ron protested the move to no avail. Unsettled and unhappy, he went into a 0-for-30 slump.

"I wouldn't say the manager's decision ruined my career, but it definitely held me back," recalled Ron. "They had hyped me to be the next superstar, but I was confused as to why a superstar would be platooned. I couldn't see what they had to lose by playing me every day."[6]

Ron reported to the Yankees' spring training camp in 1971, hopeful of sticking with the club. But he was one of the first players cut. Depressed and impatient about his future, he didn't report to Syracuse. His wife, Mara, however, convinced him to return to Syracuse. Refocused, he was determined to convince the Yankees he was ready. In a torrid stretch, he lifted his average 40 points to .326 in a couple of weeks. That was the cue for the Yankees to call him up on June 25.

Blomberg, 22, contributed immediately as a pinch-hitter, outfielder, and first baseman. He blasted a 425-foot home run and doubled in his first game. "My impressive debut started up the hype machine again, tagging me the next Mickey Mantle," he said.[7]After a couple of long-distance home runs, he earned the nickname "Boomer." Since he hadn't hit against lefties for almost two years in the minors, Yankees manager Ralph Houk continued to platoon him.

The fans and the media loved Blomberg. He was boyish, enthusiastic, engaging, and talkative. Unlike many teammates, he enjoyed talking to the media and interacting with fans. When approached by the media, he was ready with a quote, anecdote, or opinion. Some of the Yankees resented him for all the publicity he received. After all, he wasn't even a star. Yet, you couldn't tell that by fan response. He received more than 100 letters daily, many from Jewish fans. As an extrovert, he wanted to be part of the community. He volunteered at charity events, made countless public appearances, did radio and television promotions, and visited numerous synagogues. In 64 games, he batted .322 and whacked seven round-trippers. It was a performance the Yankees couldn't ignore.

Projecting Ron as their first baseman of the future, the Yankees sent him to the Instructional League to work with former Yankee Bill White, a seven-time Gold Glove winner at first base. Ron, however, was a defensive liability, regardless of where he played. Houk insisted on platooning him in 1972.

A 12-day players' strike delayed the start of the season until mid-April. Ron's towering home run off of California Angels starter Nolan Ryan on July 22 at Yankee Stadium was one of the season's highlights. The hard-throwing Ryan failed to sneak a fastball past Boomer. He rocketed it into the right field upper deck near the foul line, hitting the facade just a foot and a half from leaving the stadium. Only Mantle had hit a ball as hard.

John Mayberry of the Kansas City Royals predicted Ron would become the first player to hit a ball out of Yankee Stadium. Slowed by a sore shoulder, he finished the season with a .268 batting average, 14 home runs, and 49 RBI.

After the 1972 season, Yankees manager Ralph Houk said, "There's no doubt Blomberg has great potential. He has so many plusses going for him that it has to be only a matter of time and experience before he realizes all of his potential. With speed, power, the ability to make contact, and all the other things he has going for him, Blomberg could wake up one morning and find himself a star."[8]

Blomberg wrote his name in the record book on Opening Day, April 6, 1973, when he became the game's first designated hitter. He drew a walk off of Boston Red Sox starter Luis Tiant in the historic first-inning at-bat at Fenway Park.

By May of 1973, Houk looked like a prophet. Blomberg fashioned a 13-game hit streak, which was snapped when he went hitless in a pinch-hitting appearance. He hit safely in the next seven games to give him hits in 20 consecutive games as a starter. The hot streak (32-for- 68) lifted his average over .400, making him one of the most feared batters in the American League.

"I knew I was going to do this someday," he said. "I knew I had the ability to hit like this. I thought when I came up, I was going to be a superstar right off the bat, but now all I want to do is to play up to my ability."[9]

Blomberg and his hitting exploits were the biggest baseball news in the country. Dave Anderson of *The New York Times* wrote, "In time, the House that Ruth Built may be remembered as the House that Blomberg Remodeled."[10]

An *Atlanta Constitution* headline asked, "Is Blomberg the Next .400 Hitter?" The Yankee star quickly replied: "I'm not going to hit .400, you know that, and I know that. But I'm still trying to get a hit every at-bat.[11] He later added, "I don't care about hitting .400 or winning a batting title. I want the team to win the pennant."[12]

On June 25, the Yankee slugger, named to the All-Star team as a write-in candidate, was hitting .414. It marked the first time in more than 25 years a player hit over .400 that late in the season. Ted Williams and Stan Musial were the last players to accomplish the feat. Unlike Williams and Musial, however, Blomberg was limited to playing against right-handed pitching. Consequently, other teams saved their southpaws for the Yankees, forcing the slugger to stay on the bench. The limitation almost guaranteed he would not get the 502 plate appearances needed to qualify for the batting title.

Frustrated, Ron lobbied Houk to play every day. The veteran manager, however, refused, citing damning statistics. "Ron is something like 1-for-46, including spring training, versus left-handed pitchers," he pointed out. "If he can hit .400 against right-handed pitching, that would be the best thing for us."[13]

Thousands of fans wrote Houk, telling him what a fool he was for not playing Blomberg versus left-handed pitchers. He countered by saying he would be foolish to take a chance of losing a game by doing so. Houk believed Blomberg would learn to hit left-handed pitching. But at the time, he didn't have the same swing against lefties as righties. He pulled away from the ball and didn't break his wrists against lefties.

"Ron wouldn't be hitting .400 against southpaws," stressed the skipper. "In the minors, they let him play against lefties, and he got to where he couldn't hit righties either. We don't want that to happen to him in the majors."[14]

The 24-year-old was adamant he could hit, or learn to hit, southpaws. Since he rarely batted against lefties, it became a psychological issue. He put a lot of pressure on himself. He knew if he didn't get a hit, he would probably never face that pitcher again.

"If you can hit, you can hit," he said. He stressed that he hit left-handers and right-handers in high school and the first three years in the minors. "If I thought I would be platooned for the rest of my career, I would look for another line of work."[15]

Blomberg's incredible performance made him a media darling. He appeared on the cover of *The Sporting News* and *Sports Illustrated* (along with teammate Bobby Murcer) and made guest appearances on *The Tonight Show*, *The Dick Cavett Show*, and *Late Night with Tom Snyder*. He was the biggest thing to hit the Big Apple since Joe Namath. It helped that the Yankees played their most inspired baseball since they won the pennant in 1964. The Yankees were in first place from June 10 through August 2 before fading to 17 games behind the Orioles in 1973.

Blomberg's fairy tale season started to crumble in early July when he pulled a hamstring. The injury limited him to DHing, and his average dropped. He ended up at .329 (.338 vs. right-handers and .176 vs. left-handers) with 12 home runs and 57 RBI in 100 games.

Blomberg said Houk promised he would play every day in 1974. Those plans were scuttled when Bill Virdon replaced Houk as manager. Virdon faced the same questions Houk had. Could Blomberg hit left-handed pitching? Was he an everyday player? Could the Yankees afford to sacrifice defense with him on the field? Ron made it clear he didn't want to be the DH. But the club already had a fine defensive first baseman in Mike Hegan.

Ron put pressure on Virdon during spring training when he drove in 10 runs in his first 14 at-bats. His hits included a grand slam and a double against left-handed pitching. While he stood out on offense, he also made a couple of errors, failed to cover his position, and got thrown out on the bases. Meanwhile, he insisted he could hit if given a chance to play every day. Since he hadn't faced all kinds of pitching in four or five years, he said he wouldn't do well initially but would improve.

In June 1974, the Yankees were the weakest hitting team in the league, had lost 13 of 16, and had fallen into last place. With nothing to lose, Virdon experimented with Blomberg. Virdon played him against Baltimore Orioles and Chicago White Sox southpaws in back-to-back series. In those games, Ron faced Dave McNally, Mike Cuellar, Ross Grimsley, Grant Jackson, and Skip Pitlock. He went 3-for-14 (.214). Virdon said, "I'm very pleased with how he's done. Ron will play against left-handed pitching as long as he's hitting them. If he goes into a slump, he won't hit against them."[16]

Blomberg suffered a serious setback on the final day of the season. He tore his right shoulder tendon and fell to the ground in pain after slamming a home run. Doctors optimistically said it should heal with rest. Limited to 90 games, he batted .311 with 10 homers and 48 RBI.

Ron's shoulder was still painful at the start of the 1975 season. He tried to play through the pain, but things got worse. He hit a home run on April 20 and heard a pop in his shoulder. He rested a few games, came back, hit another homer, and heard another pop. The tendon leading to his bicep popped out of place. His season was over on July 12 after playing 34 games. It was a frustrating and wasted year.

The Sporting News wrote, "Blomberg has turned 27, and he's still not close to fulfilling his potential. In five years in the majors, he's never had an injury-free season. He has played the equivalent of just two seasons."[17]

Ron was convinced he could hit 30 to 35 homers if given a chance. He was eager to return to the Yankees' lineup in 1976. But bad luck continued to plague him. He reinjured his right shoulder in the final game of spring training. He underwent surgery in early May. He didn't play the rest of the season except for a game on September 8.

Doctors declared Blomberg 100 percent healthy as 1977 spring training approached. It was a crucial year because Ron needed to prove himself. "All I want is a chance to show what I can do," he said. "When I'm right, no one can out-hit me, not even Rod Carew."[18]

He never got that chance. The snake-bitten Yankee, who hoped to be the Comeback Player of the Year, ran into a concrete wall in a Winter Haven exhibition game. He knocked himself out, tore his cartilage, and shattered his left knee. Another surgery was required, and another season was missed.

"I realized I wasn't going to live up to my potential. I felt like I let the team, the fans, and myself down. I lost my confidence and became depressed. It was the lowest point of my career," he lamented.[19]

To make matters worse, he believed the Yankees snubbed him after his knee injury. One day, he entered the Yankees clubhouse on crutches and found his number had been removed from his locker and his personal items had been packed away in a box.

Ron tested the free agent market in the winter of 1977. He was 28 and had played just 35 games in the past three years. Yet, several clubs thought he was worth a gamble. The Mets, Braves, Indians, White Sox, and Rangers were interested. He wanted to stay in New York because the fans treated him so well, but the Mets didn't make a competitive offer.

The White Sox lost power hitters Richie Zisk and Oscar Gamble to free agency. Owner Bill Veeck looked to replace that power. Veeck developed a fondness for Blomberg. "He has the ability to pop the ball, and I don't think he's begun to approach his potential. He's going to hit a great many balls into the right field stands (at Comiskey Park) and elsewhere."[20]

Blomberg believed he was an everyday player and he could help a club. "I'm 100 percent recovered from my shoulder and knee injuries."[21] In truth, he was about 70 percent healthy, which was probably a generous estimate.

Veeck stunned the baseball world when he signed Blomberg to a four-year, no-cut contract for $600,000. Ron made $47,500 in 1977, and now he would make $150,000. Veeck lifted Blomberg from the lowest to the highest point of his career. Veeck was either a genius or a fool.

The White Sox projected Blomberg as an everyday player and a left fielder. The club also acquired free-agent outfielder Bobby Bonds. Blomberg and Bonds were expected to provide Chicago's power. Ron's knees and shoulder bothered him in spring training, but he didn't complain.

He stepped into the spotlight on Opening Day 1978 in Chicago. He smashed a two-run, upper-deck, ninth-inning homer off Boston's Dick Drago to tie the game, which the White Sox went on to win. He dedicated the dramatic homer to Veeck, who had given him a second chance. After three years of depression and multiple surgeries, Blomberg said, "It's been a long time. But this is a new year, and I have a new body. I know I can help this team."[22]

It was, however, his last hurrah. It became obvious he wasn't completely healthy. The White Sox moved him from the outfield to pinch-hitter and designated hitter. There were brief glimpses of his potential, but he was hitting .215 with 15 RBI in mid-season. He knocked five home runs and batted .231 in 61 games.

The White Sox placed Blomberg on irrevocable waivers to give him his release in the spring of 1979. The club asked him to report to its Triple-A team in Iowa, but he refused. Teams had until April 5 to claim him off of waivers. No team was interested.

"I'm poorer but not wiser," said Veeck, who clearly was not a genius in this case. "Keeping Blomberg would be compounding a stupidity. You may not grin, but you bear it. It's not the first mistake I've made, and it won't be the last." He added, "Ron and I are the only two people in the country who think he can still hit."[23]

Ron's once-promising baseball career was over at age 30. "It was a sad discovery, as I was not leaving on my own accord," he said. "I really felt like I did not fulfill my potential, and in the process, I let a lot of people down, including myself. It took me a while to get over that feeling."[24] Not living up to your potential hurts, he said. "I would have liked to have seen what I could have done."[25]

Yankees general manager Lee MacPhail, who drafted Blomberg, said, "Ron had good tools, and he was ideal for Yankee Stadium because he could really pull the ball. He should have been a great major league ballplayer."[26]

CHAPTER 12

CLINT HURDLE 1B
ROYALS

CLINT HURDLE
THE CAN'T-MISS KID

*Clint is going to be a helluva ballplayer. He's going to hit
for average with 25-40 homers a year.*
—KANSAS CITY ROYALS SCOUT BILL FISCHER

Camera crews, newspaper reporters, and radio stations swarmed the Kansas City Royals' spring training complex at Fort Myers, Fla., in March of 1978. Everyone wanted an interview or photograph of Clint Hurdle, the 20-year-old Royals rookie who graced the cover of the March 20 issue of *Sports Illustrated*. "Every time I turned around, there was a half dozen microphones in my face and another six people with notepads," he recalled.[1]

The *Sports Illustrated* cover touted him as "This Year's Phenom." The magazine described the 6-3, 195-pounder as "tall, dark, handsome and brash and able to hit a baseball nine miles."[2] Although Hurdle was the most publicized rookie in Kansas City Royals' history and perhaps the most publicized rookie in 25 years, he hadn't secured a spot on the Royals' regular-season roster.

The left-handed hitting outfielder, however, demanded serious consideration after a highly successful season at Triple-A Omaha and an impressive major league debut. When Hurdle joined the Royals on September 18, 1977, at age 20, he became the youngest player in the club's history. In his second at-bat, he unloaded a majestic 450-foot homer to right field at Royals Stadium. He played nine games and batted .305 with a pair of homers. His late-season exploits came after he was named The Most Valuable Player in the American Association. He batted .328, slammed 16 homers, and drove in 66 runs for Omaha.

Hurdle had never failed at anything in his life. Yet, he never lived up to the hype and expectations accompanying "The Can't-Miss Kid" tag. His inability to hit the long ball, inconsistency at the plate, defensive lapses, excessive nightlife, and a back injury caused the Royals to lose confidence in him before he turned 24. He played parts of 10 seasons, only two as an everyday starter.

As a baseball and football star at Merritt Island High School in Florida, Hurdle attracted attention from major league baseball teams and college football programs. He was a first-team All-State selection in baseball and an All-State quarterback. Clint signed a letter of intent to play football for the University of Miami.

The Royals signed Hurdle as their number one pick (ninth player chosen overall) in the 1975 amateur draft. The club was originally luke-warm on him, but Kansas City scout Bill Fischer changed their outlook. Fischer thought Clint could be a fantastic major leaguer. To convince the Royals' front office, he took Clint to Kansas City's spring training complex in Fort Myers. For Hurdle's hitting exhibition, he selected a field where the wind blew straight out from home plate.

The teenager put on a dazzling display with the Royals executives in the stands. Joe McGuff, the sports editor of the *Kansas City Star*, recalled that neither Mickey Mantle nor Roger Maris could have topped the distance of many of Hurdle's homers that day. Fischer called it "the greatest exhibition you ever saw."[3]

Charlie Lau, the Royals' hitting instructor, was in the stands that day. He said, "From the time he took his first swing, there was no doubt in my mind."[4] Impressed, the Royals signed Hurdle to a reported $70,000 bonus. Fischer enthused, "He'll be a helluva ballplayer. He's going to hit for average with 25-40 homers a year."[5]

The Royals assigned Clint to their rookie league team at Sarasota. He was named to the Gulf Coast League All-Star team. The following season he played for the Class-A Waterloo Royals in the Midwest League and was named Prospect of the Year. The 19-year-old began his third season at Triple-A Omaha in the American Association, where he blossomed.

Praise for Hurdle came from throughout baseball. Cincinnati Reds scout Ray Shore said, "He's the best I've ever seen. He just smashes the ball."[6] Dallas Green, head of the Phillies' minor leagues and scouting, added, "He's got speed, and he's got power. He puts the bat on the ball, and he can throw with anyone. The only thing you can't say is that he has game experience."[7]

During spring training, the Royals worked with Hurdle at first base. The club had veterans Amos Otis and Al Cowens in the outfield and highly touted rookie Willie Wilson. Tom Poquette and Steve Braun provided outfield depth. The Royals figured Hurdle, a right fielder in the minors, could replace the declining John Mayberry at first base. Hurdle, however, had played first base for only 12 games in the Venezuela Winter League.

Mayberry, 29, was the Royals' mainstay slugger for six seasons. He clouted 143 homers, including a career-high 34 in 1975. A two-time All-Star, Mayberry averaged 24 homers a season and tallied 100 or more RBI three times. He was one of the best fielding first basemen in the league. The Royals gambled and sold Mayberry to the Toronto Blue Jays a few days before the start of the 1978 season.

Hurdle was in the Opening Day lineup, playing first base and batting fifth. A notoriously slow starter in the minors, he struggled at the plate the first month of the season. He also committed three errors and was guilty of defensive lapses. He missed easy pop-ups and had other problems at first base due to inexperience. Besides the pressure of being a heralded rookie, he had to deal with learning a new position at the major league level, replacing a long-time starter, and being part of a competitive team aiming for its third consecutive AL West pennant.

At the end of May, he improved his batting average to .256 but had only two home runs. His defensive problems at first base persisted. He had neither Mayberry's bat nor glove, and the fans constantly reminded him of it. "I've been booed before, but not with the intensity like I was in Kansas City," he recalled years later. "A crowd of 30,000 to 40,000 can make a lot of noise."[8]

Hurdle was uncomfortable at bat and in the field. At bat, he felt like a yo-yo as manager Whitey Herzog urged him to pull the ball and go for the home run. Hitting instructor Charlie Lau was convinced he was more of a line-drive spray hitter. Clint constantly adjusted his stance and swing.

A frustrated Herzog told reporters, "Clint is swinging like a girl. If he doesn't start swinging like a man, I'm going to have to send him back to Omaha."[9] Herzog ended the experiment of Hurdle at first base at the end of June. Club officials believed his defensive problems were affecting his offense. "Hurdle has not hit the long ball as expected of him," declared a disappointed Herzog.[10]

Hurdle reverted to his old batting stance. "I feel comfortable again. I'm standing more straight up and down, and I'm seeing the ball better," he said.[11]

Patrolling right field in place of the injured Al Cowens, Hurdle put together a nine-game hitting streak. His best performance came on July 17 against the Boston Red Sox in Kansas City. He went 3-for-3, including a three-run homer, and drove in six runs.

"Slowly but surely, I'm learning," he said. "I'm more relaxed. I feel more comfortable in the outfield because that's where my minor-league experience is. It's not my style to pull the ball and hit homers. I don't know why people would expect a 20-year-old to come in here and take over."[12] Hurdle couldn't please everyone. "If I had done everything I was supposed to do up until now, I would be leading the league in homers, have the highest batting average, given $1,000 to the cancer fund, and married Marie Osmond," he said.[13] Hurdle was frustratingly inconsistent in 1978. He demonstrated marked improvement with the bat and the glove after he returned to the outfield. Herzog believed too much instruction hurt the potential star. "Clint's got to do less thinking and let his natural ability take care of things," he said.[14]

The Royals were in first place, one game ahead of the California Angels in the AL West at the beginning of September. Not completely satisfied with Hurdle's defense or hitting, Herzog limited his playing time. From September 10 through September 23, he batted only five times, mainly as a pinch-hitter.

"I got a crash course in the big leagues," said Clint. "I've had a bad year, but better than a lot of guys who have been around longer. It's been a learning experience."[15] He ended the regular season, batting .264, with seven homers and 56 RBI. He played 52 games at first base, 42 in right field, and 41 in left field.

The Royals finished the season in first place with a 92-70 record, five games ahead of the California Angels and the Texas Rangers. The Yankees swept Kansas City in four straight in the American League Championship Series. Hurdle didn't play in Game 1. He started in left field in Games 2 and 3, going 3-for-7. He struck out as a pinch-hitter in Game 4.

Hurdle was glad his pressure-packed rookie season was over. A pre-season favorite to win the Rookie of the Year honor, he failed to receive a single vote. Manager Whitey Herzog fired hitting instructor Charlie Lau, citing a difference of philosophies. Hurdle was at the center of that difference. With Lau out of the picture, Herzog re-emphasized his desire for Hurdle to be a home run hitter.

The Royals sent Hurdle to the Florida Instructional League to work on his long ball swing and outfield defense. "I believe Clint can hit for more power," stressed Herzog. "I want him swinging the bat the way he did in Omaha in 1977 and when he came up to us in September of that year."[16]

The work in the Florida Instructional League paid off. "I'm excited about next season," said Hurdle. "I'm trying to get my stroke back and forget about spraying the ball around. They want me to hit for more power."[17]

Royals general manager Joe Burke added, "Some rough edges showed up last summer, and we want Clint to smooth them out. We believe he has the potential to be a very, very good player."[18]

The pressures and expectations Hurdle faced were palpable when the Royals opened spring training in 1979. The good news was he now had more experience, perspective, and wisdom.

"Last year, I was supposed to be The Can't-Miss Kid," he said. "Last year was unbelievable. I was 20 and trying to play outfield and first base. What did I know?[19]

As a rookie, the cocky and good-looking Hurdle, along with teammate and fellow bachelor George Brett, enjoyed a seldom-rivaled nightlife. He saw every bright light in the American League and admittedly did some immature things. The lifestyle took its toll.

Miami Herald columnist Edwin Pope wrote, "The Can't-Miss Kid missed. It wouldn't have been a miss for a regular rookie. What he missed was being what nature never meant for any human being so young—superstar at age 20."[20]

Herzog acknowledged that intense pressure and high expectations had impacted Hurdle. "Clint had a good year. If it hadn't been for all the ballyhoo, we would be saying it was a hell of a year."[21]

Hurdle battled Tom Poquette, Steve Braun, Willie Wilson, and Joe Zdeb for the starting left fielder job in spring training. He came out on top and was in the 1979 Opening Day lineup. He was plagued by another slow start. Herzog moved him to right field in early May to replace the injured Al Cowens. At the end of May, Kansas City demoted Hurdle, batting .240 with three homers, to Triple-A Omaha.

"Clint just wasn't hitting the long ball," commented Herzog. "He's too good of a prospect not to be playing every day. But with (Willie) Wilson, (Amos) Otis, and (Al) Cowens in the outfielder, there was no place for him. We want Clint to work on pulling the ball and not taking so many pitches."[22]

Hurdle had trouble pulling the trigger on a fastball and lunging too much. He lost the stroke that brought him so much success in 1977. The Royals, however, were confident he could regain it.

Hurdle's pride was hurt, and he fumed. "I'm bitter as hell about the demotion. I understand why it happened, but it doesn't mean I have to be happy about it. They can explain it to me over and over, but all the explanation isn't going to make me happy about it."[23]

Many observers believed too much was expected of the youngster too soon. Royals veteran Hal McRae said, "Clint had too much responsibility put on him too soon."[24] Some maintained the Royals brought him up too soon and sent him back to the minors too quickly.

Hurdle vowed to work hard. But from now on, the only person he would worry about on the field was himself. He was no longer the eager rookie, anxious to please everyone.

After a month in the minors, Clint still hadn't rediscovered his stroke, and his fundamentals were terrible. He explained the reason for his offensive decline. "I was supposed to hit the long ball, really drive it. So I was trying to sit on every pitch, and that's what got my mechanics off. I was lunging at every pitch, and I lost my rhythm."[25]

Omaha fans verbally abused and booed Hurdle every game. They strongly voiced their displeasure with his failure to become their idol. In a small ballpark, Hurdle heard the fans loud and clear. Meanwhile, Royals general manager Joe Burke assured fans that Hurdle was part of the club's future. There were no plans to trade him.

After 68 games in Omaha, the Royals recalled him in mid-August. Hurdle played 17 games and failed to deliver a home run. He finished his disappointing 1979 season batting .240 with three homers and 30 RBI in 59 games.

Kansas City traded outfielder Al Cowens to California Angels for first baseman Willie Aikens, opening up right field for Hurdle. John Schuerholz, director of player personnel, said, "We've never given up on Clint. What we're saying is 'Clint you have to go out there and show us your true natural abilities. Play hard and keep the job. The job is yours.'"[26]

Hurdle had an opportunity to earn a starting job, play his natural position, and not feel as much pressure. He vowed to be ready for spring training. The Royals fired manager Whitey Herzog and replaced him with the more patient Jim Frey.

Frey discussed Hurdle: "At age 20, when most kids are learning to hit junior college pitching, Clint was expected to hit in the majors. And the media made such a big deal out of him that there was no way he could live up to it. He looks like Jack Armstrong, and everyone wanted to write about him."[27]

Frey's advice to Hurdle was to relax, let his natural abilities take over, and forget everything that had happened. It was music to Hurdle's ears.

Hurdle played right field and batted seventh on Opening Day 1980. He believed this was his make-or-break season. "I got all the hype, and I've fallen short. People have given up on me," he acknowledged.[28]

Detroit Free Press columnist Jim Hawkins wrote, "The fans haven't forgiven him for being human."[29]

The promising star hadn't lost faith in his abilities. He said, "I'm going to be a helluva ballplayer. I know it, regardless of what people say. I'm going to hit for average, and I'm going to hit homers. Just give me time."[30]

This time, Clint avoided a slow start. His bat came to life in June as he batted .432.

His offensive production lifted the Royals to an 8-game lead over the Chicago White Sox on July 1. Manager Jim Frey platooned 17-year veteran Jose Cardenal and Hurdle in right field during the season's final six weeks. Hurdle enjoyed his best season with a .294 average, 10 homers, and 60 RBI. The Royals cruised to a 97-65 record to win the AL West by 14 games over the Oakland A's.

Kansas City swept the Yankees in the American League Championship Series, three games to none. Since the Yankees used three southpaw starters, Hurdle got just two at-bats in the series. But, in the World Series against the Philadelphia Phillies, he started four games in right field. He went 5-for-12 (.417) as the Phillies won in six games.

Buoyed by his best season and a new two-year contract, Hurdle, 23, started the 1981 season as the Royals' right fielder. His goal was to match or surpass his 1980 numbers and play every day. In the third game of the season, he injured his back, sliding into third base. When the pain didn't go away in a few days, he was admitted to the hospital and placed in traction. He went on the disabled list and didn't return to the lineup until May 30. Two weeks later, major league baseball went on strike until August 9.

According to Hurdle, the Royals' medical staff did not diagnose his back problem correctly. At first, they said it was muscle spasms, then a congenital birth defect, and finally, a vertebra problem. The medical staff wanted to operate, but Hurdle nixed the idea. Finally, upon the advice of his agent Ron Shapiro, he visited his own physician, who diagnosed it as a hairline fracture of his lower back. He underwent treatment which consisted of traction and ultrasound. He missed 72 days with back pain and soreness. He was sidelined until mid-September.

In addition to his back problems, Clint went through a divorce and had to deal with ugly rumors. The rumors began when he went to a Kansas City police station to help a friend who had been arrested for being intoxicated. His presence and actions irritated one of the police officers, who falsely claimed Clint was a homosexual. The rumor spread quickly. The police officer was later reprimanded, but the damage had been done. It was an issue he addressed in every city where the Royals played.

Hurdle finished the strike-shortened season batting .329 in 28 games. It wasn't the season he had imagined. Rumors whirled about his future. The handwriting was on the wall when the club traveled to Japan for a series of exhibition games. He played the first five games and didn't play for the next three weeks.

The hammer dropped on December 11, 1981, when the Royals traded Hurdle to the Cincinnati Reds for Scott Brown, a 24-year-old, right-handed relief pitcher. It was official. Kansas City had given up on The Phenom, who was just 24.

The trade was a new lease on life for Clint. He no longer felt under a microscope where everything was magnified. He hoped the enormous pressure he had played under would subside. The Reds said the left field job was his. The club had no expectations regarding the number of home runs or batting average. They just expected him to play and hustle.

Despite the early optimism, Clint quickly fell into disfavor. He suffered through a dismal spring training and a 4-for-22 start in the regular season. He was benched before the season was two weeks old. He was batting .206 with no homers and only one RBI in 19 games when the Reds optioned him to Triple-A Indianapolis.

Reds president Dick Wagner said, "We think optioning Clint to Indianapolis will benefit him and the team. He'll have a chance to play and get his batting stroke back."[31] After trying unsuccessfully to trade him, the Reds released him on November 15.

The Seattle Mariners needed a left-handed, experienced hitter, and Hurdle signed with them in February 1983. They were his best chance to return to the major leagues. He batted .312 in spring training but was cut on the final day. Mariners manager Rene Lachmann wanted to keep him, but the front office overruled him.

Mets vice president Lou Gorman signed Clint for the Tidewater Tides, the Mets' Triple-A club. Hurdle, released by two of the worst teams in baseball, hoped for a break to get him back to the majors.

Some reporters and fans seemed delighted by the 26-year-old's downfall. *Boston Globe* reporter Jackie MacMullen wrote, "Hurdle's ego is only equaled by James Watt (Secretary of the Interior under President Ronald Reagan) and George Steinbrenner (New York Yankees owner). Hurdle was a cocky rookie who went too fast and talked too much. He deserved to be humbled."[32]

At Tidewater in 1983, manager Davey Johnson encouraged Clint to learn to play third base to increase his value. The transition was difficult, but it didn't bother him at the plate. In 139 games, he batted .285 with 22 homers and 105 RBI. That earned him a late-season call-up to the Mets.

Johnson was promoted to manager of the New York Mets the following season. With Ray Knight and Hubie Brooks at third, Johnson advised Hurdle to learn to be a catcher with the aim of being a utility player. Hurdle was realistic. "I was no golden boy. I had to start over."[33] He spent the entire season at Triple-A learning and waiting for a break.

In 1985, the Mets invited Hurdle to spring training camp as a non-roster player. He surprised everyone by hitting .345. The Mets took him North to start the season. He could play five positions: left field, right field, first base, catcher, and third base. He had gone from a budding superstar to a part-time utility player, grateful to be in the majors. Once the top dog, he was now the underdog.

A more mature Hurdle observed, "It's too bad no one can hand you maturity. But I had listened to too much of the buildup, too much of the hype. I thought it all would just happen."[34]

Filling in at catcher and right field, Hurdle played 43 games and batted .195. Although manager Davey Johnson wanted to protect him in the Rule 5 draft, the front office opted not to. The Cardinals, with Whitey Herzog as manager, claimed Hurdle. The club planned to use him as a utility player. Playing mainly first base, Clint got into 78 games and hit .195. He was granted free agency at the end of the season.

He signed with the Mets as a free agent in February 1987. He spent most of the season at Tidewater. In December, he announced he was retiring from professional baseball to manage the Class-A Port St. Lucie Mets. Hurdle, 29, became one of the youngest managers in organized baseball. He said, "I have too many things I want to do to hang on as a marginal player in the majors. This is a once-in-a-lifetime opportunity."[35]

Hurdle's once-promising playing career was over. He had played parts of ten seasons, only two as an everyday starter. He tallied 32 homers and averaged .259. He had played in a World Series, been demoted, traded, released, and relegated to the bench. He played 300 games more in the minors than the majors.

Hurdle reflected on his career many times. He once said, "The biggest mistake I ever made was trying to be what everybody told me I should be. There is no greater fight than when you're battling yourself."[36]

CHAPTER 13

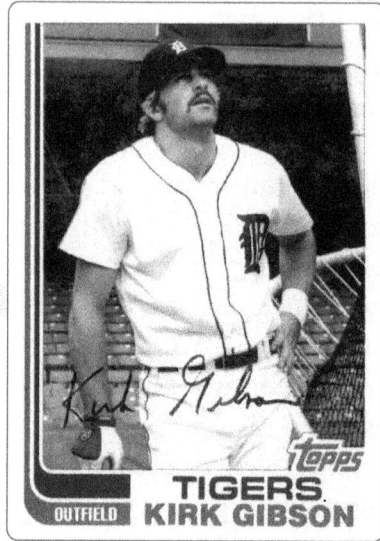

KIRK GIBSON
THE HARD-NOSED IMPACT PLAYER

I have found the next Mickey Mantle. Kirk Gibson will be a legend.
—Seattle Mariners scout Jerry Krause

Sportswriter Jayson Stark once observed that Kirk Gibson "had the physique of Gibraltar and the speed of a Porsche."[1] At 6-foot-3 and 220 pounds, Gibson possessed the rare combination of extraordinary speed and awesome power. In college, he ran the 40-yard dash in 4.28 seconds, and he could bash a baseball into the upper deck of any ballpark and completely out of some. As if that wasn't impressive enough, he played the game with the intensity of a hard-nosed football player, which he was in college.

The "next Mickey Mantle" tag was applied early, stuck with Gibson longer, and haunted him more than perhaps any other player. Despite periods of brilliance and dramatic moments, Gibson never played in an All-Star game in his 17-year career. Battling a series of injuries throughout his career, he never clouted 30 homers, drove in 100 RBI, or batted .300 in a season.

Kirk Gibson never considered a career in baseball until his junior year in college. Being a professional football player was his goal. Gibson played football, baseball, and basketball at Waterford Kettering High in Waterford, Mich. He attended Michigan State University on a football scholarship and worked hard to become an outstanding receiver. He led the Spartans in receiving yards from 1976 to 1978.

After Gibson's junior football season, MSU baseball coach Danny Litwhiler, a former 11-year major league player, asked him if he was interested in playing baseball. Initially reluctant, Kirk decided to play baseball after receiving the blessing of Darryl Rogers, MSU football coach, and his father. They figured playing baseball would increase his leverage with NFL teams at draft time.

Gibson made an impression as he batted .390, slugged 16 homers, tallied 52 RBI, and stole 21 bases in 48 games. He established school records for homers and RBI and was named to the All-American team. More than a dozen major league teams were interested in drafting him. Litwhiler said, "Kirk has more all-around ability than any baseball player I've ever seen."[2]

The Michigan native preferred to play for the Tigers, who had the 12th selection in the draft. He wanted to stay close to home and play in front of his friends and family. He used the leverage of possibly playing in the NFL (some thought he could be a first-round selection) to discourage other baseball teams from pursuing him. He was more honest with the Tigers.

Detroit invited Kirk to show off his skills in pre-game batting practice at Tiger Stadium. He recalled the unofficial tryout: "I hammered everything. I don't know how many pitches crashed into the upper deck, but during a lengthy 60-pitch session, it was more than enough to have sold the Tigers on my raw ability."[3]

He was adamant that he would return to Michigan State University to play football his senior year after being selected in the baseball draft.

He said there was no negotiation on that point. Many teams weren't willing to risk him getting injured playing football.

The MSU star garnered high praise from major league scouts. The Atlanta Braves had the first selection in the 1978 draft. Their chief scout Paul Snyder said, "Gibson stands out. If I had to compare him to anyone, he's like Mickey Mantle. You don't often see that combination of speed and power."[4]

Jerry Krause, a scout for the Seattle Mariners, told scouting director Mel Didier, "I've found the next Mickey Mantle." Krause believed Gibson would hit 50 homers a year in the Kingdome. "He'll be a legend," he enthused.[5] Didier wrote in a scouting report, "Gibson reminds me of Mickey Mantle with Pete Rose hustle. He has flair."[6]

The Atlanta Braves selected Bob Horner of Arizona State University number one. The Braves passed on Gibson because he told them his first love was football, explained Snyder. Gibson was still available when the Tigers selected with the 12th pick.

Gibson opted for baseball over football because he thought he would have a longer career, and baseball had free agency. He admitted, however, that baseball was extraordinarily difficult for him. He figured it would take him longer to excel at the professional level in baseball than in football.

The Tigers signed him for $200,000, the largest bonus in the club's history. They assigned him to Class-A Lakeland in the Florida State League. Kirk made it clear he wanted to get to the majors as quickly as possible. Detroit shared his goal but had to be careful not to rush him.

At Lakeland, he was introduced to taskmaster and manager Jim Leyland, who stated he wasn't impressed by Gibson's reputation, potential, or bonus. He expected the highly touted prospect to report to the ballpark at 8:30 every morning for a challenging workout. Gibson responded by telling him to "Bring it on." In 54 games, he batted .240, knocked eight homers, and drove in 40 runs. He struck out 54 times in 175 at-bats and made six errors.

After eight weeks in the minors, he returned to Michigan State University to play his senior year of football. He helped lead the Spartans to a share of the 1978 Big Ten Championship and a number 12 national ranking by the Associated Press. He was named first-team All-Big Ten and first-team All-American. He closed his career as MSU's all-time leader in receptions, receiving yards, and TD receptions. The St. Louis Cardinals selected him in the seventh round of the NFL draft.

The Tigers invited Gibson to their 1979 spring training camp, but he was cut early. Detroit assigned him to AAA Evansville in the American Association. Tigers great Al Kaline said, "Gibson has awesome power. He just has to get used to playing every day, seeing a lot of different pitches. I think he's going to be a super baseball player."[7]

In his first exhibition game, he collided with another outfielder, injuring his knee. Arthroscopic surgery revealed a significant bruise but no serious ligament damage. He was out of the lineup for a month.

Manager Jim Leyland, who had been promoted to Evansville, continued to work with Gibson. Years later, he recalled Gibson's work ethic: "I've never had a player who worked harder than Kirk. Some days he must have taken 500-600 swings, and he never backed off. And it didn't matter how many swings he took; he wanted to work in the outfield afterward. He was tireless, a glutton for punishment. I couldn't believe it. I got tired of loading the balls into the pitching machine before he got tired of swinging."[8] Gibson batted .245, bashed nine homers, and drove in 42 runs. He batted .429 in the league playoffs versus the Oklahoma City 89ers. The Tigers called him up on September 5, 1979. Three days later, he begged manager Sparky Anderson to let him pinch-hit in the ninth inning against Goose Gossage, the Yankees' hard-throwing right-hander. Gossage fanned him on three pitches.

Sparky Anderson said near the end of the season, "Kirk either will be one of the top stars in this game or nothing. He won't be in between that, I guarantee. He's a Mantle type. By that, I mean he'll strike out 150 times a year, but he'll make our ballpark in Detroit look like a bandbox. That's how many homers he's gonna hit."[9]

Gibson appeared on the March 24, 1980, cover of *Sports Illustrated*. He was shown rounding third base at full speed, intensely focused on scoring. The cover blurb read, "Rip Roarin' Rookie." The article made it clear the Tigers were gambling on the 22-year-old, who Leyland called "a diamond in the rough."[10] Everyone agreed he had plenty of raw ability.

The question was whether it could be harnessed and refined. When describing Kirk's raw ability, Sparky said, "He's been touched by the hand of God."[11] He said Gibson "may be as good an athlete as we've ever seen."[12] Sparky believed the youngster could turn the Detroit franchise around. Anderson planned to platoon the left-handed hitting Gibson in center field with the right-handed hitting Dave Stegman, another rookie. He didn't want to overwhelm the number one draft pick.

The *Sports Illustrated* cover and article bumped up the Mickey Mantle comparison several notches, according to Gibson. Already under a microscope, the magnification increased significantly.

The Tigers' brightest prospect was in the 1980 Opening Day lineup. He fought through a sluggish start, including an 0-for-24 slump. He saw a steady diet of curves and off-speed pitches. Kirk tried to hit every pitch over the fence. He relaxed a little at the plate as he learned to deal with the daily emotional highs and lows.

When *Detroit News* columnist Joe Falls asked Tiger players what they would write a column about, Gibson replied, "How stupid the fans are." That upset fans. *Sporting News* columnist Peter Gammons commented, "Here's a rookie who hasn't hit .250 in the minors, signed for $200,000 out of college because of people who come to Tiger Stadium, and he wants to tell fans how stupid they are."[13]

Gibson was a lightning rod for fans throughout his career. Cocky and arrogant, he refused to sign autographs, abused media members, and was a public relations disaster. Teammate Jack Morris said Gibby didn't like people or crowds, and sometimes he rubbed people the wrong way.

Gibson led the Tigers in homers and held his own in center field the first eight weeks of the season. Everyone was optimistic until Kirk tried to check his swing and heard a pop in his left wrist in early June. Experiencing pain and being unable to swing a bat, Gibson was placed on the DL. His wrist was immobilized in a cast for a few weeks. He reinjured it when he returned to batting practice. The club sent him to the Mayo Clinic for a diagnosis. Doctors recommended he undergo surgery to shorten the ulna bone in his arm and have a steel plate inserted to stabilize the area. Eight to nine months of rehabilitation was expected. None of the doctors could guarantee the surgery's success or that Gibson could play baseball again.

The surgery was performed on August 22, ending Gibson's rookie season after 41 games. His baseball career was in doubt.

Kirk was still uncertain about his return in mid-February. His wrist was still stiff and sore. He hadn't thrown a ball or swung a bat in more than six months. He was unsure if his wrist would hold up. He tested the wrist gradually in spring training and avoided any setbacks. Surprisingly, he was ready for Opening Day in 1981. He reinjured his left wrist in mid-May, sidelining him for nearly three weeks. Shortly after he returned, major league baseball went on strike on June 12. The strike lasted for 50 days.

Gibson was struggling when the strike occurred. He was hitting .235, over-swinging, chasing bad pitches, and missing good pitches. He was angry and disappointed in himself. Tiger fans were even more so. They booed his every strikeout, weak pop-up, and miscue. He later said, "I was garbage."[14]

He was a different player, however, once play resumed on August 10. He batted .375 and raised his average from .235 to .328 in the second half of the season. He batted .462 in August and .331 in September. He credited a new stance, with his hands further back to compensate for impatience, better plate discipline, and hard work for his sudden improvement. He also was fully healthy for the first time.

Sporting News columnist Peter Gammons wrote, "One bright spot since the strike is the emergence of Kirk Gibson as the near superstar his physical tools promised before his wrist injury. He beats out bunts, hits 475-foot homers, scores from first on singles, and hits lefties."[15] By this time, Gibson was no longer platooning.

Texas Rangers' manager Don Zimmer said Gibson "looks like the next superstar."[16] Boston Red Sox manager Ralph Houk called him "another Mickey Mantle," while Chicago White Sox manager Tony LaRussa termed him "awesome."[17] Tigers manager Sparky Anderson pointed out Gibby hadn't had 1,000 at-bats in the majors yet, and his potential was untapped. He predicted stardom was two years away.

Detroit had gotten a two-month glimpse of what superstar Kirk Gibson might look like, which was inebriating. Anderson was convinced he would be one of the most dominating players in the game. He said, "Gibson is the only player I've ever managed who has a chance of being another Mickey Mantle. The only guy with that combination of speed and power."[18]

Gibson was quick to dismiss the comparison. "The next Mickey Mantle? Forget it. That's just talk. I may be the next something, but not the next Mantle. Guys like Mantle only come along once in a lifetime. I'd be lying if I said I wasn't flattered to be mentioned in the same breath as Mantle. But comparing me to him is a little premature. He earned his niche. I'm still learning and have a ways to go."[19]

Tiger fans were excited about the start of the 1982 season. Gibson, however, fell flat on his face, opening the season with a 3-for-35 slump. He was plagued by intestinal problems, a badly bruised knee, and a strained calf muscle. He sprained his left wrist on July 5 and was placed on the DL. The team soon declared he would miss the rest of the season. He was limited to fewer than 100 games for the third season since he made his major league debut. In 69 games, he hit eight homers and batted .278, 50 points below his 1981 mark.

The 25-year-old Gibson faced a crucial season in 1983. Injuries had limited him to 215 games in his career, slightly less than half of the Tigers' games. His potential remained unrealized, and he was a major disappointment. Instead of being a baseball machine and the second coming of Mickey Mantle, he wasn't even an average baseball player. Additionally, his hedonistic behavior and off-field antics turned off fans, Tigers' management, and the media. He was squandering his talents.

Gibson compounded all the setbacks by being selfish and immature. He had a lot of bad habits and was surly, demanding, and unreasonable. He said, "I was fighting Sparky, the Tigers, the media, and the world at large. I knew it all. Or at least, I thought I did."[20]

"We still don't know what Kirk is capable of," commented Anderson. "There have been some good portions of years, but that's it. He must stay healthy."[21] Sparky penciled Gibson in as DH against right-handed pitchers for the season. The demotion from an everyday player upset the Tiger outfielder.

Kirk got off to an uncharacteristically quick start in 1983. In mid-April, he underwent arthroscopic surgery for a bone chip in his left knee, the result of a diving catch. After missing a week, he returned and stayed hot. He batted .308 in April.

May wasn't as kind. He plunged into a 3-for-43 slump, and his average plummeted to .198. He struck out 23 times in 70 at-bats. The boo birds were out in force as he went 28 games without a home run.

Gibson showed everyone on June 14 why the Tigers and the fans should be patient with him. He awed everyone with an exhibition of power, hustle, and speed. He slammed a towering homer over the right field roof and out of the Tiger Stadium in the fourth inning. The ball cleared Trumbull Avenue and landed on the roof of the Brooks Lumber Company. The monster home run was estimated at 540 feet. It was the 16th homer in Tiger history to leave the park.

Two innings later, with Lou Whitaker on first base, Gibby sent a ball to deep center. It bounced off Tony Armas's glove and hit the center field wall. The speedy Whitaker was thrown out at the plate, but Gibson kept charging. Umpire Larry Barnett stepped in front of catcher Rich Gedman to call Whitaker out. He had placed himself in Gibson's path. The ex-football player appeared to be out by 10 feet. He plowed into Barnett and Gedman, sending them both sprawling. Gedman dropped the ball, and the first base ump called Gibson safe.

In his book, *Bottom of the Ninth*, Gibson said the mammoth home run was "actually the worst thing that could have happened. It generated even more publicity and attention, which made me think that by this one feat, I had earned the right to play every day."[22]

He continued to struggle at the plate. At one point, he was trapped in a 9-for-78 slump. The fans were merciless, and he dreaded coming to the ballpark. Every day he fought the urge to quit. But Sparky stuck with him, putting him in the lineup and hoping he would snap out of his slump. The Tigers battled the Baltimore Orioles for first place in the American League East in mid-August. Teammate and pitcher Milt Wilcox said, "There's been so much written about Kirk's ability. But I think you can talk about ability only a certain amount of time. Now the pressure is on. He's got to come through and deliver some of the promise he has."[23]

Gibson failed to deliver on the promise. He batted .227 with 15 homers and 51 RBI. He was pressing and didn't know what was wrong. He said he was "an all-around flop" in 1983.[24]

Miserable, unhappy, and unfulfilled, he said he wouldn't wish what he had gone through on his worst enemy. He faced the prospect of being another player with great potential but never achieving it. He decided he had to change his life. His agent, Doug Baldwin, suggested he enroll at the Pacific Institute, a Seattle-based clinic for mind and soul. There, he worked with counselor Frank Bartenetti. "He (Bartenetti) helped me focus on some basic issues—who I was, who I wanted to be, what I wanted to accomplish, and how to secure the life I wanted by changing my thought processes," he recalled.[25]

After winning 92 games and finishing second in the American League East in 1983, the Tigers' outlook for 1984 was rosy. The Tigers had a solid lineup that included Lance Parrish, Alan Trammel, Lou Whitaker, and Chet Lemon. Jack Morris, Dan Petry, and Milt Wilcox anchored the starting rotation. During the off-season, the club acquired reliever Willie Hernandez from the Phillies and designated hitter Darrell Evans from the San Francisco Giants.

A big question was how much of a role the 27-year-old Gibson would play. He had something to prove and was ready for a turnaround season. Mentally, he had a new outlook on baseball and life. Physically, he shaved his beard and cut his long hair, signaling a new beginning. Sparky moved him to right field in spring training. The club designated legendary Al Kaline to work with him. Although Gibson hated right field, it was the only position open to him if he wanted to play every day.

It turned out to be an incredible season. The Tigers jumped out to a 35-5 start and led wire-to-wire. The Tigers joined the 1927 New York Yankees and the 1955 Brooklyn Dodgers as the only teams in first place the entire season.

Gibson thrived with a new approach and less pressure. American League pitchers were surveyed in late September as to what hitters they least wanted to face in the ninth inning. Gibson finished second behind Eddie Murray of the Baltimore Orioles. He emerged as one of the league's premier players. He compiled a .282 batting average, 27 homers, and 91 RBI, including 17 game-winning hits and 29 stolen bases. He became the club's first player to smack 20 homers and steal 20 bases. He also became the first left-handed hitting Tiger to record double figures in triples, doubles, and home runs since Charlie Gehringer in 1934.

It was the first year he didn't make headlines with an injury, clash with fans or media, or experience a prolonged slump. The expectation of being the next Mickey Mantle weighed less on him. He thought the buildup was unfair, particularly since he had only one year of college baseball experience. Many fans saw him as a savior. He said he just had raw talent. He asked manager Sparky Anderson to back off from the comparison to Mantle, and he had.

"That was the worst thing I could have done to him," acknowledged Anderson, discussing the comparison to Mantle. "All it did was burden him. I set him back who knows how long, probably a couple years. You'll never hear another word from me on the subject. He doesn't need the added pressure."[26]

Detroit hitting coach Gates Brown chimed in, "The Mickey Mantle comparison hurt Kirk. He tried to live up to that, and it screwed him up."[27]

The Tigers swept the Kansas City Royals in the American League Championship Series. Gibson batted .417 and was named the series' Most Valuable Player. Facing the San Diego Padres in the 1984 World Series, Gibby was on baseball's biggest stage for the first time in his career.

Gibson demonstrated he was a force to be reckoned with in Game 5, with the Tigers leading three games to one. In the first inning, with a runner on first, he clouted the first pitch from Padre Mark Thurmond over the 370-foot sign in right-center and halfway up the second deck. In the bottom of the fourth, with the score tied 3-3, he singled and advanced to third after a pair of walks. With one out, pinch-hitter Rusty Kuntz lifted a sacrifice fly to shallow right field. Tony Gwynn lost it, and second baseman Alan Wiggins caught it off balance. The heads-up Gibson scored from third base.

In the bottom of the eighth, with runners on second and third, Gibson was due to face ace reliever Goose Gossage. Padres catcher Terry Kennedy held up four fingers, signaling Gossage to walk him. But the fireballer had other ideas. San Diego manager Dick Williams visited the mound, and Gossage convinced him to let him pitch to Gibson. The Tiger slugger sent the second pitch to deep right field for a three-run homer, breaking open a 5-4 game. He ceremoniously rounded the bases, arms raised high with delight. He crossed home plate and pounded teammates with a series of high fives. The victory gave Detroit its first World Series title since 1968. No longer the target of Detroit boo birds,

Gibson was the toast of the town. He placed sixth in the American League Most Valuable Player voting, which was won by Tigers reliever Willie Hernandez.

Looking to defend its American League title, Detroit won its first six games of the 1985 season. After that, the club played .500 ball. The Tigers won 84 games and finished in third place, 15 games behind the Toronto Blue Jays. Unlike 1984, there wasn't anything magical about 1985. The club slumped in every department. Kirk Gibson, however, was one of the bright spots. He enjoyed the best year of his career, setting personal highs in games (154), at-bats (581), hits (167), doubles (37), homers (29), and stolen bases (30). He fell one homer shy of becoming Detroit's first 30-30 man.

Gibson was a free agent at the end of the season. Resigning him was the Tigers' top priority. Kirk wanted a 5-year contract for $8 million. The Tigers offered a 3-year contract at $3.6 million. Gibson was insulted by the proposal. "For me to sign a 3-year contract and then shake hands with Bill Lajoie (general manager) or Jim Campbell (president), I would vomit," he said.[28]

Although he was the premier free agent, he didn't receive an offer from any other club. In fact, none of the 62 free agents received an offer from any club but their own. Contract negotiations between Gibson and the Tigers were ugly, with both sides feeling slighted. The slugger accepted Detroit's offer of a 3-year, $4.1 million contract one minute before the deadline. A lot of hard-working Tiger fans saw him as greedy and unappreciative.

Fans' expectations rose, the attention intensified, and the pressure to perform at the highest level increased. Kirk said he brought it all on himself. "I'm flamboyant, abrasive, and I have a different personality. It draws attention."[29] *Detroit News* columnist Mitch Albom wrote that Gibson was a compelling attraction who could be the center of attention even when he was yawning.

Gibson reported to spring training in 1986 with something to prove. However, tendinitis in his left shoulder limited him to being the designated hitter. When the season opened on April 7, he was in right field. He got off to a terrific start. He was batting .359 on April 22 when he sprained his left ankle trying to get back to first base on a pick-off throw. He missed six weeks. His batting average and production dipped as he went 1-for-21 when he returned. He continued to struggle for several months.

Fans and the Tigers' front office were disenchanted with him. The club didn't believe it had received appropriate dividends on its hefty investment. General manager Bill Lajoie said, "If you take 8 or 10 games out of his stats, you wouldn't have a lot there. Unfortunately, he's more dramatic than consistent."[30] Gibson didn't make any excuses. "I outright stink," he said.[31]

In reality, Kirk had a decent season—28 homers, 86 RBI, 34 stolen bases, and a .268 batting average in 119 games. But, too often, he failed in the clutch as the Tigers finished third.

"I've failed more than it is like me in this game," he said. "I'm the one who led people to believe I could do the job in pressure situations. But there's been a lot of times this year that I haven't. It's not like me."[32]

A pulled ribcage muscle kept Gibson on the bench for the first month of the 1987 season.

In late September, the Tigers trailed the Blue Jays by three games with seven games remaining. The club won five of its remaining seven games, including a 1-0 win over the Blue Jays, to clinch the division title on the season's final day. The Tigers posted a 98-64 record, the best in baseball. The Minnesota Twins, however, captured the American League Championship Series, downing Detroit four games to one.

Arbitrator Thomas Roberts ruled on January 18, 1988, that major league baseball owners were guilty of collusion by restricting free agents in 1985. He ordered the owners to pay the players $10.5 million in damages. As part of the ruling, Gibson and six other players could offer their services to any other teams before March 1 without losing their existing contracts. Gibson signed a 3-year, $4.5 million contract with the Los Angeles Dodgers on January 29, 1988.

He preferred to stay in Detroit, but the Tigers wouldn't meet his contract demands. Leaving Detroit was one of the toughest decisions he had to make in his life. Not everyone, however, was sad to see him go. A *Detroit News* poll revealed that 70 percent of its readers wouldn't miss the slugger.

Tigers' owner Tom Monaghan, who also owned Domino's Pizza, blasted Gibson in his corporate newsletter. He called him "a disgrace to the Tigers uniform for his half beard. His best talent is hitting homers against right-handed pitchers and stealing bases, and they aren't worth $1.5 million a year, which means the best he could do for the Tigers would be to DH against right-handed pitching. He has one of the weaker arms in baseball for an outfielder and can't field well. He was a real liability in the field."[33]

The 31-year-old Gibson made it clear that winning a World Series title was his sole goal with the Dodgers. The club jumped to a 13-7 start and was in first place on Memorial Day. Gibson, free of injuries, adjusted quickly to the National League. At the end of May, he was hitting .292, leading the Dodgers in home runs, runs, and doubles, and tied for most RBI. His teammates praised his 'win-at-all-costs' attitude, aggressiveness, and leadership.

San Bernardino County Sun columnist Steve Dilbeck wrote, "Gibson plays hard and demands it for his teammates. He has brought a harder edge to the clubhouse, one that brooks no half-hearted efforts. The new team chemistry he has helped create has had a major impact on the team's success this year. The Dodgers are Kirk's team now."[34]

Los Angeles finished the 1988 season 94-67, seven games ahead of the Cincinnati Reds. Gibson nursed a pulled left hamstring in the final week of the season. He led the team in batting average (.290), runs (106), doubles (28), and home runs (25). Although his statistics weren't overwhelming, there was talk he deserved the Most Valuable Player Award. Sportswriters and fans recognized his value to the club and the intangibles he provided.

The pulled hamstring still bothered him when the Dodgers opened the National League Championship Series against the New York Mets. In Game 4, with the Mets leading two games to one, Gibson delivered the winning blow. He pounded a solo homer off Roger McDowell in the top of the 12th inning, snapping a 3-3 tie. He was 1-for-16 before his home run. The following day, he launched a three-run homer off Sid Fernandez in the fifth inning to expand a 3-0 lead. In the ninth inning, he singled and stole second base, aggravating his hamstring injury and seriously spraining his right knee. In Game 7, he delivered a sacrifice fly in the first inning, pushing across the only run the Dodgers needed en route to a 6-0 victory. His .154 average for the series belied his value to the club.

Twenty-four hours before the start of the 1988 World Series against the Oakland A's, he tried to swing a bat, but his knee was too painful. He tried to jog at home in his living room but couldn't. He arrived at Dodger Stadium so late he wasn't included in the pre-game introductions. Manager Tommy Lasorda penciled Mickey Hatcher in the lineup in left field, replacing Gibson.

Gibby figured there was no way he could play. He received a cortisone treatment and a pain killer in his knee. Hatcher staked the Dodgers to a 2-0 lead in the first inning with a home run. Oakland's Jose Canseco wiped that lead out with a grand slam in the second inning. Gibson removed the ice bags from his knees, put on his uniform, and took some practice swings in the batting cage near the clubhouse. He told Lasorda he was ready for a do-or-die effort.

Los Angeles added a run in the bottom of the sixth on Mike Scioscia's RBI single. A's relief ace Dennis Eckersley replaced Dave Stewart in the bottom of the ninth. Looking ahead, announcer Vin Scully said, "Gibson's gone from the dugout, so he won't be available if the Dodgers need him." Gibson's response was, "The hell I won't."[35] He told Lasorda he was ready to pinch hit.

Eckersley retired Scioscia on a flyout and Jeff Hamilton on a strikeout before Mike Davis walked. Gibson was announced as a pinch-hitter for pitcher Alejandro Pena, setting the stage for one of the most memorable moments in World Series history.

Gibson strode out of the dugout, swinging his bat as the fans rose to their feet. He fouled off the first two pitches from Eckersley. The tension was palpable. He dribbled the third pitch foul down the first-base line. The next pitch was outside. After another foul, Eckersley threw two pitches outside, running the count to 3-2. Davis stole second base on ball three, setting up the tying run.

Gibson called timeout and stepped out of the batter's box. He recalled the words of the Dodgers' advance scout Mel Didier, who told him that if Eckersley goes 3-and-2, he will see a back-door slider. Sure enough, Eckersley tried to sneak a back-door slider past Gibson. The slugger poked his bat out and used mainly his arm strength to send the ball towering over the right field fence, igniting a wild celebration. He limped around the bases on his two bad legs. He raised his fist high above his head when he stepped on first base, pumped his arms as he rounded second, and slowly navigated each base, celebrating each step. When he reached home, his teammates mobbed him. As the crowd continued its thunderous applause, he dished out a spate of high-fives and hugs.

"I must have been quite a sight, limping around the bases. I was moving, but barely. What I couldn't make my legs do, I let my right arm accomplish. I pumped the arm, hard, celebrating a triumph over every damn foe I had battled over the past ten years," he recalled.[36]

It would be Gibson's only appearance in the 1988 World Series, which the Dodgers won in five games. He was named the National League's Most Valuable Player after his World Series heroics. He became the fourth National Leaguer to win an MVP award without hitting 30 homers or driving in 100 runs.

Gibby's hamstring and knee still bothered him when he reported to spring training in 1989. Bursitis in his right shoulder also pained him. He was limited to six games in spring training. The Dodgers placed him on the DL on April 30, and he missed a month.

In June, he and his wife and two children were robbed at gunpoint by an intruder as they returned home. The intruder took several hundred dollars and drove off in Gibson's 1988 BMW. It was a traumatic incident. Kirk and his family moved into a hotel for the remainder of the season.

Kirk went on the DL again on July 23 due to his sprained knee. He had exploratory surgery, and doctors discovered that 50 percent of his hamstring had torn. They repaired it, and he was done for the season. He played 71 games and batted .213. The initial rehab was predicted to be ten months. Gibson didn't return to the Dodgers lineup until June 2, 1990.

He started slowly but heated up in July, raising his average to .290. With his contract set to expire, he asked the Dodgers to trade him to a team closer to his home in Michigan. Gibson battled a deep slump late in the season, going 37 games without a home run.

The Dodgers granted him free agency. He signed a two-year, $3.5 million contract with the Kansas City Royals on December 1, 1990. Manager John Wathan planned to bat him fifth and use him as a DH and an occasional outfielder. The DH role appealed to the 34-year-old. The Royals faltered out of the gate. They fired Wathan on May 22 and replaced him with Hal McRae. That move and George Brett coming off the DL changed Gibson's role. Instead of being the DH, he became the regular left fielder and batted first or second.

His first season with the Royals was a disaster. In 1991, he played in 132 games, clouted 16 homers, and batted .236. "I did a terrible job," he acknowledged.[37] During the off-season, McRae told Gibson he wouldn't be a full-time player in 1992. Unhappy, he requested a trade.

On March 10, the Royals traded him to Pittsburgh, where he was reunited with manager Jim Leyland. The Pirates acquired Gibson to help fill the void left by Bobby Bonilla's departure. The club guaranteed him $1.5 million. Gibson was hitting just .196 when the Pirates released him on May 10. He went home to ponder his future.

Feeling he could still compete and contribute, Gibson wasn't ready for retirement. There was talk the Detroit Tigers, under new ownership, were interested in bringing the aged and matured slugger back for a second stint. The Tigers resigned Gibson to a one-year, $500,000 contract with $600,000 in incentives on February 22, 1993. They figured he was worth the risk.

Gibby, aided by nine months of rest, was healthier than he had been in a long time. He contributed 13 homers and 62 RBI in 116 games while playing mainly DH and pinch-hitting. He signed a one-year, $1.5 million contract with the Tigers the following season. Manager Sparky Anderson used him against right-handed pitchers. Gibson responded with one of his best seasons. He had a chance, at age 38, to become the oldest player to record his first 100 RBI season. The players' strike on August 12 nixed that possibility. In 98 games, he racked up 23 homers, 72 RBI, and batted .276. Detroit writers named him the Tigers Player of the Year.

Playing his 17th season in 1995, Gibson slugged eight homers, including one in four consecutive games, and batted .345 in May. Then bursitis in his shoulders made it difficult and painful to swing. He surprised everyone when he announced his retirement on August 11, saying he had been traded to his family.

Detroit Free Press columnist Jerry Green wrote, "Kirk Gibson, a man of impact, drama, raging moods, and an awesome competitive streak, left in silence. He had a complex personality and a large vocabulary of cuss words. But, through it all, his work ethic, motivation, desire to improve, and competitive spirit were apparent."[38]

At his retirement press conference, Gibson noted he came into the league with a strikeout and left with a strikeout. "I came in being humble, and I leave being humble," he said.[39] He labeled himself "an average ballplayer who did exceptional things at the right time."[40] Sparky Anderson said, "Kirk will do more to win games for you than any other player I've ever seen."[41]

Although his early promise was never fulfilled, sportswriter Bob Hertzel may have explained it best after the 1984 World Series. He wrote, "For Kirk Gibson, it has always been the curse of talent, the burden of potential. Tigers' manager Sparky Anderson had looked at him and said he could be another Mickey Mantle, forgetting that there could be only one. Life is difficult enough when you're Kirk Gibson without shouldering the ghost of baseball greatness past."[42]

CHAPTER 14

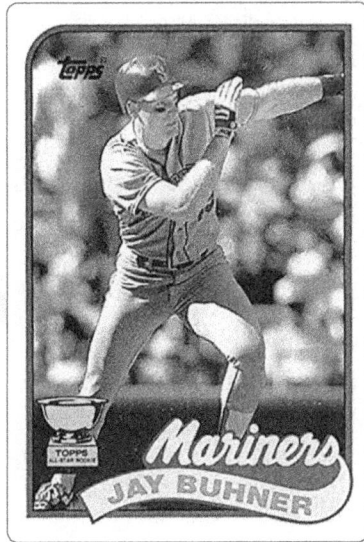

JAY BUHNER
THE UNDERAPPRECIATED PROSPECT

Jay's young, and he's going to make mistakes. But, when he's done developing, which he will because he'll get every chance with the Mariners, he has the makings of greatness.
—SEATTLE MARINERS MANAGER JIM SNYDER

In 1996, 31-year-old Jay Buhner smashed 44 home runs and tallied 138 RBI while batting .271 for the Seattle Mariners. The 6-foot-3, 220-pound right fielder also was named to the American League All-Star team and won a Gold Glove.

That season belies the fact that as a younger player, the highly touted Buhner was traded twice before the age of 24. The Pittsburgh Pirates and the New York Yankees lacked the patience to develop the young slugger, who the Yankees had envisioned as the "next Mickey Mantle."

After joining the Mariners at age 23, Buhner was given the opportunity to play every day. He developed into a feared slugger, defensive standout, and team leader. He enjoyed a productive 14-year career in Seattle.

The Texas resident was quickly noticed after he graduated from high school. He played college baseball for McLennan Community College in Waco, Texas. In 1983, his freshman year, the team made its fourth consecutive appearance in the Junior College World Series in Grand Junction, Colo., and won its first national championship. The Atlanta Braves selected Jay in the ninth round of the 1983 draft, but he opted not to sign. The Pittsburgh Pirates selected him in the second round of the secondary phase of the free agent draft the following year.

The 19-year-old signed his first pro contract in late May in the visitors' locker room at the Astrodome. He had wrapped up a home-run-hitting exhibition for Pirates manager Chuck Tanner and club executives. "The Pirates wanted me to show power and pull the ball. After hitting a couple of grounders, I hit one 410 feet over the center field fence," he said.[1] The Pirates didn't need any more convincing.

Pittsburgh sent him to the New York-Penn Class-A short-season league to play for Watertown, N.Y. He excelled immediately. In 65 games, Jay tied for the league lead with 58 RBI, clouted nine homers, and batted .323.

The Pirates sent Buhner, one of their brightest prospects, to the Winter Instructional League. Bucs' legend and hitting instructor Willie Stargell befriended him. He saw Jay's potential as the next Stargell or Dave Parker. He tried to convince the Bucs' front office to keep Buhner.

But, on December 20, 1984, the Pirates traded Buhner, along with infielder Dale Berra and pitcher Alfonso Pulido, to the New York Yankees for infielder Tim Foli, outfielder Steve Kemp and $800,000. Stargell called Buhner and said he did everything he could to keep the club from trading him. "I told the Pirates you were going to make it," he said.[2]

Buhner had mixed feelings about the trade. "The Pirates said they were real high on me; then they traded me. To be traded for major league players is a pat on my back, but here I am, 20 years old and already traded."[3] He didn't hold any grudges against the Bucs because his goal was to get to the majors, and he didn't care with whom.

The Yankees assigned Buhner to Class-A Ft. Lauderdale in the Florida State League. Former Yankee hero Bucky Dent was his manager. Dent recognized the gem he had in uniform. "At least for the moment, you would have to call the trade a steal," he said. "You have to wonder how an organization lets a player with Jay's potential go so easily."[4]

Buhner was a raw talent with a lot of rough edges. He had trouble controlling his temper and intensity, lacked concentration on defense, and was undisciplined at the plate, resulting in frequent strikeouts. Additionally, he was cocky and egotistical. He and Dent butted heads on several occasions. Dent pushed the potential star hard because he knew what it took to get to the majors.

"I told him not to accept just being good because he had the potential to be great," said Dent.[5] He added, "Jay has all the tools. I'm sure he'll play in the big leagues someday. He's a definite prospect. He's got a real good arm, and he hits with power to all fields."[6]

Buhner, in a rush to make the majors, made his case. The 20-year-old banged 11 homers, drove in 76 runs, and batted .296 in 117 games. He established himself as one of the Yankees' brightest prospects. Yankees owner George Steinbrenner praised the young star: "Buhner reminds me of Mickey Mantle, the way he stands in center field with his shoulders drooping. He gets a great jump on the ball, and he hits the hell out of it."[7]

The Yankees' 1986 spring training camp was abuzz as writers, fans, and club executives wanted to get a look at the up-and-comer. Buhner was assigned temporarily to the Hollywood, Fla., training complex as the club decided where to place him. Five days after arriving at the complex, he suffered an injury that threatened to sideline him for the season. Buhner slid into second on a hit-and-run play and threw his arm up to prevent getting hit in the face with the relay throw. The shortstop kicked him in the right arm, snapping it on impact. For six weeks, he wore a plastic cast that extended from his elbow to his wrist. Next, he wore a shorter fiberglass cast for another four weeks. Finally, he spent two weeks in a movable cast and was required to rest for two weeks.

The Yankees placed him back with Class-A Ft. Lauderdale when he returned. Knowing he was rusty from the layoff, they saw no need to rush him by moving him up to Class AA. The youngster picked up where he left off. He hit seven homers and batted .302 in 36 games.

Peter Jameson, Yankees assistant director of player development, said, "Buhner has an above-average arm and is a line-drive hitter with home run power. He is one of our top prospects in the outfield. A lot of people thought he was a throw-in in the Pirates trade."[8]

The 22-year-old slugger opened the 1987 season with Class-AAA Columbus in the International League. He appeared to be ready for the majors. He batted .349 with five homers and 13 RBI after 22 games. The maturing Buhner capitalized on what manager Bucky Dent taught him. Dent, working with Buhner for the third consecutive year, focused on improving his mental approach and eliminating his self-criticism.

"When Jay hits them, he hits hard line drives that take off. You can't help but to think he's going to make it because he's such a good kid and a hard worker," said Dent.[9]

Yankees owner George Steinbrenner was enamored with Buhner. He promised not to trade him, at least not until he had a chance to prove what he could do at the major league level. Steinbrenner had a weakness for veteran players. He often dealt younger players to acquire them. Buhner was the possible heir to Dave Winfield, the Yankees' 35-year-old right fielder embroiled in a feud with Steinbrenner.

Buhner appeared destined for the Yankees' starting lineup when he led the International League with 31 homers and 20 outfield assists. He made his major league debut on September 11, 1987. The following day, he collected his first hit, a single off Toronto Blue Jay Jimmy Key.

Buhner started the 1988 season at Class-AAA Columbus. The Yankees recalled him on May 13. Manager Lou Piniella used him mainly in center field. In the first month, he batted .300, slugged his first major league homer, unloaded an opposite-field grand slam against the Baltimore Orioles, and powered a homer over Fenway Park's Green Monster. His range in the outfield, strong throwing arm, and ability to hit the ball long distances generated more comparisons to Mickey Mantle. The comparisons flattered and embarrassed Buhner. "It was fun because we have some similarities," he said. "But there was only one Mickey Mantle. I always knew that."[10]

Chris Chambliss, hitting instructor, and Clyde King, special advisor to George Steinbrenner, praised him. Chambliss termed him "an aggressive hitter with some pop in his bat.[11] King said, "He's shown he can hit the ball out of the park in both directions. And, he's one of the few guys who throws them like he hits them."[12]

The previously untouchable prospect slipped into a deep slump. He went 0-for-27 with 13 strikeouts. His average dropped from .300 to .179. The slump painfully highlighted his offensive weaknesses. New York fans were brutal, booing him nearly every at-bat. The Yankees shipped him back to Class-AAA Columbus.

The Yankees, trailing the Detroit Tigers by three games in the American League East, debated their needs. Some in the front office favored more pitching, while others believed the team needed a left-handed power bat. On July 21, 1988, the Yankees traded the 23-year-old Buhner and a player to be named later to the Seattle Mariners for 33-year-old designated hitter Ken Phelps. Phelps was the Mariners' all-time home run leader with 104. He knocked 20-plus homers in three of the past four seasons, with a career-high of 27 in 1987.

The trade surprised and confused people. "I was stunned by the deal," admitted Buhner, who went 18-for-91 (.198) with three homers, 14 RBI, and 30 strikeouts in his two stints (32 games) with New York. "All I've heard was hands off; he's untouchable. I had no idea that something like this was going to happen. I have trouble making sense of the trade. I'm 23, and Phelps is 34 (he would turn 34 in less than a month). I hate to leave New York. I'm disappointed in a way, but I guess it was time to move on."[13]

Buhner looked forward to playing every day without the pressure of wearing pinstripes. Phelps was stressed because he didn't know what to expect moving to the pressure cooker of New York City.

Jay didn't believe the Yankees had given him a fair chance. Yankees manager Lou Piniella disagreed. He said it made it difficult to get a rookie into the lineup with players such as Rickey Henderson, Dave Winfield, Jack Clark, and Don Mattingly on the team.

Moss Klein, a Yankees beat reporter, pointed out that Phelps, a designated hitter, was a defensive liability, didn't have a natural position and seldom played against left-handed pitching. He was most likely on the downside of his career.

Yankees general manager Bob Quinn explained, "We had to look at the deal from the standpoint of improving the club now. Buhner wasn't with us. He has great tools, but there's no guarantee he'll make it."[14]

The Mariners had never experienced a winning season. They were excited to welcome the young slugger, who also was a defensive asset. "He's the real thing," gushed Mariners manager Jim Snyder. "What he's got is pure instinct. You can refine it, but you can't bestow it on someone. It has to be there from the start. Jay's young, and he's going to make mistakes. But, when he's done developing, which he will because he'll get every chance with the Mariners, he has the makings of greatness."[15]

Seattle made Buhner their everyday right fielder. In August, the Mariners defeated the Yankees in five of seven games. The Yankees witnessed first-hand the terrible blunder they had made. Buhner blasted a pair of monstrous homers, clubbed four doubles, and went 11-for-24 (.458). He made several fine catches and displayed a rifle arm.

Besides his powerful bat and flashy glove, Buhner brought a rare intensity and vocal leadership to the team. Seattle had been accused of being too complacent and accepting of its losing ways. Mariners catcher Scott Bradley said, "The attitude Jay has brought to the Mariners is just great. He's just lifted the entire team. He's a throwback to the old days. He plays hard every day. He can do it all."[16]

The Jay Buhner-for-Ken Phelps was a fiasco for the Yankees. It is considered one of the worst trades in the Yankees' history and one of the worst trades in baseball history. Buhner bashed 307 homers in a 14-year career with the Mariners. He recorded three seasons of 40-plus homers and 100-plus RBI. Phelps played parts of two seasons with the Yankees. He batted .240 and knocked 17 home runs before being traded to the Oakland A's in 1989 for a minor leaguer.

A 1996 episode of the popular television comedy *Seinfeld* immortalized the trade. Actor Jerry Stiller, playing Frank Costanza, yells at an actor playing George Steinbrenner, "What the hell did you trade Jay Buhner for? He had 30 home runs and over 100 RBI last year. He's got a rocket for an arm. You don't know what the hell you're doing." The Steinbrenner character replies, "He was a good prospect, no doubt about it, but my baseball people loved Ken Phelps. They kept saying Ken Phelps, Ken Phelps."[17]

Buhner smacked 10 homers, drove in 25 runs, and batted .224 in 60 games with the 1988 Mariners. The team finished seventh in the American League West. Buhner arrived at spring training the following season, thinking the right field job was his. He led the team in home runs with four and tallied 12 RBI in pre-season. Despite his performance, Jay didn't make the opening-day roster. The Mariners shipped him to Class-AAA Calgary in the Pacific Coast League. The demotion was a slap in the face. "I should be in Seattle. I'm not pleased to be in Calgary, to say the least," he complained.[18]

First-year Mariners manager Jim Lefebvre wanted Buhner to improve his on-base percentage while at Calgary. Lefebvre was building his team around on-base percentage, not home run percentage. Seattle lit a fire under its potential star.

Buhner vowed to do whatever it took to get on base. He focused on improving his self-discipline, taking more pitches, and drawing more walks. His goal was to have as many walks as strikeouts. He reached base at a .456 clip, drew a team-leading 15 walks, and batted .328 in his first 17 games with Calgary.

The Mariners recalled him on June 1. Reflecting on his stint in Calgary, he said, "I wasn't a happy camper when I was sent down, but it may have done me a lot of good. It was humiliating, and my pride was hurt. But it also made me bear down."[19]

Buhner's improvement pleased manager Jim Lefebvre. His big outfielder was more relaxed, self-assured, and more of a professional hitter. Seattle placed Buhner on the 21-day disabled list on July 4 with a sprained ligament in his right wrist. He injured it when he slammed into the outfield wall to rob an opponent of an extra-base hit. Limited to 58 games, Jay hit nine homers and batted .275. He improved his on-base percentage to .341.

Injuries plagued Buhner in 1990. He tore ligaments in his ankle in spring training. He was on the disabled list until the Mariners assigned him to Calgary for a 20-day rehabilitation. He came off the disabled list on June 1 but went back on the list two weeks later. A pitch hit him and broke a bone in his right forearm. The 25-year-old longed for a chance to show the Mariners what he could do if he played full-time.

He got that chance in 1991. He played 137 games, slugged a team-high 27 homers, tallied 77 RBI, and batted .244. The team, with young stars such as Buhner, Ken Griffey Jr., Edgar Martinez, and Randy Johnson, posted its first winning season and finished fifth in the American League West.

He credited batting coach Gene Clines for rebuilding his confidence and making him a better hitter. Clines changed Jay's stance from a crouch to a more upright position. He got him to rock back and forth before the pitch to get in a rhythm to swing. "He's got me seeing the ball better and in a good frame of mind," said Jay.[20]

Clines took a slow, steady, and patient approach with Buhner. He convinced Buhner he was a hitter, not just a home run hitter. He emphasized using hits, walks, and other kinds of production to fill in between his home run streaks. Instead of just swinging, Buhner went to the plate with a plan.

Buhner, nicknamed "Bone," became a Seattle stalwart. His shaved head, goatee, and large personality endeared him to fans. His father, David, explained that "Bone" was short for "Bonehead." It is related to a childhood incident. "When he was in high school, Jay lost a fly ball in the lights, and it hit him square on the skull. The coach ran out to see if he was OK, and Jay was fine. The coach said, 'It's a good thing you've got a bony head.' Ever since then, he's been Bonehead."[21]

Buhner's arrival as a star was reinforced when he went to arbitration and was granted a salary of $1.4 million. He was paid $247,000 the previous year. Determined to prove he was worth the money, he forged three solid seasons, featuring 20-plus homers, from 1992-94. Under manager Lou Piniella, the Mariners finished seventh, fourth, and third (in the strike-shortened 1994 season).

Buhner and the Mariners entered the 1994 season at a financial standoff. He asked for $4.7 million per year, while the Mariners offered $4 million yearly. The outfielder was close to signing with the Baltimore Orioles as a free agent before teammate Ken Griffey Jr. got involved.

Griffey, one of the game's brightest young stars, went to management and said, 'If he goes, I go.' Taking the threat seriously, Seattle upped its offer. Buhner signed a three-year contract for $15.5 million in December 1994. Griffey kept his part of the bargain. He signed a four-year contract extension with the Mariners for $34 million.

After Griffey's intervention, Buhner said, "Do I know how to pick my friends?"[22]

Griffey added: "Jay's as important to our team as anyone, maybe more important than anyone."[23]

Manager Lou Piniella echoed Griffey's opinion. "Jay's an integral part of our team. He's outstanding in the fourth spot and has a lot of qualities in the clubhouse. Because of those factors, it was important to get him re-signed."[24]

Buhner was a major cog in the explosive 1995 Mariners offense. He slammed 40 homers and drove in 121 runs on just 123 hits. The club won the American League West. Buhner clouted a club-record 13 homers in September as the Mariners overtook the division-leading California Angels. Leading the Mariners to their first-ever playoffs was his biggest thrill in baseball.

Buhner was a thorn to the Yankees in the American League Divisional Series. He went 11-for-24 (.458) as Seattle won in five games. He slugged three homers and batted .308 in the American League Championship Series against the Cleveland Indians. Seattle lost in six games.

Buhner was one of the premier players in the game from 1996 through 1997. In 1996, he clouted 44 homers and drove in 138 RBI. Ken Griffey Jr. added 49 homers and tallied 140 RBI. Twenty-year-old shortstop Alex Rodriguez contributed 36 home runs and 123 RBI while leading the league with a .358 average. Despite their dynamic offense and 245 home runs, Seattle finished second in the American League West.

Buhner discussed his increased home run production. "I have become more consistent. I've learned about the little things and picked up knowledge about pitchers," he pointed out. "My swing has improved, and I've gotten more mature. I've always been a confident player."[25]

In 1997, he blasted 40 homers and drove in 109 runs. Griffey Jr. powered 56 homers and drove in 147 runs. Buhner became the 10th player to hit 40-plus homers in three consecutive seasons (something Mickey Mantle never accomplished). Although he led the league in strikeouts in 1996 and 1997, his run production made up for the whiffs. He averaged 100 walks in those seasons. The team walloped a then-record 264 homers in 1997. Every starter finished in double figures. The Mariners won the American League West before falling to the Baltimore Orioles in four games in the American League Division Series.

Over the next four seasons, a series of injuries and surgeries turned Buhner into a part-time player. He appeared in 100 or more games just once. In 2001, his final season, the Mariners won a record-tying 116 games. He played in only 19 games because of plantar fasciitis in his right foot.

The 36-year-old Buhner announced his retirement at the end of the 2001 season. His passion for playing and disregard for outfield walls sent him to the disabled list ten times, costing him hundreds of games. Buhner's body could no longer take the punishment of professional baseball.

"I think I will toot my own horn," he said. "I did leave it on the field, and that's the reason I have to retire. I'm beat and battered, but I'm a realist, and I realize there's no greater time for me to go out."[26] When he hung up his cleats, he had played 15 years, slammed 310 home runs, driven in 965 runs, and batted .254. He was one of the most popular and beloved athletes in the Pacific Northwest. Buhner was inducted into the Seattle Mariners Hall of Fame in August 2004. It was appropriate they played the *Seinfeld* clip on the Safeco Field video board during the ceremony.

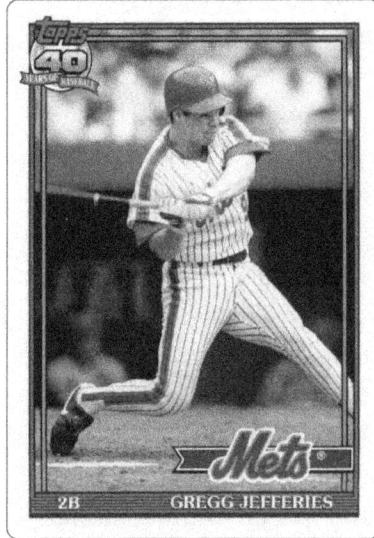

2B   GREGG JEFFERIES

GREGG JEFFERIES
THE WUNDERKIND

Some players are labeled 'can't miss.' Gregg's better than that.
He's inevitable.
—New York Mets manager Davey Johnson

Gregg Jefferies was the most hyped rookie in New York Mets history. If you paid attention to the hype emanating from the Big Apple, you knew Jefferies, a 20-year-old switch-hitter with power from both sides of the plate, was a legend in waiting, a player who already had his ticket punched for the Baseball Hall of Fame, a crown jewel around which the Mets could build a dynasty.

Make no mistake, Jefferies owned impressive, almost God-like, minor-league credentials. He inspired breathless comparisons to Mickey

Mantle. In 1987, a minor league baseball writer wrote, "The likes of the 19-year-old, full-blooded phenom have not been seen since Mickey Mantle blew in off the Oklahoma prairie 40 years ago."[1]

Jefferies was the subject of a *Sports Illustrated* feature while still in the minor leagues. The magazine focused on his intense 8-hour-a-day, six-days-a-week baseball workouts with his father. "He is arguably the best baseball player not on a major league roster," offered *SI* writer Jill Lieber.[2]

There was nothing beyond Jefferies' reach—a batting title or two, Most Valuable Player, or even *People's* Sexiest Man Alive award. But New York City wasn't Kingston, Tennessee, Jackson, Mississippi, Lynchburg, Virginia, or Tidewater, Virginia, some of his minor league stops. It was unlike anything he could have imagined.

New York Met Darryl Strawberry, 1983 Rookie of the Year, issued a prophetic word of caution: "All those writers every day, nothing can prepare you for that. You can't compare a 20-year-old to a Hall of Famer because he'll only disappoint."[3]

Even though Jefferies was a two-time All-Star in his 14-year career, he was a major disappointment to Mets' fans, their front office, and those who staunchly believed talent was the sole determinant of success.

The 5-foot-10, 175-pounder was drafted 20th in the 1985 major league amateur draft after a stellar career at Junipero Serra High School in San Mateo, Calif. Some players drafted ahead of him included B.J. Surhoff, Will Clark, Barry Larkin, and Barry Bonds. The 17-year-old received a signing bonus of $110,000. The Mets assigned him to the Appalachian Rookie League in Kingsport, Tennessee. He played short-stop and batted .343 before being promoted to Class-A Columbia, South Carolina.

The following season, he played for Class-A Columbia and Lynchburg and Class-AA Jackson. He compiled a .353 average, 16 homers, 111 RBI, and 57 stolen bases. He was named the 1986 Carolina League Player of the Year and *Baseball America's* Minor League Player of the Year.

He continued to awe fans and the Mets' front office in 1987 when he batted .367 with 20 home runs, 101 RBI, and 26 stolen bases for Jackson, Miss., in the Texas League. He was named Texas League Player of the Year and once again *Baseball America's* Minor League Player of the

Year. It was the first time any player earned the *Baseball America* award in back-to-back years. The feat wasn't duplicated until Andruw Jones accomplished it in 1995 and 1996.

Mets' special assignment scout Darrell Johnson observed, "Gregg Jefferies was the best 18-year-old hitter I ever saw, and he was the best 19-year-old hitter I ever saw."[4]

New York called him up from Class-AA Jackson for six games to finish the 1987 season. He fouled out in his first at-bat, eliciting a "Go back to Jackson (the Mets' AA team)" yell from a fan. The 19-year-old rapped three hits in six at-bats, stirring up even more excitement about the future.

The Mets invited the youngster to spring training camp in 1988. Although the infielder batted .333 (10-for-30 in 12 games), the club sent him to Class-AAA Tidewater, where he could get more experience. Mets manager Davey Johnson said, "I hated to send the kid down. I enjoy watching him play. Some players are labeled 'can't miss.' He's better than that. He's inevitable."[5]

While Jefferies didn't put up gaudy numbers like he had his first two seasons, he notched a 24-game hitting streak and batted .282. He continued to struggle in the field. He committed more than 100 errors in three seasons, playing mostly shortstop.

The first-place Mets promoted Jefferies on August 28. The wunderkind was expected to pinch hit and give the club extra bench strength down the stretch. Many of the Mets resented the hype Jefferies received. That resentment was fueled when the club gave Jefferies the locker next to Keith Hernandez, the team's leader. Veteran Wally Backman, a fan favorite and member of the 1986 World Champion team, was displaced and forced to take a locker elsewhere.

Manager Davey Johnson plugged him into the starting lineup. Some of the veteran infielders were upset. They didn't think the team needed the rookie's help. Gregg stunned everyone as he went 24-for-52 (.462) in his first 13 games. He lashed 14 extra-base hits, including 7 doubles, 2 triples, and 5 homers. He batted .321 in 29 games. He committed just two errors, playing second base and third base. The Mets went 22-7 to finish 100-60, 15 games ahead of second-place Pittsburgh.

Jefferies was too good not to start in the National League Championship Series against the Los Angeles Dodgers. The Dodgers were massive underdogs. They beat the Mets just once in 11 games during the regular season. Although they were 94-67, they had no .300 hitter, 100-RBI, or 30-home run slugger. Pitching was their forte, and Orel Hershiser (23-8) was their ace. Darryl Strawberry (39 home runs, 101 RBI) and Kevin McReynolds (27 home runs, 99 RBI) powered the Mets. Starters David Cone (20-3), Dwight Gooden (18-9), and Ron Darling (17-9) troubled hitters all year long.

The Mets, winner of the 1986 World Series, looked to redeem themselves after a disappointing second-place finish in 1987. They wanted to prove they were a dynasty in the making.

The Mets' Dwight Gooden faced the Dodgers' Orel Hershiser in the opener. The Dodgers' right-hander was the hottest pitcher in baseball, riding a record-setting 59 consecutive innings scoreless streak. Hershiser extended his streak to 67 consecutive innings with eight scoreless innings. The Mets trailed 2-0 going into the top of the ninth. Jefferies started the Mets' rally with a single, his third of the game. He advanced to second on Keith Hernandez's ground-out. Darryl Strawberry doubled, sending Jefferies home and knocking Hershiser out of the game. Reliever Jay Howell walked Kevin McReynolds, struck out Howard Johnson, and surrendered a two-run double to Gary Carter. Mets' reliever Randy Myers held the Dodgers scoreless in the bottom of the ninth to secure the 3-2 win. Jefferies played a key role in a pressure-packed game in front of 55,582 fans in Dodger Stadium against the toughest pitcher in baseball.

The Mets and the Dodgers split the next two games to set up Game 4, which turned out to be a 12-inning nail-biter. Jefferies, hitless in the game, figured in two crucial situations. He failed to advance a runner into scoring position when he popped up a bunt attempt to the catcher in the bottom of the 10th inning with the score tied 4-4 and no outs.

Dodger Kirk Gibson unloaded a dramatic solo homer off Roger McDowell in the top of the 12th to snap the 4-4 tie. In the bottom of the inning, Mackey Sasser and Lee Mazzilli singled, setting the stage for Jefferies. The rookie flied out to left field. Keith Hernandez walked, and Darryl Strawberry popped out. With two outs, ace Orel Hershiser relieved Jesse Orosco and retired Kevin McReynolds.

The clubs split the next two games to set up Game 7. The pitching matchup featured the Mets' Ron Darling against the Dodgers' Orel Hershiser. The Dodgers' bulldog dominated the New Yorkers, surrendering just five hits (two by Jefferies). Los Angeles led 6-0 after the second inning and coasted to the win.

The New York Mets dynasty would have to wait (it never came). The future, however, would include 21-year-old Gregg Jefferies, who batted .333 (9-for-27) in the series. He proved he was a rare talent and belonged in the major leagues.

Jefferies was one of the hottest commodities in baseball during the off-season. He was in high demand for autograph shows, commanding as much as $13,000 for three hours of signing. Collectors gobbled up his Fleer rookie card for as much as $10. One overly enthusiastic Hartford, Conn., card dealer speculated Jefferies' rookie card could be worth as much as $100 in four years. Today, you can buy it for $5.99. Posters, plaques, and other baseball memorabilia featuring Jefferies were produced in outrageous quantities. All the attention galled many of the veteran Mets.

Jefferies was a player without a position, despite his outstanding performance at the end of 1988. He played mainly shortstop in the minors, but it was clear he was no major league shortstop. He played third base throughout the NLCS, forcing Howard Johnson to move to shortstop. Kevin Elster replaced Johnson at shortstop midway through the series.

The Mets had a surplus of young infielders. Wally Backman, 28, and Tim Teufel, 29, platooned at second base. Elster, 23, handled shortstop, and Johnson, 27, held down the hot corner. Dave Magadan, 25, could play first base or third base. Kevin Miller, 25, played second, short, and third. Veteran Keith Hernandez started at first base. Jefferies took playing time away from the veterans and was a threat to practically every infielder. Although where he would play was a question, Mets' vice president Joe McIlvaine said, "When Gregg's ready, we'll create a position for him."[6] The 1989 New York Mets were only three years removed from the 1986 World Champion team. Author Jeff Pearlman described the 1986 team as "an X-rated clubhouse of booze hounds, skirt chasers and bar fighters. They played hard and partied even harder."[7] They were arrogant, cocky, intimidating, bullies and tormentors. They were as reprehensible as they were talented, and they were extremely talented. Jefferies called his parents every night, and didn't smoke, drink or chase women. He was like a choir boy riding with the Hell's Angels.

The Mets were favored to win the National League East. One sportswriter predicted they would win 110 games and stamp themselves as legends like the 1927 Yankees and the 1976 Cincinnati Reds. The Mets declared they were the best team in baseball. Manager Davey Johnson said the club would be in the hunt for the World Series. He looked for the team to win its second world championship in four years. That would put them in the discussion as one of the greatest teams of all time.

Jefferies was the center of attention when spring training opened in Port St. Lucie, Fla. The hype entered another stratosphere. Mets' vice president Al Harazin said, "Only God had a bigger buildup."[8] Jefferies deflected as much attention as possible. "People are making me out to be the next Mickey Mantle or Pete Rose," he said. "I just want to be the next Gregg Jefferies."[9]

One of the sure bets for the upcoming season was Gregg Jefferies would win the 1989 National League Rookie of the Year. The Mets had been careful not to let their young star exceed 130 at-bats, preventing him from qualifying as a rookie (He had 115 at-bats before the 1989 season).

All the distractions in spring training contributed to Gregg hitting .108. The perfectionist put excruciating pressure on himself. Bill Robinson, the Mets' hitting instructor, had battled the 'next Mickey Mantle' label as a New York Yankee. He understood what Jefferies was going through. "He's a good player and a good hitter, but he might be a little too critical of himself. If he doesn't get a hit every time up, he gets mad."[10]

Jefferies was in the Mets' starting lineup on Opening Day. He batted second and played second base. He collected two hits, made an error, and missed a relay throw as New York beat St. Louis. He was uncomfortable at second base, but it was his only infield option.

Third baseman Howard Johnson's home run, RBI, and batting average had dropped significantly during the 1988 season. The club sought to trade him, but that never happened. Unhappy with platooning, second baseman Wally Backman requested a trade and was shipped to the Minnesota Twins.

The first two months of the 1989 season were a disaster for Gregg. At the end of May, he was batting .187 with no home runs and 13 RBI. He lost his confidence, swung at bad pitches, and took every out personally. He tried to pull every pitch to hit homers but didn't adjust to pitchers. Whenever he made an out, he threw his helmet, tore off his batting gloves, and sulked. That behavior didn't go over well with his teammates, the fans, or the media. Howard Johnson observed, "Gregg has been built up by some people in New York as a certain Hall of Famer. That's a joke."[11]

The Mets perceived Jefferies as an arrogant and overrated spoiled kid who received too much attention. They felt he was selfish and cared more about his statistics than the team's success. His teammates said he took himself too seriously. In the clubhouse, he constantly swung one of his specially made bats that reportedly cost $100 each. He polished them daily with alcohol and kept them locked up.

Players thought manager Davey Johnson coddled Jefferies. He stuck with him through a deep slump when other players would have been benched. Johnson started to platoon the slumping Jefferies with Tim Teufel. He quickly returned to Jefferies as a starter, saying he was concerned about his feelings and fragile psyche. Teufel wondered if his feelings counted.

Johnson demonstrated how to turn the double play and other finer points of the position to Jefferies. Some of the players wondered what coaches were for. Jefferies played a timid second base, avoiding contact on the double play. He was consistently out of position when taking throws on stolen base attempts. He was a self-described "butcher at second base."[12]

Fans and the media debated whether he should be sent down to AAA Tidewater. Some Mets wondered why he was still on the team, much less in the lineup. What was the rush to make a 21-year-old the cornerstone of the club? When the lineup card, which included Jefferies batting about .180, was posted one day, a Met wrote "Are we still trying?" next to his name.

Jefferies strongly opposed being demoted. He thought it would mean he was a failure. Johnson and others in the Mets' front office wondered if the demotion would crush the perfectionist. Was it better for him to play in a circus-like atmosphere where every at-bat and ground ball came with extraordinary pressure and expectations? Did it matter that his teammates resented him?

On June 15, the Mets had a lackluster 32-30 record and were tied for third place. Underachieving at bat and in the field, Jefferies was blamed for the poor start.

"It's stupid and ridiculous to keep centering on a rookie as if his problems are why we're struggling," declared manager Davey Johnson. "I'm sick and tired of everybody talking about a rookie and putting that kind of pressure on him."[13]

Jefferies irritated Johnson with his pouting and slow walks back to the dugout after making an out. But Johnson believed the Mets' jealousies and resentments were petty and overdone.

Johnson benched Jefferies for nearly two weeks at the beginning of August. When he returned, Johnson moved him into the leadoff position. Jefferies responded with an 11-game hitting streak. The benching was a turning point in the season. Jefferies batted .308 in the final two months.

"I'm relaxed, and the game is fun again," he said. "I felt no pressure, and that immediately allowed me to enjoy myself more. Early in the season, I felt every loss. I took them all to heart, blamed myself for every defeat. The other difference is that I got into bad habits and was swinging at bad pitches. Now, I'm taking pitches, getting ahead in the count, and things have turned around."[14]

The hostility toward Jefferies visibly surfaced on September 27, the final Mets home game of the season against the Philadelphia Phillies. With two outs in the bottom of the ninth, Roger McDowell trotted in from the bullpen to face Jefferies, his former teammate. McDowell had been one of Jefferies' main tormentors. He was rumored to have been the player who sawed several of his precious bats in two. McDowell and centerfielder Lenny Dykstra were traded to the Phillies on June 18.

Jefferies grounded out to second base to end the game. As the out was being made, McDowell said something to Jefferies, who charged the mound and wrestled his former teammate to the ground. That ignited a bench-clearing brawl.

Phillies' manager Nick Leyva snidely remarked, "There were 30 of our guys rooting for Roger and 20 of their guys rooting for him."[15]

Years later, McDowell said, "Gregg Jefferies killed us (the Mets). He was treated as an outcast because he was an arrogant kid who thought he was better than everyone else. Other than wearing a uniform, he was not part of our club."[16]

Jefferies' nightmarish year ended with him batting .258 with 12 homers and 56 RBI in 141 games. The once highly touted rookie placed a distant third in the 1989 National League Rookie of the Year voting behind the Chicago Cubs' Jerome Walton and Dwight Smith.

New York finished a disappointing second with an 87-75 record. Many Mets and their fans blamed Jefferies for the club's failure. They said the club stuck with the slumping rookie too long, accommodated him too much, and suffered because of his poor defense. The wunderkind failed to deliver.

It was a hellish and nightmarish season for Jefferies. The best thing about his rookie season was that it was over. He arrived at spring training in 1990 with a new attitude. He consciously tried to improve relationships with his teammates and tone down his temper. He accepted some blame for how things had gone in his rookie season.

There was less tension in the clubhouse. Pitchers Roger McDowell and Randy Myers had been traded, in part, because of their problems with Jefferies. Management's strong message was that players better learn to accept the upcoming star. First baseman Keith Hernandez signed with the Cleveland Indians as a free agent. He cited Jefferies as one of the reasons he didn't re-sign with the Mets.

Veterans like relief pitcher Bob Ojeda vowed to nip Jefferies' bad behavior in the bud. "We don't hate Gregg. We just don't like some of the things he did," said Ojeda, who felt the Mets didn't deal with Jefferies correctly in the past.[17]

Manager Davey Johnson said Jefferies had been very immature and handled himself poorly the previous year. Keith Hernandez added that although Jefferies was a rookie, "He acted as if he had won three batting titles."[18]

The Mets were favored to win the National League East. The club got off to a 20-22 start, and manager Davey Johnson was fired at the end of May. Coach Bud Harrelson took the reins and guided the New Yorkers to an overall 91-71 record and a second-place finish.

Jefferies' sophomore season was like Disney World compared to his rookie year. The budding star was hitting .300 as late as September 2. But he tired and faltered the final month. With less pressure, tension, and backstabbing, the 22-year-old batted a respectable .283 with 15 homers and 68 RBI. He led the National League in doubles with 40. The Mets, however, still tolerated his antics of throwing his helmet, ripping off his batting gloves, and pouting after nearly every out. He continued to rub teammates the wrong way.

Jefferies reported to spring training in 1991, declaring he had matured and grown up. Yet, he said he didn't want to play second base, and he didn't want to hit second in the lineup. To teammates, it was the sound of a selfish prima donna. Manager Bud Harrelson moved Jefferies to third base and Howard Johnson to shortstop late in the season. Jefferies wanted to stay at the hot corner. He preferred to bat third, where he wouldn't have to take so many pitches or hit-and-run as much.

The season opened with Jefferies playing third base and batting second behind speedy Vince Coleman. Thirty-five-year-old Tommy Herr, acquired from the St. Louis Cardinals at the end of the 1990 season, played second base. When Harrelson replaced Herr with Jefferies early in the season, there was a lot of grumbling from Mets' pitchers. They preferred Herr's defense. Jefferies' shoddy defense led one New York sportswriter to write, "Watching Jefferies play second base is like watching a house painter put a second coat on the Sistine Chapel."[19]

Tension and backstabbing once again filled the Mets' clubhouse. The atmosphere was as toxic as it was in 1989. Tired of the criticism by his teammates, the fans, and the media, Jefferies penned a nine-paragraph letter to WFAN radio. The letter fueled the flames of resentment and animosity.

"I have never claimed to be the future of the Mets; this was a label that was put on me," he wrote. "I can only hope that one day those teammates who have found it convenient to criticize me will realize that we are all in this together. If only we can concentrate more on the games rather than complaining and bickering and pointing fingers, we would all be better off."[20]

Jefferies hoped to clear the air and correct misunderstandings. The letter did neither. It solidified his reputation as an immature crybaby and whiner. The letter triggered a closed-door team meeting. His teammates treated him like a leper for the rest of the season. Years later, he admitted the WFAN letter was probably the worst thing he could have done.

"I never said I would hit .340. I never claimed to be Mickey Mantle. You can only take this for so long," he told reporters.[21]

A month later, Bob Ojeda, a former teammate and critic who had been traded to the Los Angeles Dodgers, piled on. He said, "The organization (the Mets) started going downhill when it decided to build the team around Jefferies. They made bad trades. They moved people around, and they ticked off veterans. How many moves were dictated by Jefferies?"[22]

The 1991 season ended with the Mets buried in fifth place. The club fired Bud Harrelson and replaced him with Mike Cubbage. The New Yorkers were no longer a talent-laden squad. A shakeup loomed, and Jefferies was trade bait.

On December 11, 1991, Jefferies was traded to the Kansas City Royals along with Kevin McReynolds and Kevin Miller for infielder Bill Pecota and two-time Cy Young Award winner Bret Saberhagen. After the trade, Mets' vice president Al Harazin said, "We still think Gregg Jefferies will be a great player."[23]

Joining the Royals gave Jefferies a clean slate and a refreshing environment. No one was touting him as the next superstar, batting champ, or Most Valuable Player. Going from New York, where a horde of media analyzed your every move, to small-media-market Kansas City, where a handful of reporters covered the games, was a welcomed change.

The Royals had been active in the trade market after finishing sixth in the American League in 1991. But hopes of improving their record disappeared with a horrendous 1-16 start. The Royals accepted Jefferies, and the season was relatively drama free.

The highlight of the season for Jefferies was an 18-game hitting streak. Offensively, he delivered a respectable season. He batted .285, tying George Brett for the team high; he led the Royals in RBI with 75 and stolen bases with 19. Defensively, he was a liability at third base. He made 26 errors to top all American League third basemen.

On February 22, 1993, the Royals traded him and a minor leaguer to the St. Louis Cardinals for outfielder Felix Jose and infielder Craig Wilson. Kansas City parted with Jefferies because they felt Keith Miller was an adequate replacement at third base and needed a power-hitting outfielder.

Cardinals' manager Joe Torre admired Jefferies for years, and he pushed for the deal. "I really covet the kid. I liked him with the Mets. He was such a good hitter, then he got caught up in the whole New York thing, and that can be rough."[24]

St. Louis planned to play the erratic infielder at first base, a position he had never played. Torre figured since the position was less demanding defensively, it would allow Jefferies to be more relaxed and play better.

Torre nurtured the 25-year-old, and it paid off. In mid-June, Gregg led the Cardinals in batting average, hits, home runs, runs, and stolen bases. He was the club's best overall player. In two weeks in June, the Cardinals' number three hitter raised his average by 53 points with one four-hit game, five three-hit games, and a pair of two-hit games.

Baseball was fun again. He was batting .343 and contending for the National League batting title at the All-Star break. He made the All-Star team as an alternate due to an injury to the San Francisco Giants' Robby Thompson.

He played up to his potential for the first time in his major league career. He batted .342, finishing fourth in the National League batting race behind Andres Galarraga (.370), John Olerud (.363), and Tony Gwynn (.358). He added 16 home runs, 83 RBI, and 46 stolen bases as the Cardinals finished in third place. He was only the fifth player to bat .340 with an on-base percentage of at least .400, a slugging average of at least .450, and 40 stolen bases. The other players were Tony Gwynn and Paul Molitor in 1987, Rod Carew in 1973, and Kiki Cuyler in 1929.

Jefferies earned $2.65 million in 1993. He asked for a raise to $4.6 million, while the Cardinals offered $3.7 million. He won the arbitration case and became the club's first $4 million player. St. Louis offered

Jefferies a 4-year, $20 million contract midway through the 1993 season. He rejected it because it lacked a no-trade clause. Additionally, he wanted a $1.5 million signing bonus.

Jefferies had a strong start in 1994, but the Cardinals never got untracked. When the players' strike halted action on August 12, Gregg was batting .325 and had been named an All-Star for the second year in a row. St. Louis was mired in third place.

Jefferies signed a four-year, $20 million contract as a free agent with the Philadelphia Phillies on December 14, 1994. Phillies general manager Lee Thomas said, "We got Gregg because we felt he was the best pure hitter available."[25] The deal shocked many observers. Jefferies was neither a marquee player nor a home run hitter. He was the only player making $5 million a year who hadn't tallied 100 RBI, 100 runs, or 20 home runs.

The Phillies expected him to spark the offense. He had a reputation as a solid clutch hitter who seldom struck out. The club felt he would make the adjustments needed to play left field.

The Phillies believed the 27-year-old Jefferies was on the verge of reaching his prime. He entered the 1995 season with 959 hits. Only two active players had more hits and were younger—Roberto Alomar (1,174 hits, 27 years, 2 months) and Ken Griffey Jr. (972 hits, 25 years, 5 months).

The pressure on Jefferies to prove he was worth $5 million a year was palpable. The Phillies jumped to a great start, but their newest addition struggled. On May 25, he was batting .235, including .120 with runners in scoring position. He reverted to his childish behaviors of throwing his helmet, pouting, and being self-centered.

Teammate Jim Eisenreich observed later in the season, "If he got his hits, he was OK. One time, Gregg said, 'It's good we're winning because I'm sure stinking it up. It's kind of a double negative.'"[26]

Jefferies, 27, collected his 1,000th hit on June 11, 1995. It was an encouraging milestone. Pete Rose was 27 when he notched his 1,000th hit. The Phillies placed Gregg on the 15-day disabled list with an inflamed left thumb on June 18. Philadelphia reached its high-water mark of the season on June 25 as they raised their record to 37-18, good for a 4.5-game lead over second-place Montreal Expos.

A strained right hamstring bothered Gregg all season. It limited his ability to run, cover ground in left field, and steal bases. Additionally, the artificial turf at Veterans Stadium was hard on his legs. Manager Jim Fregosi moved him to first base on July 18, which ignited an impressive turnaround.

Jefferies' behavior continued to irritate and alienate his teammates. He angrily tossed his batting helmet into the right-field bullpen at Wrigley Field, nearly hitting one of the Phillies' relief pitchers. In a closed-door meeting a couple of days later, Fregosi loudly criticized him for acting unprofessionally. Gregg promised to stop throwing his helmet and better control his emotions. His teammates labeled him a crybaby.

Although a wealth of injuries and slumps sent the Phillies into a nosedive in the second half of the season, Jefferies batted .347 after the All-Star break. He drove in twice as many runs as he had in the first half. On August 25, he became the first Phillie since Johnny Callison in 1963 to hit for the cycle. He completed the rare feat with no outs in the fifth inning.

The once-promising Phillies finished tied for second place, 21 games behind the Atlanta Braves. Jefferies closed with a .307 batting average. While he didn't show much power, his 11 home runs tied Charlie Hayes for the team high.

The 1996 season started poorly for Jefferies. In the third game of the season, he slid headfirst into third base after hitting a triple, tore the ligament in his left thumb, and fractured his right pinky finger. He was sidelined for two months. When he returned, the club was 28-28, nine games out of first place. With the Phillies going nowhere, Jefferies was on the trading block. He failed to meet expectations as one of the highest-paid players in the game. His .292 average did little to help the Phillies. They finished 67-95 in last place, 29 games out of first.

"Although Jefferies is probably the Phillies' best pure hitter, there is a strong belief throughout the clubhouse that the Phils will never win anything with Jefferies as the focal point of the club," wrote Bob Brookover, a *Camden Courier* reporter. "Jefferies' perception of himself is the polar opposite of how he's perceived by many of his teammates and other club personnel."[27]

Gregg reported to spring training in 1997, vowing to work on controlling his emotions and rehabilitating his image as an immature and selfish player. It was sad commentary for a player who had been in the major leagues for almost ten years. He considered his first two years with the Phillies disappointing.

First-year manager Terry Francona moved him back to left field. Hot prospect Scott Rolen manned third base, and Rico Brogna was at first. The team was terrible (they were 32 games out of first place at the All-Star break), and Jefferies was a $5 million-a-year albatross. The *Wilmington News Journal* labeled him as perhaps the worst $5 million per year player ever. He was benched for a couple of weeks in June, on the disabled list in August, and sat out the season's final three weeks with a bad hamstring. He batted .256 with 48 RBI in 130 games, the worst year of his career. "If I hit .250 again, I'll quit," he declared.[28] The Phillies' failed to protect Jefferies in the 1997 expansion draft. The veteran cooperated by waiving his protection rights and his no-trade clause. Neither the Arizona Diamondbacks nor the Tampa Bay Devil Rays selected him.

The forecast for the 1998 Phillies was gloomy. Jefferies was in the final year of his four-year contract, and it was clear he would not return. General manager Ed Wade said, "Gregg's career here never met expectations. A lot of his desirability was based on what he had accomplished in St. Louis."[29]

The Phillies traded Jefferies to the Anaheim Angels on August 28 for a player to be named later. The Angels led the American League West. They hoped Jefferies' bat and experience would help their stretch run. He batted .347 in 19 games, but the club faltered in September, finishing in second place.

Granted free agency, he signed a two-year, $4.8 million contract with the Detroit Tigers. The club planned to use him as a full-time designated hitter and pinch-hitter He had trouble adjusting to the DH role and battled a strained hamstring. He batted just .200 in 70 games in 1999.

A strong performance in spring training lifted Jefferies' spirits. Manager Phil Garner moved him back to the infield, splitting his time between first and second base. Jefferies was getting around on the ball, spraying line drives, and was one of the club's most consistent hitters.

In late May 2000, he ran out a ground ball and stopped suddenly after feeling like he had been shot. Initially, it was thought he had torn his right hamstring and would be out for four to six weeks. Later tests revealed he had severed his right hamstring. "My doctor and trainer said, 'We can't fix your hamstring.' It was devastating."[30]

Jefferies' career was abruptly over at age 32. He planned on playing until he was 40, but now he had no option. In 14 years, he played in 1,465 games, rapped 1,593 hits, and compiled a .289 lifetime average. He committed the unpardonable baseball sin of being good when greatness was predicted. He would forever wear the label of an underachiever and an outcast in the clubhouse.

Near the end of his career, he said, "When I broke in 1987, I was supposed to be the next Mickey Mantle. I can't live up to that. You're talking about one of the greatest players of all time."[31]

Mark Carreon, who played with Jefferies in New York, summed up the one-time wunderkind's career: "I think a different time, a different place, he could have made a run at the Hall of Fame. He was that kind of hitter."[32]

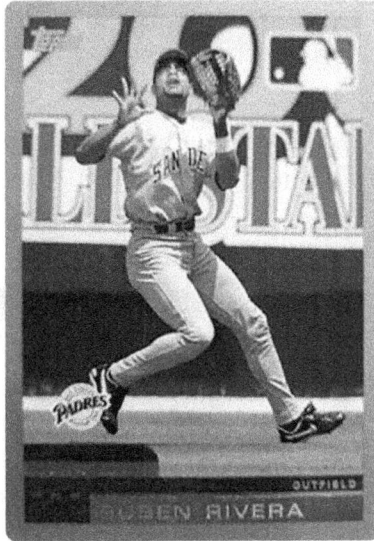

RUBEN RIVERA
THE COLOSSAL MYSTERY

*Of all the next Mickey Mantles, none had the full quota of
God-given talent to bring an entire ball field of players, coaches,
and scouts to attention the way Ruben Rivera has.*
—BILL MADDEN OF THE *NEW YORK DAILY NEWS*

There's the Mystery of the Great Sphinx, and then there's the Mystery of
Ruben Rivera.

Both have baffled experts. While Egyptologists wrestle with the age
of the Great Sphinx, why and how it was built, baseball men are puzzled
how a five-tool player, who was once compared to Mickey Mantle, Dave
Winfield, Barry Bonds, and Ken Griffey Jr., failed miserably at the big
league level. Instead of achieving predicted greatness, Rivera batted .216
in a nine-year, trouble-filled career, playing for five teams.

Rivera spent more time playing soccer than baseball as a youth in Panama. The New York Yankees signed the 17-year-old in 1990. There are two versions of how Latin American scouting director Herb Raybourn signed the youngster. One says Chico Heron, the Yankees area scout, alerted Raybourn to Rivera. After watching Rivera in a private tryout, Raybourn signed him for $3,000, plus $70 for a missed day of wages on a fishing boat.

The second version is less likely to be true. Raybourn returned to Panama seeking more talent after he signed Mariano Rivera, Ruben's cousin, who was four years older. He asked Mariano if there were any other good players. He replied, "Yes, my cousin. He can play."[1]

Rivera spent his first two seasons with the Gulf Coast Yankees in the Rookie League and Oneonta in the New York Penn League, where he was named the league's Most Valuable Player. He broke out in 1994 as a 20-year-old with Class-A Greensboro in the South Atlantic League and Class-A Tampa in the Florida State League. In 139 games, the 6-foot-3, 190-pound right-handed hitter bashed 33 homers, drove in 101 runs, and batted .281. On the negative side, he struck out 163 times. He was named the Most Valuable Player in the South Atlantic League and a finalist for *Baseball America's* Minor League Player of the Year Award.

That fall, he played for the Peoria Javelinas in the Arizona Fall League, where he was the consensus best prospect. Rivera appeared on the December 25, 1994, cover of the over-sized *Baseball America* magazine with the intriguing question: "Yankees' Ruben Rivera: The Next Mickey Mantle?" The publication rated Rivera as the Yankees' number one prospect, ahead of Derek Jeter, Jorge Posada, Andy Pettitte, and Mariano Rivera, his cousin.

Javelinas manager John Stearns, a former New York Mets catcher, showered Rivera with unbridled praise."The Yankees haven't had a talent like this guy since Mickey Mantle," he exclaimed. "He does more things than (Andre) Dawson could do at this age and more things than a young (Dave) Winfield could do. Winfield hit between 20 and 30 homers. Rivera could hit between 40 and 60 homers. Winfield has a good arm; Rivera has a great arm."[2]

In an interview with Bill Madden of the *New York Daily News*, Stearns added, "Ruben is the best player I've seen in my 22 years in baseball. He is the total package, including 40-homer power."[3]

Stearns admitted Rivera was not yet ready for the majors, saying he needed another 500 to 1,000 at-bats. But, he predicted Rivera would be a number three hitter like Mantle when he made it to the majors. After all the praise, Stearns offered one important disclaimer: "He has yet to do it."[4]

Stearns wasn't the only one impressed with Rivera. Madden wrote, "Of all of the next Mickey Mantles, none had the full quota of God-given talent to bring an entire ball field of players, coaches, and scouts to attention the way Ruben Rivera has."[5]

Yankee great Reggie Jackson enthused, "Looking at him is like looking at Secretariat as a one-year-old. He looks bigger and better than anyone else on the field. A blind man could see his skills. He's got everything."[6]

When a reporter asked Rivera if he felt any pressure to live up to the legacies of Joe DiMaggio or Mickey Mantle, the youngster shyly admitted he didn't know who they were. He asked, "Were they as good as Ken Griffey Jr.?"[7]

Although the Yankees agreed with Stearns' assessment, they were much less vocal about it. Stearns, a member of the Cincinnati Reds organization, wasn't concerned about putting too much pressure on the potential star. However, Bill Livesey, Yankees vice president of player development, said, "The next DiMaggio or Mantle tag will only put undue pressure on the kid."[8]

The Yankees invited Rivera to their 1995 spring training camp. He impressed manager Buck Showalter with his outfield speed and arm strength. He was assigned to Class-AA Norwich in the Eastern League. He started slowly and didn't show some offensive pop until after 50 games.

In May 1995, *Baseball America* listed Rivera as its number two minor league prospect, behind Seattle's Alex Rodriguez. The list included Chipper Jones, Derek Jeter, Shaun Green, Charles Johnson, Norma Garciaparra, and Andruw Jones. Actually, *Baseball America* listed Rivera among its Top 10 prospects from 1995 through 1997.

The 21-year-old earned a promotion to AAA Columbus in the International League after batting .293 with nine homers in 71 games with Norwich. Manager Jimmy Johnson observed, "Ruben is a five-tool player. He's as good as everyone says he is. He's going to hit the ball well."[9]

At Columbus, Ruben added 15 homers while hitting .270. The Yankees called him up, and he made his major league debut on September 3, 1995, as a pinch-runner. He struck out against Oakland's Dennis Eckersley in his only plate appearance. He got into four more games but didn't bat in any of them.

Cousin Mariano Rivera assessed Ruben, saying he needed to gain maturity and learn to hit the curveball. If he didn't learn to do it, he would have a hard time. His advice to Ruben: "Be consistent, be patient at the plate and wait on your pitch."[10]

Manager Buck Showalter and the Yankees front office expected Rivera and shortstop Derek Jeter to compete for starting positions in 1996 and become the nucleus of many Yankee teams in the future. Jeter was the Yankees' starting shortstop on Opening Day. He would go on to be named Rookie of the Year. Rivera opened the season at AAA Columbus. The 22-year-old failed to dominate AAA the way many thought he would. He got off to a slow start, going 7-for-40 (.171).

Yankees general manager Bob Watson said the poor start might have been good for Rivera. "It lets him know this game isn't easy, lets him know he was to work at it. Like so many youngsters, he's coping with hitting the ball hard and watching it being caught."[11]

The Yankees were forced to call Rivera up in late May as outfielders Bernie Williams and Tim Raines went on the disabled list. The club preferred to keep him in Columbus, where he could hone his raw skills. *New York Daily News* writer John Giannones termed Rivera's promotion "a necessary evil."[12] Watson was adamant that Rivera would not have been called up if it wasn't for the injuries. He insisted once Raines was healthy, Rivera would be shipped back to AAA.

Before his first major league start against Oakland at Yankee Stadium on May 23, team advisor Reggie Jackson offered Ruben encouragement in Spanish. It must have worked. Rivera responded with a walk, a two-run double, a single, and a hit-by-pitch. He also scored the winning run.

Afterward, Jackson said, "Ruben's just a tremendous talent. I saw that the first time I saw him play in Tampa in 1994. He did everything that day—hit a homer, stole a couple bases, made a great catch in center field, and got a couple more hits. All he needs to do is to mature, which I'm trying to help him do."[13]

In his first four starts, Rivera went 5-for-10 with five RBI, reaching base in 10 of 15 plate appearances. It was enough to convince manager Joe Torre to keep him on the roster instead of sending him back to Columbus. Torre acknowledged that Ruben still was maturing, but he needed experience. The idea was to watch him carefully, get him more at-bats, and not bury him on the bench. Torre wanted Rivera to be more selective at the plate, keep from getting overwhelmed by 0-1 and 0-2 counts, and try not to pull the ball all the time. Despite Ruben's shortcomings, Torre said, "When he hits the ball, it just explodes off of his bat, and that's something you can't teach. That excites me."[14]

Jackson and Torre agreed Ruben was comparable to Barry Bonds and Ken Griffey Jr. Yankees outfielder Bernie Williams said, "If Ruben stays off injuries and stays out of trouble, he has the potential to be one of the greatest players in baseball history."[15] Williams' allusion to trouble referred to Rivera's attraction to the nightlife, women, and late hours, which often caused him to lose his focus on baseball. In their quest to keep Rivera out of trouble, the Yankees assigned Reggie Jackson to be part bodyguard, part mentor, and part psychologist to the youngster.

Rivera was batting .277 after 15 starts when the Yankees shipped him back to AAA Columbus on June 24. Although Torre and his staff had a better idea of his capabilities, Rivera was upset by his demotion. When he returned to Columbus, he sulked and angered his teammates with his lack of hustle. Some said he had a case of major league-itis. After an early ejection, he cleaned out his locker and left the stadium. He was suspended for seven games for insubordination. Rivera denied any wrongdoing. He accused manager Stump Merrill of not giving him a chance to tell his side of the story. According to Ruben, he went to the hotel, stayed there, and returned to the field early the next day. He had some stuff in his locker that he had to clean out. Although Merrill thought he had left the team, he said he never left his room.

Rivera's actions upset Torre and Yankees general manager Bob Watson. "There's some maturity that needs to take place," stressed Torre, who added the team had gone out of its way to work with him. "Like most young people, Ruben is impatient and thinks he doesn't have anything to learn. This was the year he was supposed to make the jump, and he hasn't done it."[16]

Despite his pouting at Columbus, the Yankees recalled him in late August. General manager Bob Watson favored keeping Rivera in the minors. He made the move after talking with Torre and Yankees owner George Steinbrenner. The plan was to use him as a backup outfielder and a possible late-inning defensive replacement.

The youngster helped the Yankees during the pennant race. On September 10, in Detroit, Rivera entered the game as a defensive replacement in right field. In the ninth inning, he made a diving catch of a line drive with two runners on base to preserve a one-run lead. On September 18, in New York, he rapped a 10th-inning, walk-off single to propel the Yankees over the rival Baltimore Orioles. Rivera, however, also showed his immaturity. He made a pair of impressive, unnecessary throws from right field on September 25 in a 14-1 romp. As the crowd roared with approval, he threw lasers to third base and home plate. The throws aggravated his right shoulder injury, resulting from running into an outfield wall earlier in the month. His late-season heroics caused the Yankees to re-evaluate him. The club decided he needed to be a starting outfielder in 1997.

The Yankees clinched the AL East, four games ahead of the Baltimore Orioles. Rivera could barely throw a ball and tried to play through the injury. He was limited to one unsuccessful pinch-hitting appearance in the American League Division Series against the Texas Rangers. He was not physically able to play in the American League Championship Series against the Orioles or the World Series against the Atlanta Braves, which the Yankees won in six games.

In late February, Rivera was scheduled to have surgery on his shoulder. It was bad news. Ruben, and others, worried it could be career-threatening. A series of tests revealed inflammation in the bursa sac and rotator cuff and a deep bone bruise in his right shoulder. His cousin,

Mariano, wondered why the Yankees waited so long to do the surgery. Although Ruben had undergone four previous MRIs since October, it wasn't until February that he started complaining of shoulder pain. He was expected to miss two or three months of the season.

The Yankees reportedly assigned a full-time chaperone to their budding star to keep him out of trouble. The club was disturbed by his off-the-field activities, which leaned toward the wild side. The chaperone encouraged a quieter, more restricted lifestyle. The club hoped Ruben would spend less time out on the town. One Yankee official said, "If anything is going to ruin Ruben, it's going to be the ladies."[17]

The Yankees were determined to get Ruben 400 at-bats in 1997. That meant possibly trading Paul O'Neill or Tim Raines. Other teams were interested in Rivera. The Phillies were rumored to be offering pitcher Curt Schilling for the Panama prospect. The club resisted all offers, proclaiming 1997 would be Ruben's breakthrough season. "We're talking about a guy who has a chance to be the next Ken Griffey Jr.," said a Yankee official.[18]

Yankee higher-ups and veteran players believed Rivera would either be a superstar beyond reproach or a bust. The consensus, however, was he would never mature. That thinking led to trading him to the San Diego Padres for 27-year-old Japanese pitcher Hideki Irabu on April 22, 1997. The Yankees also sent minor league pitcher Rafael Medina and $3 million to the Padres. In turn, San Diego included three minor leaguers and Irabu, whose boyhood dream was to pitch for the pinstripes. New York Mets manager Bobby Valentine had managed Irabu when he pitched for the Chiba Lotte Mariners in 1995. He called him "one of the ten best pitchers in the world."[19]

Rivera was not thrilled about going to San Diego. "I think the Yankees are making a mistake," he said. "I say that because I have confidence in my ability. I'm going to be a great player."[20]

Rivera's rehab program from his shoulder injury took longer than the Padres anticipated. He played 18 games in the minors before joining the Padres in mid-August. He was limited to 20 at-bats in 17 games as he was used mainly as a pinch-hitter and pinch-runner.

The Padres sent Ruben to the Dominican Winter League since he hadn't played regularly in almost a year. Ten days into the season, he fractured his pinky finger and was out a month. He returned to help lead his team to the playoffs.

General manager Kevin Towers and the Padres' front office wrestled with the decision of whether Rivera should start the 1998 season in the majors or in the minors. They sent him to Class-AAA Las Vegas in the Pacific Coast League. Once again, Rivera was despondent, and he sulked. In his first 104 at-bats in Las Vegas, he struck out 42 times while batting .144. Despite his discouraging stats, he was promoted to San Diego in mid-May. Back where he wanted to be, Ruben turned his game around. In his first 17 games, he showed discipline at the plate as he batted .316. He also played stellar defense. Despite his fast start, his average plummeted to .209 at the end of the season, and he struck out 52 times in 172 at-bats.

San Diego won the National League West and defeated the Houston Astros in the National League Division Series, three games to one, and the Atlanta Braves in the National League Championship Series, four games to two. Facing the New York Yankees in the 1998 World Series, the Padres were swept in four games. Rivera increased his value in the post-season, particularly in the World Series. He delivered a pinch-hit RBI double in the eighth inning of Game 2. In Game 4, he rocked Yankee starter Andy Pettitte for a single and double and added a ninth-inning single off his cousin Mariano Rivera.

The Padres granted starting center fielder Steve Finely, 33, his free agency. This potentially opened up a starting job for Rivera. Finley had averaged 20 homers, batted .276, and won two Gold Gloves in his four-year stint with the club. San Diego cast its lot with the 25-year-old Rivera. General manager Kevin Towers figured Ruben, who he likened to a young Dave Winfield, would make up for the loss of Finley. He had raw power, a better arm, more speed, and was at least his equal in the outfield. What Rivera hadn't proven, however, was that he could hit consistently.

Although Ruben played well in spring training, he appeared clueless at the plate once the 1999 season started. He didn't raise his average above .200 until mid-June. *The Sporting News* correspondent Tom Krasovic observed Ruben often started his swing late, pulled his hands down toward the pitch, lunged, and dissipated his power.

In trying to explain his struggles, Rivera said, "Sometimes, I try too hard. I pull everything. When I'm relaxed, I can see the ball and react, whether it's inside or outside. Sometimes, I try to kill the ball and only use left field."[21] He had offered that reason before, but frustratingly he hadn't corrected it.

Observers felt he had regressed, offensively and defensively. He wasn't hitting ordinary, 87-miles-per-hour fastballs, and his swing looked worst than it did the previous season. In August, he batted .139 with no homers and three RBI. He went homerless for 41 games. His defense was average instead of stellar, and runners had begun challenging his arm, which had been considered one of the best in baseball.

Rivera batted .195 with 23 homers. He whiffed 143 times in 411 at-bats (1 strikeout per 2.87 at-bats). Towers remained tantalized by his raw power and potential despite his lackluster performance.

The Padres hired Ben Oglivie as hitting coach to unlock Rivera's offensive potential. The former 16-year major league veteran and three-time All-Star was from Panama and spoke Spanish. The team said Ruben's English wasn't good enough to convey his thoughts to previous coaches. Oglivie's task was to make the youngster's swing more compact and improve his focus. He tried to get Rivera to simplify his swing, eliminate his double toe tap with his front foot, and lay off junk pitches. Despite his efforts, the Padre center fielder showed little improvement. He remained erratic and inconsistent. His swing was too long and often late. He failed to make solid contact and struck out at an alarming rate. He was overmatched at the plate. The rest of the team soured on Oglivie, and the Padres fired him midseason.

For the second consecutive season, Rivera faded down the stretch. He batted .161 in August and September with four homers. He finished with a .208 batting average and 17 home runs. Another unimpressive season. To add to San Diego's disappointment, Steve Finley, the former Padre, averaged 34 homers, 100 runs scored, and 100 RBI in his two seasons with Arizona. He also won two Gold Gloves and earned an All-Star berth.

Towers was frustrated with Rivera but refused to give up on him. The Padres signed him to a $1 million contract for 2001. The contract represented a $300,000 raise. Towers figured it was worth the risk. After all, how often does a five-tool player come along? And $1 million was worth the gamble for a 20-plus homer season. No Padre outfielder slugged 20 or more homers in the previous season. Although Towers hated to give up on power, he had tried unsuccessfully to trade Rivera.

Towers was out of answers. He clung to the hope of something clicking to unlock Ruben's potential. *North County Times* sportswriter Shaun O'Neill opined, "The Padres would need baseball's version of the Rosetta Stone to translate Rivera's raw skills into big-league success."[22] Other than occasional flashes of power, he had been a miserable failure at the plate.

The Padres' infatuation with the underachiever ended on March 14, 2001, when the club released him. "It's frustrating," said Towers. "He's such a talent. You see moments or flashes of greatness. There's just no consistency."[23]

Padres teammate Eric Owens said, "It's very hard to live up to expectations. People sometimes expect too much. Then, when you don't live up to expectations, it is hard for the person to deal with it."[24]

The Cincinnati Reds signed Rivera as a free agent a week later. General manager Jim Bowden hoped a change of scenery, along with the tutelage of manager Bob Boone and hitting coach Ken Griffey Sr., would transform the 27-year-old enigma.

Rivera carried a lot of baggage with him to Cincinnati. *Dayton Daily News* columnist Hal McCoy wrote, "Rivera is a body full of talent and a dossier of trouble."[25] He wrote that he resisted when the Padres wanted him to cut down on his swing. When they wanted him to play shallower in the outfield, he resisted. When they tried to tone down his nightlife, he resisted.

In San Diego, Rivera refused to work extra to cut down on his strikeouts and make better contact. Tony Gwynn tried to work with him, but he gave up. "You have to do it every day, and Ruben doesn't want to do it," lamented Gwynn.[26] According to Ruben, all his problems were related to trying too hard.

Ruben got off to a 9-for-22 start (.346) and added to the club's bench strength as a pinch-hitter and defensive replacement. He avoided trouble with the Reds, batted .255 (54 points above his career average), and knocked 10 home runs in 117 games. His 83 strikeouts in 263 at-bats were still alarmingly high. He surprisingly declined a one-year option with the Reds, accepting a $350,000 buyout. If he had accepted the option, the Reds would have paid him $1 million for 2002. At the time, the Reds were reportedly working on a deal to send Rivera to the Boston Red Sox for a minor-league player and cash.

On February 14, 2002, he signed as a free agent with the New York Yankees. Manager Joe Torre said, "He could be a find for us."[27] Catcher Jorge Posada added, "He's been a five-tool player forever. He just has to put it all together. He's putting some good swings on the ball. He just has to keep opening their eyes."[28]

A second chance with the Yankees was snuffed out in mid-March when Ruben was placed on unconditional release waivers. He had been accused of stealing teammate Derek Jeter's bat and glove from his locker and selling it for $2,500 to memorabilia dealers. Rivera admitted to the crime in a meeting with general manager Brian Cashman, manager Joe Torre and team advisor Reggie Jackson. Some of the Yankees were livid over the theft. Rivera's actions were puzzling, particularly since he had negotiated a $1 million contract with the Yankees.

Ruben returned the stolen equipment to Jeter. He said, "I didn't kill anyone. I just made a mistake, and I've repented. I did it without thinking because it wasn't for the money. It was just an instant where I wasn't thinking, and I made a mistake that I'm paying for."[29]

The Texas Rangers signed Rivera as a free agent. They sent him to Class-AA Tulsa and later promoted him to Class-AAA Oklahoma City. The Rangers called him up at the All-Star break. In 69 games with the Rangers, he batted .209 with four homers. He was released at the end of the season.

He signed a minor league contract with the San Francisco Giants in January 2003 and was invited to spring training. He made the club but was released in mid-June after hitting .180 in 31 games. It marked the last stop in the major leagues for the 29-year-old. He played in the minor leagues for the Baltimore Orioles (2003), the New York Yankees (2005), and the Chicago White Sox (2006). He competed in the Mexican League during the winter of 2004 and continued through 2019. He also played in the World International Baseball Classic for Panama in 2006 and 2009.

In his nine-year major league career, Rivera batted .216 with 64 home runs. He fanned 510 times in 1,586 at-bats (1 strikeout every 3.1 at-bats). In 2001, *Sports Illustrated* called Rivera "one of the most over-hyped busts of his generation."[30]

The failure of Ruben Rivera shocked countless scouts, general managers, and players. In 2015, New York Yankees general manager Brian Cashman said Rivera was overrated because of the lack of analytics. He said to a scout's eye Rivera possessed all the physical tools and was impressive. But today's analytics would have painted a different picture.

"In today's world, Rivera wouldn't be packaged as the next Mickey Mantle," he declared. "He would be packaged as a lot of swing and miss. Feasting on garbage pitching at the lower levels. And, he would have had predictable trouble at the higher levels. There would have been predicted failure. I guarantee it."[31]

Whether Rivera would have met expectations today or not, he is forever known for underachieving. Perhaps, New York Yankee Jim Leyritz summed it up best, "Ruben was probably the best five-tool player in the game who never matured to use his talents. The guy had every ability there was but just couldn't mentally get it together. It was a shame."[32]

CHAPTER 17

MIKE TROUT
THE COMPLETE PACKAGE

Mike Trout is a player people will be talking about 100 years after we're dead.

—FREDDIE FREEMAN, ATLANTA BRAVES

Mike Trout is baseball royalty. His achievements put him in a class with Hall of Famers Ty Cobb, Jimmie Foxx, Mel Ott, Ted Williams, Stan Musial, Joe DiMaggio, and Mickey Mantle. If the 31-year-old retired from baseball tomorrow, he would still likely be a first-ballot Hall of Famer.

The 6-foot-3, 230-pound Los Angeles Angels outfielder began to forge his regal status in 2012 when he became the youngest player (20 years old) to be named unanimous Rookie of the Year in the American

League. He also finished second to Triple Crown winner Miguel Cabrera of the Detroit Tigers in the American League Most Valuable Player balloting.

Entering the 2022 season, Trout owned three Most Valuable Player Awards. He has been runner-up four times, fourth once, and fifth once. He appeared in eight consecutive All-Star Games from 2012-2019 and was named the Most Valuable Player twice.

Combining speed and power, Trout has led the American League in on-base percentage (OBP), on-base percentage plus slugging average (OPS), runs scored four times, slugging average and walks three times, RBI and stolen bases once.

Former Angels manager Mike Scioscia said, "Mike's a special player. There isn't anything he can't do. He hits for average, gets on base, can steal a base, hits for power, and is a tremendous defensive asset."[1]

Trout distinguished himself as one of baseball's all-time elite players from the outset.

In 2018, Arizona Diamondbacks pitcher Zack Greinke observed, "He's been the best player since he's been in the majors. He's never not been the best player."[2]

In retrospect, it's surprising Trout wasn't selected until the 25th pick in the 2009 major league amateur draft. Twenty-one teams passed on him. The Washington Nationals and the Arizona Diamondbacks passed on him twice. Six players selected ahead of him never made it to the major leagues.

Trout began attracting attention from traveling team baseball coaches when he was 11. Although he played on one of the premier traveling teams in the Northeast and competed in several high-profile showcase tournaments, his baseball schedule was limited, particularly compared to players in warm-weather states.

As a senior at Millville (New Jersey) Senior High, Trout, a center fielder, batted .531 with a state-record 18 homers and 45 RBI in 26 games. An all-around athlete, he also played football and basketball. Before his senior year, he pitched (he once threw an 18-strikeout no-hitter) and played shortstop. He signed a letter of intent to play baseball at East Carolina University.

While he was on the scouts' radar, he didn't jump out as clearly superior to other prospects. Angels scout Greg Morhardt, however, felt he had found a so-good-it's-hard-to-believe diamond. He claimed Trout was the fastest and strongest 17-year-old he had ever seen.

"I think I have Mickey Mantle up here," he told one scout.[3] He initially gave Trout such a high overall future potential (OFP) grade that he intentionally downgraded it for fear he wouldn't be taken seriously by the organization.

Trout was built like a linebacker with explosive speed, power, good instincts, and plate discipline. He was timed from home to first base in 3.9 seconds, impressive for a right-handed batter.

Despite his traits and performance, a Northeast bias may have worked against him in the draft. Ten of the 11 high school players selected ahead of him were from warm-weather states, where year-round baseball was common. Besides a limited high school schedule, Trout's competition was of questionable quality. New Jersey wasn't known for producing top-notch prospects. Third baseman Billy Rowell of Pennsauken, N.J., selected ninth by the Baltimore Orioles in the 2006 draft, was floundering in the minors and his chances of reaching the major leagues looked slim.

After being drafted by the Los Angeles Angels, Trout quickly signed for a $1.2 million bonus. Confident of his abilities, the 17-year-old was eager to start his professional baseball career. The draft supplied him with extra motivation. Although he didn't discuss it at the time, he reflected on his draft position years later. "A lot of people doubted me," he said. "I just try to prove them wrong each and every day."[4]

The Angels assigned him to the Arizona Rookie League, where he batted .360 in 39 games before being promoted to Class Low A Cedar Rapids in the Midwest League for five games.

Before the start of the 2010 season, *Baseball America* ranked Trout the 85th top prospect. By midseason, however, he had rocketed to the number two prospect on the publication's rankings. Playing for Cedar Rapids, the young outfielder blistered opposing pitchers. In early July, he led the Midwest League in batting, runs, hits, stolen bases, on-base percentage (OBP), second in on-base percentage plus slugging (OPS), and fourth in slugging. He had not made an error and had thrown out six runners. He also was named to compete in the 2010 Futures Game at Anaheim Stadium on July 11. After the game, the Angels promoted him to Class High A Rancho Cucamonga Quakes in the California League.

Cedar Rapids General Manager Jack Roeder said, "I've been in the minor leagues for 30 years, and he's the best player I've been associated with. He's a five-tool player. He's the total package."[5]

Trout's quick, overwhelming success surprised many people, even those in the Angels organization. Abe Flores, the Angels' director of player development, said Trout's incredible mental game and winning attitude, combined with phenomenal tools, made him a future star. "Mike's intangibles exceed his abilities, and that's special," he said.[6]

The Angels' prospect appeared on the cover of the July 12-25 issue of *Baseball America*. He is shown chasing a fly ball under the headline "Angel in the Outfield." In the article, Cedar Rapids hitting coach Brent Del Chiaro compared him to Tigers centerfielder Austin Jackson and Hall of Famer Rickey Henderson.

At Rancho Cucamonga, Trout batted .306 in 50 games and helped lead the Quakes to the playoffs. At the end of the season, he was named 2010 Midwest League MVP and Prospect of the Year. He also earned the Topps Minor League Player of the Year Award. At 19 years and two months, he became the youngest player to win the award. Additionally, he was named a *Baseball America* All-Star and a Topps Class-A All-Star.

Trout opened the 2011 season with the Class-AA Arkansas Travelers in the Texas League. The Angels had high expectations for him but didn't want to rush him to the major leagues. He had little trouble adjusting to Class-AA competition. He was named to the Texas League All-Star team and was due to be promoted to Class AAA.

The Angels, however, called Trout up on July 8 after center fielder Peter Bourjos strained his hamstring. He was batting .324 with nine homers in 75 games for Arkansas when he got the call. At 19 years and 335 days, he was the youngest player in the major leagues and the youngest Angel player since pitcher Andy Hassler in 1971. Angels general manager Tony Reagins cited Trout's maturity, preparation, and performance as reasons for his promotion.

The teenager struggled as he combated a case of the jitters while adjusting to a new environment, new teammates, and unfamiliar pitchers. In 14 games from July 8-29, he batted .163 with one home run and six RBI. When Bourjos returned to the lineup, Mike rejoined Arkansas. However, his stay in the minors was brief, as Los Angeles called him up again on August 19.

Not as nervous this time, he hit safely in seven of his first eight games. On August 30, Trout slugged a pair of home runs off Seattle's Anthony Vasquez. At 20, he became the youngest Angel to clout two homers in a game. In 40 games with the Angels, he batted .220.

Angels teammate Torii Hunter was impressed with Trout. He saw a bright future for him. "I've seen a lot of young players who thought they were special, but they lacked the mental makeup and desire to keep learning. They die out about age 25, and you wonder what happened to them."[7]

Despite spending much of July and August with Los Angeles, Trout led the Texas League in batting average, OBP and OPS. *Baseball America* named him the 2011 Minor League Player of the Year.

Mike attended the Angels' spring training in Tempe, Arizona, in 2012. But a viral infection and a shoulder issue limited him to just six at-bats. Los Angeles assigned him to the Class-AAA Salt Lake Bees in the Pacific Coast League. After 20 games, he batted .403 with a .467 OBP and a 1.091 OPS. The Angels called him up on April 28 after they released veteran Bobby Abreu.

This time, he was ready for the major leagues. The 20-year-old awed everyone. In his first 77 games, he collected 111 hits and 49 RBI. He also stole 31 bases. According to the Angels, only Ty Cobb in 1911 matched those numbers in his first 77 games of a season. As if that wasn't enough, Trout made highlight-reel catches in left field. He combined speed, power, and defense.

At the All-Star break, the newest Angel was batting .350. Although he wasn't on the original All-Star ballot, he was named to the All-Star team as a reserve. In his lone All-Star at-bat in the bottom of the sixth inning, he singled off R.A. Dickey of the Mets. In August, he appeared on the cover of *Sports Illustrated,* holding a bat under the headline "The Supernatural." At the time, he led the American League in batting, runs, stolen bases, slugging percentage, and on-base-plus-slugging percentage.

Mike enjoyed a sensational rookie season in 2012. Playing in 139 games, he batted .326, slugged 30 homers, drove in 83 runs, scored a league-leading 129 runs, and stole 49 bases in 54 attempts. He became the first player in baseball history to bash 30 homers, score 125 runs, steal 45 bases, and bat higher than .320 in a season. He didn't appear to have any weaknesses.

The rookie produced an eye-popping 10.5 WAR (Wins Above Replacement). He became the only position player to register a 10-plus WAR at age 20 or younger. Jayson Stark of ESPN observed that "no player in baseball history had combined so much excellence in so many areas in the same season."[8]

Mike was the unanimous choice for the 2012 American League Rookie of the Year, becoming the youngest to win the award. He also received serious consideration for the American League Most Valuable Player Award. He received six first-place votes as he finished runner-up to Triple Crown winner Miguel Cabrera of the Detroit Tigers (44 homers, 139 RBI, and a .330 batting average).

What Trout accomplished at age 20 was historic. Keith Law of ESPN said, "Very few people in baseball history have come anywhere close to what he's done, even at their peak level."[9]

Observers and teammates gushed with praise. Hall of Famer Al Kaline compared him to Mickey Mantle; Phillies coach Larry Bowa called him the best player he had seen in 30 years; teammate Mark Trumbo said he was an unreal total package.

Angels outfielder Torii Hunter didn't mince words. "What you guys are witnessing is greatness," he said. "This guy is one of the best players to play the game right now."[10]

Teams who passed on Trout in the 2009 draft pondered how they misjudged him. Phillies assistant general manager Mike Arbuckle explained. "I think everyone underestimated his makeup. I don't think we realized how exceptionally good he is in his attitude, work ethic, and competitiveness."[11]

As the 2013 season opened, baseball fans and officials wondered if Trout could maintain his excellence. Could he adjust to how hurlers would pitch him? Could he handle the exorbitant media attention and fame? Would he fall victim to the sophomore jinx?

Angels manager Mike Scioscia, however, did not doubt that Trout was the real deal. "Mike is not doing anything he isn't capable of. He's playing to his potential at a very young age. His challenge will be consistency. He has the ability to do what he did for a long time. That's what's exciting about him."[12]

Trout started the season slowly, heated up in May, and didn't cool down until September. On May 21, the 20-year-old touched Seattle hurlers for a single, triple, double, and home run to become the youngest American League player to hit for the cycle. Mike proved he was a bona fide star as he batted .323, clouted 27 homers, and drove in 97 runs. He also led the league in runs (109) and walks (110). After just two full seasons, many considered him the best player in baseball. Once again, the young star finished second to Detroit's Miguel Cabrera (.348, 44 home runs, and 137 RBI) in the Most Valuable Player voting.

In February 2014, the Angels and Trout agreed to a $1 million, one-year contract for the upcoming season. Three days before Opening Day, the club signed him to a 6-year, $144 million contract extension, which would run from 2015-2020. Trout was one of just four players to hit .320 with 50 homers and 200 runs in their first two full seasons. The others are Ted Williams, Joe DiMaggio, and Albert Pujols.

Before the 2014 All-Star Game, *The Star Tribune* of Minneapolis, Minn., polled two baseball writers from each MLB city, asking them to rank the three top all-around players in their league based on the five-tool criteria: hitting for average, hitting for power, speed, arm, and fielding. Trout finished number one in the American League, far ahead of the Orioles' Adam Jones and Manny Machado. Jeff Passan of yahoo.com said, "Trout is the best player in baseball. It's not even close."[13]

Trout appeared in his third consecutive All-Star game on July 16, 2014, in Minneapolis. He sandwiched a first-inning triple between Derek Jeter's double and Miguel Cabrera's home run to give the AL a 3-0 lead. The NL tied the game in the fourth inning. Trout broke the tie in the bottom of the fifth with an RBI double, and the AL went on to win 5-3. The Angel outfielder was voted the Most Valuable Player of the game, joining Ken Griffey Jr. as the only players to win the award before the age of 23.

In 2014, Trout led the Angels to capture the American League West to a 98-64 record, a 20-game improvement over the previous year. The slugger's first playoff appearance in the American League Division Series against the Kansas City Royals was a dud. The Royals swept the Angels in three games, and Trout's lone hit was a home run in Game 3. He went 1-for-12 (.083). He finished the season batting .287 with 36 homers and a league-leading 111 RBI and 115 runs. The only blemish was a league-high 184 strikeouts.

This time there was no doubt about his Most Valuable Player status. He was the unanimous winner and the youngest player to sweep all the first-place votes. Angels hitting coach Don Baylor said, "Mike's loaded with talent, loves to play the game, and walks the walk. He's held up under pressure and has done it with great humility. This may be his first MVP, but it won't be his last."[14]

Mike entered the 2015 season determined to cut down on his strike-outs. He said the problem was that he chased too many high pitches out of the strike zone. On April 15, 2015, he became the youngest player (23 years and 253 days) to reach 100 home runs and 100 stolen bases. Named to his fourth consecutive All-Star game, Trout electrified the Cincinnati crowd when he became the first player in 38 years to lead off the game with a homer. He was named the All-Star Most Valuable Player for the second consecutive year, becoming the only player to accomplish the feat. In his first four All-Star games, he went 5-for-10 with four extra-base hits.

Milwaukee Brewers manager Ned Yost said, "Mike can do anything anyone can do on a baseball field. He can hit with power, he can run, and he can drive the gap. He's a great defender. He's just special. He's one of the best players on the planet."[15]

Washington Nationals' 22-year-old outfielder Bryce Harper, en route to an MVP year in the National League, said, "Mike Trout is the best player in baseball, and I don't think anyone can argue it."[16]

Despite his .299 batting average, 41 homers, and 90 RBI in 2015, Trout finished second to Toronto Blue Jays Josh Donaldson (.297, 41 homers, and 123 RBI). Donaldson, aided by a strong final two months of the season, collected 23 first-place votes, while Mike garnered seven. Once again, the fact he wasn't a member of a playoff team seemed to hurt him in the voting. The Blue Jays went 93-69 and defeated the Detroit Tigers in the ALDS before losing to the Kansas City Royals in the ALCS. The Angels were 85-77 and finished third in the AL West.

Trout placed second or higher in MVP voting for the fourth consecutive year. He joined Yogi Berra, Stan Musial, and Barry Bonds as the only players to do so. Richard Justice of MLB.com said, "If there's something Mike doesn't do better than almost everyone, we haven't seen it yet."[17]

Trout entered the 2016 season with the same goal he had every year: To be the best player in the American League. In June, *The Sporting News* named him baseball's best (active) player. According to FanGraphs, he accumulated more WAR through his age-24 season than any other player since 1913. Trout racked up 45 WAR, while Mickey Mantle was second with 41.1. Mel Ott, Jimmie Foxx, and Ted Williams completed the Top 5.

While Mike continued his excellent play, the Angels faltered early. The club, plagued by injuries, trailed the Texas Rangers in the AL West by 18.5 games on July 4. With the retirement of 14-time All-Star Derek Jeter in 2014, many people thought Trout would become the face of baseball. However, his opportunity for national exposure was limited to the All-Star Game. In San Diego, Trout went 1-for-3 to help the American League to a 4-2 victory.

Trout didn't put up spectacular numbers in 2016, but he played consistently well in virtually every category. He batted .315, knocked 29 home runs, and drove in 100 runs. The Angel outfielder led the league in runs (123), base on balls (116), and OBP (.441). He also stole 30 bases. That production resulted in an impressive 10.5 WAR season.

Although the Angels finished 74-88 and in fourth place in the AL West, Los Angeles skipper Mike Scioscia believed Trout was the obvious AL MVP. "What Mike does and what Mike accomplished this year has more impact than the fact we're a sub-.500 team," he said. "His numbers are incredible. You can't deny that they're a notch above anybody else that's there."[18] The voters agreed with Scioscia. Trout captured 19 first-place votes compared to nine for runner-up Mookie Betts of the Boston Red Sox. The Angel slugger became just the eighth player from a non-winning team to earn the award.

"Winning MVP one time is hard to do," he said. "Twice is something special. It was one of the best feelings I've ever had. This one has got to be the biggest one."[19]

Scioscia called Trout "the consummate team player."[20] The club's general manager Billy Eppler praised his "ferocious work ethic."[21]

In his first five full seasons, Trout never finished lower than second in the Most Valuable Player voting, led the American League in WAR each season, and played in every All-Star Game, twice being named the game's Most Valuable Player.

In 2010, when Trout was an 18-year-old dominating Class-A pitching, *Baseball America* compared him to Mickey Mantle. Trout kept being compared to Mantle. Now, after six seasons, their hitting statistics were strikingly similar. After each had completed their age-24 season, Trout had played in 811 games, compared to Mantle's 808. Trout had more hits (917 to 910) and doubles (175 to 136). Mantle led in home runs (173 to 168), runs (642 to 600), RBI (575 to 497), walks (524 to 477), batting average (.306 to .304) on-base percentage (.412 to .405), and slugging percentage (.570 to .557).

Trout had won two Most Valuable Player awards, while Mantle had one. The Yankee star won the Triple Crown in 1956, his age-24 season. By then, he had appeared in five World Series and clouted eight homers in 92 at-bats. Trout's post-season experience consisted of three games in which he batted .083.

At the beginning of the 2017 season, Oakland A's general manager Billy Beane said, "Mike Trout is the best player I've ever seen."[22] Beane lamented that the A's, and many other teams, failed to select him in the 2009 draft.

Trout was batting .337 with 16 homers and a 1.203 OPS on May 28 when he tore the ulnar collateral ligament in his left thumb on a head-first slide. He had surgery three days later. He missed the 2017 All-Star

Game because he was rehabbing at Class-A Inland Empire. He returned to the Angels lineup on July 14.

Mike notched his 1,000th career hit on August 7, his 26th birthday. He became the 23rd player to reach 1,000 hits during their age-25 season. Only six players who made their debut in the past 50 years reached the milestone quicker. He joined Mel Ott, Jimmie Foxx, and Mickey Mantle as the only players to have 1,000 hits, 500 runs, and 500 walks in their age-25 season.

Limited to 114 games in 2017, Trout batted .306, slammed 33 home runs, and drove in 72 runs. Although he led the league in OBP (.442), slugging percentage (.645), and OPS (1.071), he slipped to fourth in the MVP voting.

Before the start of the 2018 season, *Sports Illustrated* named Trout the number one player in baseball. He was cruising along with another MVP-worthy season when he reached a career WAR of 60.7 at the end of June. It was better than 74 position players in the Hall of Fame.

He was blindsided by controversy at the 2018 All-Star Game in Washington. In comments to *USA Today*, major league baseball commissioner Rob Manfred said it was Trout's fault that he and baseball were not as popular as they could be. "Mike has made decisions on what he wants to do, doesn't want to do, how he wants to spend his free time or not spend his free time," said Manfred hours before the All-Star Game. "I think we could help him make his brand very big. But he has to make a decision to engage. It takes time and effort."[23]

In the same article, Trout said, "I try to do as much as I can, but keep it to a point where I can still play baseball."[24] The Angels' star regularly signed autographs, engaged with fans, and participated in community events. He preferred to spend his off-season with friends and family, hunting, fishing, and attending Philadelphia Eagles football games. He turned down requests from *60 Minutes* and HBO for profile interviews and chose not to participate in the All-Star Game Home Run Derby.

The Angels quickly defended their star, issuing a press release. They applauded him for prioritizing his personal values over commercial self-promotion. They said his talent and solid character create a perfect role model for young people everywhere. His main job was playing baseball, which he did at a high level. Trout later issued his own statement. He said he just wanted to get back to playing baseball and encouraged everyone to move on.

Interestingly, Manfred, not Trout, came under fire. Mark Whicker of the *Orange County Register* wrote, "It's refreshing and nostalgic to see a great player who doesn't chase popularity, has no trademark pose, shimmy or dance."[25]

Players praised Trout for being a down-to-earth, regular-guy superstar who didn't seek out the cameras or was aloof from his teammates. They admired and respected his humility, workman-like approach, and focus on the game.

Trout emphasized his point on the field when he homered in the third inning as the American League won 8-6 in 10 innings. He joined Hall of Famers Al Kaline and Mickey Mantle as the only players to homer twice in the All-Star Game before the age of 27.

On August 1, he jammed his right wrist while sliding headfirst into third base. While he was sidelined, his brother-in-law Aaron Cox, 24, died. Cox had been a prospect in the Angels' farm system. It was a heavy loss for Mike, who made an emotional return on August 24. It was Players Weekend, and Trout wore "A. Cox" on the back of his uniform. He tripled in his first at-bat.

Despite missing 22 games, he batted .312 with 39 home runs and 79 RBI in 2018. He led the league in walks (122), OBP (.460), and OPS (1.088). According to the voters, it was a respectable season but not an MVP one. He finished a distant second behind Mookie Betts of the Boston Red Sox (.346, 32 homers, and 80 RBI). Betts collected 28 of the 30 first-place votes. It marked the seventh consecutive year Trout finished in the Top 4 in the MVP voting, tying Yankee great Yogi Berra.

Free agency was expected to dominate the off-season as Manny Machado of the Baltimore Orioles and Bryce Harper of the Washington Nationals sought new, record-breaking contracts. The 26-year-olds were two of the brightest stars in baseball. Trout, who was scheduled to become a free agent after the 2020 season, kept a close eye on how the negotiations unfolded. The San Diego Padres signed Machado to a 10-year, $300 million contract, and the Philadelphia Phillies inked Harper to a 13-year, $330 million contract in February.

As good as Machado and Harper were, Trout was better. His WAR value was more than Machado and Harper combined. He had seven Top 5 finishes in the MVP voting, while Machado and Harper had three between them. He was the consensus pick as the best player in the game.

In late March 2019, Trout and the Angels agreed to a 12-year, $426.5 million contract extension, the largest contract in professional sports in terms of overall money. Why would the perennial All-Star sign with a club that had made only one playoff appearance since 2012 and hadn't had a winning season since 2015?

Trout said he was disheartened by how other teams froze out Machado and Harper and how they were treated. It raised a red flag for him. He had a good relationship with Angels general manager Billy Eppler and others throughout the organization. The two-time MVP felt respected and valued. He was confident about the club's future because they had done everything to make him part of it. Mike was comfortable in Los Angeles, and he was loyal.

Ted Berg of *USA Today* said Trout was a "massive bargain" at $426.5 million.[26] He had the highest WAR (64.3) of any position player through the age-26 season. The four players directly behind him were Ty Cobb, Mickey Mantle, Rogers Hornsby, and Alex Rodriguez. He set career highs in walks, at-bats per home run, on-base percentage, and OPS in 2018. Berg added the staggering fact that since Trout became an everyday player in 2012, he had not gone more than two straight games without reaching base.

With his future secured and settled, Trout opened the 2019 season determined to maintain his high level of play. Tragedy struck Mike and his Angels teammates on July 1 when 27-year-old pitcher Tyler Skaggs was found dead in his hotel room. The cause of death was later listed as alcohol, fentanyl, and oxycodone intoxication. Mike was emotionally devastated by the death of his friend, who had been his roommate in the minor leagues. A week later, Trout, 27, played in his eighth consecutive All-Star Game in Cleveland, twice as many as any other position player on the AL or NL squads.

The Angel star was enjoying one of his best all-around years ever. When he turned 28 on August 7, he had 278 home runs, more than all but six players at that age. Alex Rodriguez topped the list with 332 homers, while Mickey Mantle was sixth with 280. He became the first player to accumulate 70 WAR before his 28th birthday. Oakland A's manager Bob Melvin said, "Mike is the best player in the game. I don't think there's any doubt about that."[27]

In early September 2019, a nagging, painful foot problem, Morton's neuroma, required season-ending surgery. The condition is a thickening of the tissue around a nerve leading to the toes.

Playing in 134 games, Trout batted .291, slugged a career-high 45 homers, tallied 104 RBI, drew 110 walks, and scored 100 runs. He led the league in OBP (.438), slugging (.645), and OPS (1.083). He captured his third Most Valuable Player Award as he edged Alex Bregman of the Houston Astros. Trout garnered 17 first-place votes, while Bregman captured 13 first-place votes.

He became the 10th player to win three Most Valuable Player awards. Only Stan Musial was younger when he accomplished the feat. Barry Bonds is the all-time leader with seven MVP awards.

"This was my best season ever," he offered. "I felt the most consistent at the plate."[28] With the death of his friend Tyler Skaggs, it was also his toughest season. "I just tried to come to the ballpark and step up as a leader. I felt like it was my time."[29]

The Sporting News named Mike Trout MLB Athlete of the Decade in December 2019. The publication said his greatness came from his steady excellence. Angels pitcher Andrew Heaney told *The Sporting News*, "I wouldn't say there's just one (standout) moment. But that's what makes him great. He doesn't have moments. He just does it every day."[30]

Because of the coronavirus, the 2020 baseball season didn't start until July 24 and was limited to 60 games. Trout's season highlight occurred on September 5, when he smacked his 300th career home run. He became the Angels' career home run leader, passing Tim Salmon.

He batted .281 with 17 homers in 53 games and placed fifth in the MVP voting.

Trout got off to his best start ever in 2021. He was batting .407 with eight homers, an OBP of .514, a slugging average of .779, and an OPS of 1.293 on May 4. Two weeks later, he suffered a right calf strain. Although he was expected to be sidelined for 6-8 weeks, complications caused him to miss the entire season.

Trout missed more than a month of the 2022 season with what was originally diagnosed as back spasms. It was later diagnosed as a rare condition called costovertebral dysfunction at T5 (a misalignment of one of the ribs). Physicians told Trout his condition would have to be monitored for the rest of his career.

He returned to the lineup on August 19 and quickly regained his form. He smashed a home run in seven consecutive games from September 4 to September 12, falling one game shy of tying the record. Limited to 119 games, he slugged 40 homers and batted .283. It was the third time he reached the 40-homer mark.

Arguably the best player in the game for his entire career, the Angels star has awed the baseball world with his consistency and skills. In 2019, Angels manager Joe Maddon said, "Mike is a one-of-a-kind player. His complete skill set is generational and stands up to every era that participated in our game."[31]

Mike Trout is a sure lock for the Baseball Hall of Fame and worthy of "the next Mickey Mantle" title.

CHAPTER 18

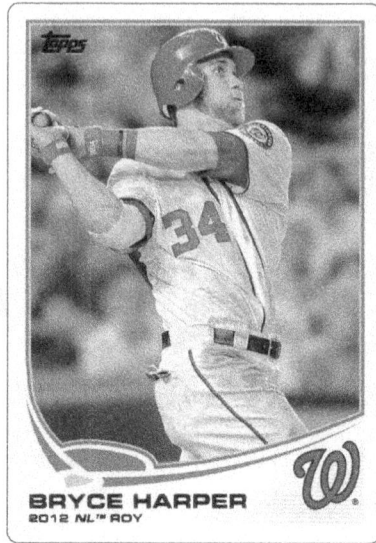

BRYCE HARPER
THE TEEN WHO WAS DESTINED TO BE A STAR

*I have only scouted three outfielders in my life with the full 5-tool
package at this level: Barry Bonds, Ken Griffey Jr., and Bryce Harper
are the only three that I could project as Hall of Famers the day they
were promoted to the majors.*
—Nationals General Manager Jim Bowden

Bryce Harper has been a head-turning, attention-grabbing, hard-to-
imagine baseball phenom since he picked up a bat at age seven. Bryce,
tutored by his iron-worker father, Ron, exhibited skills far beyond his
age. When he was seven, a coach for a team of 10-year-olds recruited him
for a traveling squad. By the time he was nine, he was flying across the
country three weekends a month and playing about 130 games a year. He

played for travel teams in California, Arizona, Oklahoma, and his home state Nevada.

When he was 12, he played in a tournament in Alabama with a 250-foot fence. The youngster proved he was in a different league, going 12-for-12 with 11 home runs and a double. In 2009, at age 16, he powered a 502-foot home run in Tropicana Field, home of the Tampa Bay Rays, during a Power Showcase. It was the longest home run in the history of the stadium.

As a Las Vegas High School sophomore, he batted .626 with 14 home runs and won *Baseball America*'s High School Player of the Year Award. No junior had won the honor, much less a sophomore.

That summer, *Sports Illustrated* featured the sensational teen on the cover of its June 8, 2009, issue. "The Chosen One: Bryce Harper is the Most Exciting Prodigy Since LeBron," declared the headline to the left of his photo. The article opened with writer Tom Verducci recounting the 15-year-old high school freshman's home run that supposedly traveled 570 feet. According to Sam Thomas, his high school baseball coach, the ball traveled over the right field fence, two trees, another fence, a sidewalk, five lanes of traffic, and another sidewalk before landing.

Labeled as a "once-in-a-generation talent," Harper was supremely confident, some would say cocky. When asked about his baseball goals, he replied, "Be in the Hall of Fame, definitely. Play in the pinstripes. Be considered the greatest baseball player who ever lived. I can't wait."[1] The *Sports Illustrated* issue introduced Harper to the rest of the country, put a target on his back, increased the pressure to an unprecedented level, created admirers and distracters, and put him under a national microscope. It left baseball fans, team front office officials, and scouts wondering if he could really be that good.

Harper left high school at age 16, earned his General Equivalency Diploma (GED), and enrolled at the College of Southern Nevada in 2009. The plan was for him to face high-level competition that would challenge him. Obtaining his GED meant he would be eligible for the baseball draft one year earlier than he would have been. His goal was to make the major leagues as quickly as possible.

Major league baseball scouts flocked to watch the left-handed hitting catcher. Harper, 6-3, 225 pounds, tried to prove he was the best player in the land on every pitch. He thrived on the attention. In his one year at the College of Southern Nevada (CSN) he batted .443, slammed 31 homers (crushing the school's previous record of 12), drove in 98 runs, and stole 20 bases. In a game that catapulted CSN into the Jr. College World Series, Harper went 6-for-6 with four homers, a double and triple, and 10 RBI.

The 2010 amateur baseball draft was rich in talent, but Harper was the consensus number one pick. One scout said he hadn't seen anyone like him in 30 years. The *New York Times* labeled him the best hitting prospect since Mickey Mantle. The 59-103 Washington Nationals, who drafted pitcher Stephen Strasburg with the first selection in 2009, tabbed the teen to lead off the draft. Other players drafted in the first round in 2010 included Jameson Taillon, Manny Machado, Matt Harvey, Christian Yelich, Noah Syndergaard, and Chris Sale.

Being the number one draft choice was "what I've wanted since I was seven years old," said Harper.[2] The 17-year-old college freshman became the first player from a two-year college to be drafted number one. One of the most celebrated and hyped picks in draft history; Harper was expected to switch from catcher to the outfield, likely right field. The Nationals signed him to a $9.9 million, five-year contract. Then they assigned him to the Arizona Fall League, where he batted .343 in nine games.

A flock of autograph seekers awaited Bryce when he arrived at the Nationals training camp in Viera, Florida, in February 2011. He captivated the crowd in batting practice when he took about 40 swings and cleared the fence four times.

No one, with the exception of Harper himself, expected him to make the team. He refused to believe it wasn't realistic. "Everybody said I couldn't do it last year at the College of Southern Nevada. I know this is a totally different level, totally different people, and I respect that. I'm going to come out here every day and play as hard as I can. And until they send me down to the minors, I'm going to try to make it hard."[3]

He kept his word, batting .389 (7-for-15) with three doubles and five RBI in 13 games. The Nationals, however, punched his ticket for

Low-A Hagerstown (Maryland) in the South Atlantic League. Bryce was shocked he didn't make the team.

Nationals manager Jim Riggleman said, "He's a special young player, but minor league baseball is tough. He'll get tested, believe me. We have every indication he's going to pass those tests."[4]

Harper played all three outfield positions at Hagerstown, made some adjustments against left-handed pitching, and wielded a hot bat. Hagerstown batting coach Marlon Anderson said, "Nobody has seen an 18-year-old who can do some of the things he's doing. He should be in high school getting ready to graduate, but he's out here hitting bombs all over the place."[5]

Nationals general manager Mike Rizzo told the media Harper would not play in the majors in 2011. He wanted his potential star to play in the minors at all three levels (A, AA, and AAA). Rizzo considered his number one draft pick a work in progress. He needed to refine some aspects of his game, such as base running, base stealing, and defense.

Although most baseball officials agreed Bryce was mature beyond his years, the teenager exhibited some immaturity on June 7, 2011, when he homered against Greensboro. He took some time to admire the blast before he left the batter's box. Greensboro pitcher Zachary Neal didn't care for his antics and let him know it as he rounded the bases. Harper responded by puckering up and blowing a kiss in Neal's direction when he reached home plate. Few people realized Harper had gotten hit by a pitch the day before. In his next at-bat, relief pitcher Grant Dayton backed him off the plate with a high and inside pitch.

However, Harper's raw power stood out to Hagerstown manager Brian Daubach. "When Bryce is taking batting practice, it's like watching a major leaguer," he said.[6]

The media recorded, analyzed, and hyped Harper's every move. New York *Daily News* columnist Wayne Coffey labeled him "a staggering package of talent."[7] Harper, who had spent most of his life ahead of schedule and hell-bent on greatness, was laser-focused on his goal of making the major leagues as soon as possible. He batted .318 with 14 homers in 72 games before being promoted to Class-AA Harrisburg (Pennsylvania) in the Eastern League in early July.

"Right about now, Bryce needs another challenge," said Nationals manager Davey Johnson, who had replaced Jim Riggleman. "And Double-A is the perfect spot."[8] At 18, he was the youngest player in Double-A baseball.

In Harrisburg, he played mainly left field and continued to refine his game. In late August, he suffered a strained right hamstring. The Nationals placed him on the seven-day disabled list and then decided to shut him down for the season. He batted .256 and hit three home runs in 18 games.

Harper went to spring training in 2012 with the same goal he had in 2011—to make the Washington Nationals. He was impatient, confident, and convinced he belonged on the team; age be damned. He figured he would make the team if he just played his game.

"I talked to Bryce when he was 15," said Davey Johnson. "He was cocky then, and he's cocky now."[9]

Baseball America rated him an 80 on the scouts' 20-80 scale. According to the publication, "Harper looks like a sure-fire superstar in the making, and he has a very real chance to develop into the best all-around player in baseball."[10]

Harper opened the 2012 season playing for AAA Syracuse in the International League. He played just 21 games before the Nationals called him up on April 27. The move occurred after the team placed third baseman Ryan Zimmerman on the 15-day disabled list. Harper made his major league debut the following day against the Dodgers in Los Angeles. He was 19 years and 195 days old, making him the youngest player in the majors by almost two years.

According to Nationals general manager Mike Rizzo, calling Bryce up to the major leagues was a difficult decision. The club wasn't sure he was ready, and the move didn't fit their developmental plan.

"We aren't dumb," offered Rizzo, explaining the somewhat unexpected move. "We feel Bryce has a chance to really impact the ballclub. He's a special talent."[11]

Nationals manager Davey Johnson thought Harper earned the right to get the opportunity. He said, "Bryce belongs here right now. He fits."[12]

Former Nationals general manager Jim Bowden said, "He's a game changer. Comparisons to Mickey Mantle, Barry Bonds, and Ken Griffey Jr. are not exaggerations."[13]

Thomas Boswell of the *Washington Post* never saw a player relish his first 10 games in the majors as much as Harper. He was more comfortable in the major leagues than in the minor leagues, where he constantly tried to prove himself. Bryce reveled in the games, wearing his emotions on his sleeve. His emotional displays irked some veteran players and fans of opposing teams.

Boswell witnessed Harper in batting practice and wrote that "it sounds like a thunderstorm." When the veteran baseball writer asked manager Davey Johnson if he had ever heard anyone swing so hard in BP while maintaining his balance and mechanics, Johnson replied, "Mantle."[14]

In his eighth major league game, Harper faced southpaw Cole Hamels of the Philadelphia Phillies. Hamels plunked him square in the back with a 93-mph fastball in the bottom of the first inning. Harper moved to third base on a single and then brazenly stole home as payback. He collected two hits in the 9-3 loss. Hamels later admitted he intentionally hit the rookie as part of an old-school way of indoctrinating him to the big leagues. The Philadelphia hurler was suspended for five games and fined an undisclosed amount.

The teen struggled in his first 20 games, batting .230 with two homers and five RBI. However, in the next 21 games, he batted .370 with five home runs, 14 RBI, and 19 runs scored. He posted a .446 on-base percentage and a .667 slugging average.

By the end of May, his OPS (on-base percentage plus slugging percentage) was .816. The only 19-year-olds with at least 100 plate appearances and a higher OPS were Jimmie Foxx (1927), Mel Ott (1928), and Tony Conigliaro (1964).

Teammate Ryan Zimmerman said, "I'm not surprised. As talented as he is and mature as he is, baseball-wise. I didn't really think he was going to have a problem hitting."[15]

At the All-Star break, Harper was batting .282 with eight home runs and 25 RBI in 63 games. He was starting for the first-place Nationals, playing right field and batting second. Harper was named to the 2012 All-Star team as a replacement for Miami's Giancarlo Stanton, who had surgery on his knee. At 19, he became the youngest American League position player to be an All-Star. However, many fans, players, and media members didn't believe he merited being an All-Star.

Harper slumped in July, batting .222, but he finished strong the last two months of the season. He completed his rookie year with a .270 batting average, 22 home runs, 59 RBI, and 18 stolen bases. The Nationals outfielder had been scrutinized more than any rookie in the past 50 years. He not only survived, but he also thrived.

He didn't fall victim to the incredible hype or rest on his reputation to Harper's credit. He worked hard, devoured every bit of information he could, watched countless videos to analyze his swing, and vowed to get better every day. Bryce promised to give his best every day, whether he was sick, hurt, or on his deathbed. He said the fans, the team, and the city deserved it. His intense love for the game was obvious.

His 22 homers erased Mel Ott's National League record of 18 four-baggers as a teenager in 1928. Only Tony Conigliaro of the Boston Red Sox clouted more homers as a teen (24 in 1964). Harper added National League Rookie of the Year to his credentials. At 20 years and 27 days, he was only 24 days older than New York Mets pitcher Dwight Gooden was when he won the award in 1984.

"I didn't reach my personal expectations," he said. "I'm never satisfied with my numbers. My biggest goal is to win a World Series. This is amazing to win this award, but I want to bring a title back to DC, and we didn't reach that."[16]

The Nationals won the National League East with a 98-64 record in 2012. But the club fell to the St. Louis Cardinals in the NL Division Series, 3 games to 2. Harper collected three hits in 23 at-bats (.130) and struck out eight times.

In 2013, Harper arrived at the Nationals' spring training camp more mature, more confident, and 20 pounds heavier, resulting from an intense off-season weightlifting program. He embraced the attention, pressure, and expectations. He wasn't overwhelmed. Instead, he liked the challenge. General manager Mike Rizzo said, "He's just scratching the surface. He has a ceiling that is really unprecedented by the measures of most players. This kid has one of the highest baseball IQs of anyone I've ever been around."[17]

Frequently compared to Mickey Mantle, Harper discussed his idol in spring training. "I love Mantle. He was unbelievable, incredible. Mantle was always my favorite player. I have watched his games on ESPN Classic. I've always tried to model my game after his, how he played and what he accomplished."[18] He explained he wore number 34 because 3 plus 4 equals 7 (Mantle's number).

Harper was batting .303 with 10 home runs on May 14, 2013, when he ran face-first into the outfield wall while chasing a line drive at Dodger Stadium. He lay on the ground dazed for several minutes before he got up under his own power. He suffered a cut on his face, a sore knee, and a banged-up shoulder, forcing him to miss 31 games.

Despite his time on the disabled list, the Nationals outfielder became the youngest hitter to start the All-Star game since Ken Griffey Jr. in 1990. He was the first player to start two All-Stars before age 21.

Harper played 118 games in 2013, 21 fewer than in his rookie season. Still, he almost matched his rookie home run (20 compared to 22) and RBI (58 compared to 59) totals. The accolades continued to pour in. Nationals manager Davey Johnson said, "I compare Bryce to Pete Rose with power. He's a dynamic player."[19]

Harper underwent surgery during the off-season to repair the bursa sac in his left knee, an injury suffered when he collided with the outfield wall in Los Angeles. In March 2014, he signed a $145 million, 6-year contract with Washington.

Thomas Boswell of the *Washington Post* wrote, "In his third season, it's time for him to be part of the team, not an attention magnet symbol of it before he's earned that distinction."[20] Boswell thought Harper was still a raw talent who received more attention and called more attention to himself than his play deserved. A poll of major league baseball players, who voted Harper the most overrated player in the game, supported Boswell's view.

On April 25, 2014, Harper tore ligaments in his left thumb on a head-first slide into third base. He had surgery four days later and was expected to be out of the lineup until July. A month after he returned, his thumb started to feel better, and he batted .305 with nine home runs from August 12 until the end of the season. Washington captured the NL

East pennant with a 96-66 record. Bryce was near the top of his game when the National League Division Series against the San Francisco Giants opened. Although the Nationals lost 3 games to one, Harper shined on the national stage. He batted .294 (5-for-19), slugged three homers, drove in four runs, and scored four runs.

In an injury-marred 2014 season, Harper was limited to 100 games and produced ho-hum results. He was a lightning rod for criticism and a constant topic for second guessers. In August, some detractors suggested he be demoted. After three seasons, some fans were convinced he was more flash than substance. General manager Mike Rizzo reminded critics that Harper had two great seasons compared to anything other players had accomplished at ages 19 and 20.

Marc Normadin of sbnation.com wrote, "Bryce Harper isn't over-rated and never was. If anything, baseball doesn't appreciate this incredible talent enough. He's only played 139 games in the minors, with most of his education coming against the best players in the world in the majors."[21]

The Bryce Harper everyone had been waiting for showed up in May 2015. He entered the month batting .286 but then caught fire. On May 6 against the Miami Marlins, he slammed three home runs and tallied 5 RBI. A solo shot in the second inning traveled 393 feet. He added a 442-foot, two-RBI blast in the third and a 445-foot solo round-tripper in the fifth. Two days later, he walloped two more homers and drove in 5 runs against the Atlanta Braves. Harper became the youngest player to knock 5 home runs in back-to-back games. He added another home run and two RBI in the following game. The baseball world was buzzing about his 6 home runs and 12 RBI outburst in three games.

Gabe Lacques of *USA Today* wrote, "The promise of more always trumped the historic nature of his accomplishments. Now, however, the hype and promise have been met and perhaps exceeded by power and production."[22]

For two weeks (May 5 to 22), Harper was hotter than any other player over the same period in the last 65-plus years, according to Ben Lindbergh of Grantland.com. Harper batted .575 with a 1.450 slugging average during that span. For the month, he batted .360 (31-for-109), swatted a franchise-record 13 home runs, and drove in 28 runs. He homered once every 6.6 at-bats.

Being more selective, pulling the ball more, and handling outside pitches and breaking balls better fueled his breakout. He hit the ball harder than ever. Many of his home runs seemed effortless.

Teammate Ryan Zimmerman observed, "It's hard for a young kid who has the weight of the world on his shoulders to produce at this level. This year, we're starting to see Bryce take a deep breath and let his talent take over."[23]

Healthy for the first time in several seasons, the Nationals outfielder enjoyed a monstrous year in 2015 as Washington finished second in the NL East. He batted .330, slammed a league-best 42 homers, tallied 99 RBI, scored 118 runs, and walked 124 times. He also led the majors in on-base percentage (.460), slugging percentage (.649), and OPS (1.109). Ted Williams was the only player 22 or younger who topped Harper's 1.109 OPS. Harper was voted the unanimous National League Most Valuable Player. At 22, he was the fourth youngest player to win an MVP award. Only Stan Musial, Johnny Bench, and Vida Blue were younger.

Fans wondered what Harper could do for an encore in 2016. New Nationals manager Dusty Baker, who replaced Matt Williams, wasn't putting any unrealistic expectations on the young star. He said, "I expect Bryce just to continue to grow as a man and a player. How many players 23 have been where he has been? Let's not forget he's 23. I'm not putting any limitations on him. I'm not going to put any pressure on him. I'm just going to let him be Bryce."[24]

Harper said he couldn't care less about anyone's expectations because his expectations were higher. He looked like he would continue his 2015 form in the first month of the new season as he slammed nine home runs, drove in 24 runs, and batted .286. No pitcher wanted to face him. In a 4-game series at Wrigley Field in early May, the Cubs walked the slugger 13 times. In a 13-inning game on May 8, the Cubs walked him 6 times, 3 times intentionally, and hit him once in seven plate appearances.

Kevin Acee of the *San Diego Union-Tribune* attempted to capture the beauty of Harper's swing. He wrote, "If Hemingway saw Harper's swing and was asked to describe it, via the written word, Papa would simply break down in tears."[25]

The 2015 MVP, however, proved inconsistent in 2016. He batted only .200 in May, .176 in July, and .210 in September. Despite Harper's struggles, the Nationals won the NL East with a 95-67 record. The Nationals star compiled a .243 average in the regular season with 24 homers and 86 RBI. It was a decent season by most standards but a disappointing one by Harper's.

In the National League Division Series, Washington lost to the Los Angeles Dodgers, 3 games to 2. Harper contributed little on offense, going 4-for-17 (.235) with no home runs and one RBI.

In his first five seasons, Harper compared favorably to Mickey Mantle and Johnny Bench, who made their major league debuts at age 19. He and Mantle each slugged 121 home runs, while Bench recorded 114. Mantle (445) and Bench (387) drove in more runs than Harper (334). His early production was just one of the reasons why Washington was already looking ahead to how they could retain the budding superstar. Harper would be eligible for arbitration in 2017 and free agency after the 2018 season. It was going to be an expensive, perhaps record-setting, proposition.

Harper had a lot to prove entering the 2017 season. But before he stepped on the field, he and the Nationals agreed to a $13.6 million one-year contract in January. The deal avoided arbitration and more than doubled his salary. Only 24, Harper was already a four-time All-Star and one of the most coveted stars in the game.

Rumors whirled that Harper had hurt his shoulder in 2016, and that's why he had a subpar season. But neither Harper, Nationals general manager Mike Rizzo nor manager Dusty Baker ever confirmed he was injured. The Nationals star, however, appeared completely healthy in April 2017. He blasted nine home runs, drove in 26 runs, and batted .391. Baker said Harper was more settled than in the past, more focused, more patient, and hitting to the opposite field more.

"Last year sucked," said Harper. "It just wasn't feeling right. I wasn't able to get to the gym and do things I wanted to do and really do it with a clear mind."[26]

In mid-May, Harper and the Nationals agreed on a $21.6 million contract for the 2018 season, his last before free agency.

On August 7, 2017, Harper, at 24 years, 295 days, clouted his 150th career home run. Among active players, only Albert Pujols and Giancarlo Stanton reached 150 home runs at an earlier age. Of the ten non-active players with 150 home runs before their 25th birthday, only Orlando Cepeda and Johnny Bench failed to hit 400 homers in their careers.

A week later, Harper injured his left knee trying to beat out an infield hit. The game was delayed by rain for three hours and played in wet conditions. Bryce hit the bag awkwardly and flew into the air. When he landed, he writhed in pain on the field, clutched his left knee, and had to be helped off the field. An MRI revealed a significant bone bruise, which was expected to keep him out of the lineup for four to six weeks.

Harper returned on September 26. Although he was limited to 111 games, he finished the 2017 season with 29 homers, 87 RBI, and batted .319, 76 points higher than the previous year. Washington won the NL East with a 97-65 record and faced the Chicago Cubs in the 2017 National League Division Series. The Cubs won 3 games to 2. Harper's sole highlight came in the second game when he blasted a 2-run homer. He went 4-for-19 and batted .211 in the series. For the fourth time, the Nationals were knocked out in the first round of the playoffs.

Two big questions confronted Washington as it kicked off the 2018 season. Would they be able to sign Bryce Harper as a free agent? And could they finally advance past the first round of the playoffs? Harper insisted he was focused solely on helping his team win, not on free agency.

Neither the Nationals nor the heavily scrutinized Harper got off to a decent start. At the All-Star break, Washington was 48-48 in third place in the NL East, 5.5 games out of first. Harper was batting .214. Yet, he was still dangerous at the plate. He had powered 23 home runs and drawn 78 walks, surpassing his 2017 totals.

He claimed the stress of free agency and trying to lead the Nationals to the World Series didn't bother him. "Should I be hitting .280 or .300? Yeah, absolutely. But I am where I am. Hopefully, the only way I can go is up," he said.[27] Observers felt he had been hampered by defensive shifts and pitchers not giving him much to hit.

Washington (82-80) finished a disappointing second. Harper contributed 34 homers and drove in 100 runs for the first time. He also scored 103 runs, drew a league-leading 130 walks, and batted .249. His career numbers before age 26 made him the most attractive free agent heading into the 2019 season.

He had staked his claim as one of the best young players in baseball history. Harper's agent Scott Boras pointed out that Alex Rodriguez, Mike Trout, and Tony Conigliaro were the only other players with six 20-home run seasons by age 25. Boras believed his client was almost a sure lock for the Hall of Fame.

Harper was a rare talent, and Boras wanted to shatter the record for the richest contract (13 years for $325 million) Giancarlo Stanton signed in 2014 with the Miami Marlins. Harper reportedly turned down a 10-year, $300 million contract from the Nationals at the end of the season.

Philadelphia Phillies owner John Middleton publicly declared he was ready to spend "stupid money" to acquire Harper. His club, winners of the 2008 World Series, hadn't had a winning season since 2011. The Los Angeles Dodgers, the Chicago Cubs, and the San Francisco Giants were the other front-runners for Harper's services.

Harper and the Phillies agreed to a 13-year, $330 million contract on February 28, 2019. It was the most lucrative contract in baseball history. The contract included a no-opt-out clause and a no-trade clause at Harper's request. He wanted to spend the rest of his career in Philadelphia.

Only 11 players had more home runs than Harper's 184 before age 26, and seven are in the Hall of Fame. By comparison, Phillies Hall of Famer Mike Schmidt, who finished with 548 homers, slugged just 93 home runs entering his age 26 season.

Schmidt applauded the Phillies' acquisition of Harper, who he considered a star in every way. He, however, viewed Harper realistically. "Bryce is in his 8th season, and for several reasons, he has not been the player he was expected to be. With the exception of his 2015 MVP season, he has fallen short of his expectations and everyone else's. There have been injuries and inconsistencies due to strikeouts and pitchers working around him, but nonetheless, he has maintained his status as one of the league's stars."[28]

Expectations, pressure, and scrutiny reached feverish levels as Harper donned the Phillies uniform. His high profile was underscored in July when ESPN ranked him the 99th most famous athlete worldwide based on internet searches, endorsements, and social media engagement. He was the only baseball player to crack the Top 100.

Bryce's first year in Philadelphia was a solid one. He slammed 35 home runs, drove in 114 runs, scored 98 runs, walked 99 times, and compiled an .882 OPS while batting .260. However, his presence in the lineup made little difference to the Phillies' record. The 2019 club finished 81-81, one more win than 2018, and fourth in the NL East.

The coronavirus prevented the 2020 season from opening until July 24. The season was shortened to 60 games. Entering his ninth season, Harper was considered one of the most polarizing players in baseball. Fans either loved him or hated him. He continued to deal with jealousy among other players and barbs from the media. Some of his teammates said he was misunderstood. Former player and Phillies announcer Kevin Frandsen said, "Bryce is misunderstood because he's been in the spotlight since he was 15. Anything he does or says gets blown up when he's just trying to be normal."[29]

Assessing Harper, *Philadelphia Inquirer* reporter Scott Lauder wrote, "He isn't the best player in baseball, and he might not be in the Top 5. But he's far more substance than style, with unbridled passion for the game and an investment in the Phillies' success that matches the team's considerable stake in him."[30]

Harper played like an MVP for most of the 2020 season. His batting average reached a high of .367 on August 18. Back soreness, however, started to bother him, and his batting average dropped from .317 on August 26 to .268 on September 27.

Entering the 2021 season, lots of questions still surrounded the 28-year-old. The Phillies outfielder got off to a slow start but sizzled in the final two months. After the All-Star break, he rapped 49 extra-base hits and drew 65 walks. He closed the season with a .309 batting average, 100 walks, 100 runs, 84 RBI, 35 homers, and a league-leading 42 doubles. He became only the fourth outfielder to tally 100 walks, 100 runs, 40 doubles, and 35 homers in a season. The others are Babe Ruth

(1921 and 1923), Stan Musial (1949), and Barry Bonds (1998). He also led the league in slugging average (.616) and OPS (1.044).

His effort culminated in winning his second National League Most Valuable Player Award. He collected 17 first-place votes while Washington's Juan Soto tallied six and San Diego's Fernando Tatis Jr. garnered two.

After Harper won the MVP, former Phillies manager Gabe Kapler said, "Bryce is a generational talent, and his work ethic, effort level, and determination are second to none."[31] The second MVP award erased many questions surrounding Harper, elevated his position in baseball history, and increased his Hall of Fame worthiness.

Harper was forced to DH for most of the 2022 season because a torn ulnar collateral ligament in his right arm made it difficult to throw. On June 25, Padres Blake Snell hit Harper's hand with a fastball, breaking his thumb and sidelining him for two months when he was batting .318 with 15 home runs, 48 RBI, and a .984 OPS.

Bryce returned to the lineup on August 26 and helped the Phillies to a playoff berth, their first since 2011. He played 99 games, knocked 18 home runs, and batted .286. Harper sizzled in the playoffs. He collected 18 hits, slammed five homers, drove in 11 runs, and batted .418. He was named NLCS MVP and carried the underdog Phillies into the World Series against the Houston Astros.

ZIPS, a projection system developed by Dan Szymborski of Fangraphs, predicts Harper will finish his contract with the Phillies with 521 home runs (equal to Hall of Famers Ted Williams and Frank Thomas) but shy of 2,400 hits and 1,600 RBI.

A P P E N D I X
CAREER STATS

The following player career stats are from Baseball-reference.com.

MICKEY MANTLE

Year	Age	Tm	Lg	G	PA	AB	R	H	2B	3B	HR	RBI	SB	CS	BB	SO	BA	OBP	SLG	OPS
1951	19	NYY	AL	96	386	341	61	91	11	5	13	65	8	7	43	74	.267	.349	.443	.792
1952	20	NYY	AL	142	626	549	94	171	37	7	23	87	4	1	75	111	.311	.394	.530	.924
1953	21	NYY	AL	127	540	461	105	136	24	3	21	92	8	4	79	90	.295	.398	.497	.895
1954	22	NYY	AL	146	651	543	*129*	163	17	12	27	102	5	2	102	*107*	.300	.408	.525	.933
1955	23	NYY	AL	147	638	517	121	158	25	11	37	99	8	1	*113*	97	.306	.431	.611	1.042
1956	24	NYY	AL	150	652	533	*132*	188	22	5	*52*	*130*	10	1	112	99	*.353*	.464	*.705*	1.169
1957	25	NYY	AL	144	623	474	*121*	173	28	6	34	94	16	3	*146*	75	.365	.512	.665	1.177
1958	26	NYY	AL	150	654	519	*127*	158	21	1	42	97	18	3	*129*	*120*	.304	.443	.592	1.035
1959	27	NYY	AL	144	640	541	104	154	23	4	31	75	21	3	93	*126*	.285	.390	.514	.904
1960	28	NYY	AL	153	644	527	*119*	145	17	6	40	94	14	3	111	125	.275	.399	.558	*.957*
1961	29	NYY	AL	153	646	514	131	163	16	6	54	128	12	1	*126*	112	.317	.448	*.687*	1.135
1962	30	NYY	AL	123	502	377	96	121	15	1	30	89	9	0	*122*	78	.321	*.486*	*.605*	*1.091*
1963	31	NYY	AL	65	213	172	40	54	8	0	15	35	2	1	40	32	.314	.441	.622	1.063
1964	32	NYY	AL	143	567	465	92	141	25	2	35	111	6	3	99	102	.303	*.423*	.591	*1.015*
1965	33	NYY	AL	122	435	361	44	92	12	1	19	46	4	1	73	76	.255	.379	.452	.831
1966	34	NYY	AL	108	393	333	40	96	12	1	23	56	1	1	57	76	.288	.389	.538	.927
1967	35	NYY	AL	144	553	440	63	108	17	0	22	55	1	1	107	113	.245	.391	.434	.825
1968	36	NYY	AL	144	547	435	57	103	14	1	18	54	6	2	106	97	.237	.385	.398	.782
18 Yrs				2401	9910	8102	1676	2415	344	72	536	1509	153	38	1733	1710	.298	.421	.557	.977

Bold season totals indicate player led league. *Italic* season totals indicate player led major leagues.

TOM TRESH

Year	Age	Tm	Lg	G	PA	AB	R	H	2B	3B	HR	RBI	SB	CS	BB	SO	BA	OBP	SLG	OPS
1961	22	NYY	AL	9	8	8	1	2	0	0	0	0	0	0	0	1	.250	.250	.250	.500
1962	23	NYY	AL	157	712	622	94	178	26	5	20	93	4	8	67	74	.286	.359	.441	.800
1963	24	NYY	AL	145	614	520	91	140	28	5	25	71	3	3	83	79	.269	.371	.487	.857
1964	25	NYY	AL	153	621	533	75	131	25	5	16	73	13	0	73	110	.246	.342	.402	.743
1965	26	NYY	AL	156	668	602	94	168	29	6	26	74	5	2	59	92	.279	.348	.477	.825
1966	27	NYY	AL	151	637	537	76	125	12	4	27	68	5	4	86	89	.233	.341	.421	.762
1967	28	NYY	AL	130	509	448	45	98	23	3	14	53	1	0	50	86	.219	.301	.377	.678
1968	29	NYY	AL	152	590	507	60	99	18	3	11	52	10	5	76	97	.195	.304	.308	.612
1969	30	TOT	AL	139	538	474	59	100	18	3	14	46	4	3	56	70	.211	.294	.350	.644
1969	30	NYY	AL	45	161	143	13	26	5	2	1	9	2	1	17	23	.182	.269	.266	.534
1969	30	DET	AL	94	377	331	46	74	13	1	13	37	2	2	39	47	.224	.305	.387	.692
9 Yrs				1192	4897	4251	595	1041	179	34	153	530	45	25	550	698	.245	.335	.411	.746

JOE PEPITONE

Year	Age	Tm	Lg	G	PA	AB	R	H	2B	3B	HR	RBI	SB	CS	BB	SO	BA	OBP	SLG	OPS
1962	21	NYY	AL	63	141	138	14	33	3	2	7	17	1	1	3	21	.239	.255	.442	.697
1963	22	NYY	AL	157	615	580	79	157	16	3	27	89	3	5	23	63	.271	.304	.448	.752
1964	23	NYY	AL	160	647	613	71	154	12	3	28	100	2	1	24	63	.251	.281	.418	.698
1965	24	NYY	AL	143	580	531	51	131	18	3	18	62	4	2	43	59	.247	.305	.394	.699
1966	25	NYY	AL	152	621	585	85	149	21	4	31	83	4	3	29	58	.255	.29	.463	.753
1967	26	NYY	AL	133	545	501	45	126	18	3	13	64	1	3	34	62	.251	.301	.377	.678
1968	27	NYY	AL	108	421	380	41	93	9	3	15	56	8	2	37	45	.245	.311	.403	.714
1969	28	NYY	AL	135	546	513	49	124	16	3	27	70	8	6	30	42	.242	.284	.442	.726
1970	29	TOT	NL	131	533	492	82	127	18	7	26	79	5	4	33	43	.258	.304	.482	.786
1970	29	HOU	NL	75	299	279	44	70	9	5	14	35	5	2	18	28	.251	.298	.470	.767
1970	29	CHC	NL	56	234	213	38	57	9	2	12	44	0	2	15	15	.268	.313	.498	.811
1971	30	CHC	NL	115	460	427	50	131	19	4	16	61	1	2	24	41	.307	.347	.482	.830
1972	31	CHC	NL	66	233	214	23	56	5	0	8	21	1	2	13	22	.262	.309	.397	.706
1973	32	TOT	NL	34	134	123	16	34	3	0	3	19	3	1	9	7	.276	.328	.374	.702
1973	32	CHC	NL	31	122	112	16	30	3	0	3	18	3	1	8	6	.268	.32	.375	.695
1973	32	ATL	NL	3	12	11	0	4	0	0	0	1	0	0	1	1	.364	.417	.364	.780
12 Yrs				1397	5476	5097	606	1315	158	35	219	721	41	32	302	526	.258	.301	.432	.733

ROGER REPOZ

Year	Age	Tm	Lg	G	PA	AB	R	H	2B	3B	HR	RBI	SB	CS	BB	SO	BA	OBP	SLG	OPS
1964	23	NYY	AL	11	2	1	1	0	0	0	0	0	0	0	1	1	.000	.500	.000	.500
1965	24	NYY	AL	79	245	218	34	48	7	4	12	28	1	1	25	57	.220	.298	.454	.752
1966	25	TOT	AL	138	418	362	44	84	14	4	11	43	3	3	48	88	.232	.324	.384	.708
1966	25	NYY	AL	37	49	43	4	15	4	1	0	9	0	0	4	8	.349	.396	.488	.884
1966	25	KCA	AL	101	369	319	40	69	10	3	11	34	3	3	44	80	.216	.314	.370	.684
1967	26	TOT	AL	114	299	263	34	65	15	2	7	28	6	4	31	57	.247	.326	.399	.725
1967	26	KCA	AL	40	101	87	9	21	6	1	2	8	4	2	12	20	.241	.340	.402	.742
1967	26	CAL	AL	74	198	176	25	44	9	1	5	20	2	2	19	37	.250	.318	.398	.716
1968	27	CAL	AL	133	426	375	30	90	8	1	13	54	8	7	38	83	.240	.309	.371	.680
1969	28	CAL	AL	103	255	219	25	36	1	1	8	19	1	3	32	52	.164	.270	.288	.558
1970	29	CAL	AL	137	463	407	50	97	17	6	18	47	4	2	45	90	.238	.317	.442	.760
1971	30	CAL	AL	113	360	297	39	59	11	1	13	41	3	5	60	69	.199	.333	.374	.707
1972	31	CAL	AL	3	3	3	0	1	0	0	0	0	0	0	0	2	.333	.333	.333	.667
9 Yrs				831	2471	2145	257	480	73	19	82	260	26	25	280	499	.224	.314	.390	.704

RICK REICHARDT

Year	Age	Tm	Lg	G	PA	AB	R	H	2B	3B	HR	RBI	SB	CS	BB	SO	BA	OBP	SLG	OPS
1964	21	LAA	AL	11	38	37	0	6	0	0	0	0	1	0	1	12	.162	.184	.162	.346
1965	22	CAL	AL	20	81	75	8	20	4	0	1	6	4	1	5	12	.267	.321	.36	.681
1966	23	CAL	AL	89	361	319	48	92	5	4	16	44	8	4	27	61	.288	.367	.480	.846
1967	24	CAL	AL	146	545	498	56	132	14	2	17	69	5	3	35	90	.265	.32	.404	.724
1968	25	CAL	AL	151	601	534	62	136	20	3	21	73	8	7	42	118	.255	.328	.421	.749
1969	26	CAL	AL	137	557	493	60	125	11	4	13	68	3	6	43	100	.254	.319	.371	.691
1970	27	TOT	AL	116	321	283	43	71	14	2	15	47	2	4	26	69	.251	.33	.473	.804
1970	27	CAL	AL	9	10	6	1	1	0	0	0	1	0	0	3	0	.167	.400	.167	.567
1970	27	WSA	AL	107	311	277	42	70	14	2	15	46	2	4	23	69	.253	.328	.480	.808
1971	28	CHW	AL	138	544	496	53	138	14	2	19	62	5	10	37	90	.278	.335	.429	.764
1972	29	CHW	AL	101	328	291	31	73	14	4	8	43	2	2	28	63	.251	.321	.409	.730
1973	30	TOT	AL	87	309	280	30	70	13	3	6	33	2	4	19	57	.250	.298	.382	.680
1973	30	CHW	AL	46	164	153	15	42	8	1	3	16	2	3	8	29	.275	.315	.399	.714
1973	30	KCR	AL	41	145	127	15	28	5	2	3	17	0	1	11	28	.22	.279	.362	.641
1974	31	KCR	AL	1	1	1	0	1	0	0	0	0	0	0	0	0	1.000	1.000	1.000	2.000
11 Yrs				997	3686	3307	391	864	109	24	116	445	40	41	263	672	.261	.326	.414	.740

BOBBY MURCER

Year	Age	Tm	Lg	G	PA	AB	R	H	2B	3B	HR	RBI	SB	CS	BB	SO	BA	OBP	SLG	OPS
1965	19	NYY	AL	11	42	37	2	9	0	1	1	4	0	0	5	12	.243	.333	.378	.712
1966	20	NYY	AL	21	73	69	3	12	1	1	0	5	2	2	4	5	.174	.219	.217	.437
1967			Did not play in major or minor leagues (Military Service)																	
1968			Did not play in major or minor leagues (Military Service)																	
1969	23	NYY	AL	152	625	564	82	146	24	4	26	82	7	5	50	103	.259	.319	.454	.773
1970	24	NYY	AL	159	680	581	95	146	23	3	23	78	15	10	87	100	.251	.348	.420	.768
1971	25	NYY	AL	146	624	529	94	175	25	6	25	94	14	8	91	60	.331	**.427**	.543	**.969**
1972	26	NYY	AL	153	654	585	**102**	171	30	7	33	96	11	9	63	67	.292	.361	.537	.898
1973	27	NYY	AL	160	672	616	83	187	29	2	22	95	6	7	50	67	.304	.357	.464	.821
1974	28	NYY	AL	156	679	606	69	166	25	4	10	88	14	5	57	59	.274	.332	.378	.710
1975	29	SFG	NL	147	632	526	80	157	29	4	11	91	9	5	91	45	.298	.396	.432	.828
1976	30	SFG	NL	147	624	533	73	138	20	2	23	90	12	7	84	78	.259	.362	.433	.796
1977	31	CHC	NL	154	649	554	90	147	18	3	27	89	16	7	80	77	.265	.355	.455	.810
1978	32	CHC	NL	146	585	499	66	140	22	6	9	64	14	5	80	57	.281	.376	.403	.779
1979	33	TOT	MLB	132	525	454	64	121	16	1	15	55	3	4	61	52	.267	.354	.405	.760
1979	33	CHC	NL	58	231	190	22	49	4	1	7	22	2	3	36	20	.258	.374	.400	.774
1979	33	NYY	AL	74	294	264	42	72	12	0	8	33	1	1	25	32	.273	.339	.409	.748
1980	34	NYY	AL	100	345	297	41	80	9	1	13	57	2	0	34	28	.269	.339	.438	.777
1981	35	NYY	AL	50	130	117	14	31	6	0	6	24	0	0	12	15	.265	.331	.470	.801
1982	36	NYY	AL	65	156	141	12	32	6	0	7	30	2	1	12	15	.227	.288	.418	.707
1983	37	NYY	AL	9	23	22	2	4	2	0	1	1	0	0	1	1	.182	.217	.409	.626
17 Yrs				1908	7718	6730	972	1862	285	45	252	1043	127	75	862	841	.277	.357	.445	.802

Bold season totals indicate player led league. *Italic* season totals indicate player led major leagues.

STEVE WHITAKER

Year	Age	Tm	Lg	G	PA	AB	R	H	2B	3B	HR	RBI	SB	CS	BB	SO	BA	OBP	SLG	OPS
1966	23	NYY	AL	31	124	114	15	28	3	2	7	15	0	0	9	24	.246	.306	.491	.798
1967	24	NYY	AL	122	472	441	37	107	12	3	11	50	2	5	23	89	.243	.283	.358	.641
1968	25	NYY	AL	28	68	60	3	7	2	0	0	3	0	1	8	18	.117	.221	.150	.371
1969	26	SEP	AL	69	130	116	15	29	2	1	6	13	2	0	12	29	.25	.323	.440	.763
1970	27	SFG	NL	16	30	27	3	3	1	0	0	4	0	0	2	14	.111	.167	.148	.315
5 Yrs				266	824	758	73	174	20	6	24	85	4	6	54	174	.23	.283	.367	.650

BILL ROBINSON

Year	Age	Tm	Lg	G	PA	AB	R	H	2B	3B	HR	RBI	SB	CS	BB	SO	BA	OBP	SLG	OPS
1966	23	ATL	NL	6	11	11	1	3	0	1	0	3	0	0	0	1	.273	.273	.455	.727
1967	24	NYY	AL	116	381	342	31	67	6	1	7	29	2	2	28	56	.196	.259	.281	.539
1968	25	NYY	AL	107	378	342	34	82	16	7	6	40	7	6	26	54	.24	.294	.380	.674
1969	26	NYY	AL	87	239	222	23	38	11	2	3	21	3	1	16	39	.171	.226	.279	.505
1972	29	PHI	NL	82	195	188	19	45	9	1	8	21	2	3	5	30	.239	.258	.426	.683
1973	30	PHI	NL	124	487	452	62	130	32	1	25	65	5	4	27	91	.288	.326	.529	.855
1974	31	PHI	NL	100	304	280	32	66	14	1	5	29	5	3	17	61	.236	.28	.346	.626
1975	32	PIT	NL	92	217	200	26	56	12	2	6	33	3	1	11	36	.28	.313	.450	.763
1976	33	PIT	NL	122	416	393	55	119	22	3	21	64	2	4	16	73	.303	.329	.534	.864
1977	34	PIT	NL	137	544	507	74	154	32	1	26	104	12	6	25	92	.304	.337	.525	.862
1978	35	PIT	NL	136	552	499	70	123	36	2	14	80	14	11	35	105	.246	.296	.411	.707
1979	36	PIT	NL	148	455	421	59	111	17	6	24	75	13	2	24	81	.264	.302	.504	.805
1980	37	PIT	NL	100	294	272	28	78	10	1	12	36	1	4	15	45	.287	.32	.463	.783
1981	38	PIT	NL	39	94	88	8	19	3	0	2	8	1	0	5	18	.216	.258	.318	.576
1982	39	TOT	NL	66	155	140	14	35	9	0	7	31	1	2	12	34	.25	.303	.464	.768
1982	39	PIT	NL	31	77	71	8	17	3	0	4	12	0	1	5	19	.239	.286	.451	.736
1982	39	PHI	NL	35	78	69	6	18	6	0	3	19	1	1	7	15	.261	.321	.478	.799
1983	40	PHI	NL	10	8	7	0	1	0	0	0	2	0	0	1	4	.143	.250	.143	.393
16 Yrs				1472	4730	4364	536	1127	229	29	166	641	71	49	263	820	.258	.300	.438	.738

TONY SOLAITA

Year	Age	Tm	Lg	G	PA	AB	R	H	2B	3B	HR	RBI	SB	CS	BB	SO	BA	OBP	SLG	OPS
1968	21	NYY	AL	1	1	1	0	0	0	0	0	0	0	0	0	1	.000	.000	.000	.000
1974	27	KCR	AL	96	279	239	31	64	12	0	7	30	0	3	35	70	.268	.361	.406	.767
1975	28	KCR	AL	93	275	231	35	60	11	0	16	44	0	1	39	79	.260	.369	.515	.884
1976	29	TOT	AL	94	329	283	29	74	13	0	9	42	1	1	40	61	.261	.348	.403	.750
1976	29	KCR	AL	31	77	68	4	16	4	0	0	9	0	0	6	17	.235	.286	.294	.580
1976	29	CAL	AL	63	252	215	25	58	9	0	9	33	1	1	34	44	.270	.367	.437	.804
1977	30	CAL	AL	116	386	324	40	78	15	0	14	53	1	3	56	77	.241	.349	.417	.766
1978	31	CAL	AL	60	110	94	10	21	3	0	1	14	0	0	16	25	.223	.336	.287	.624
1979	32	TOT	MLB	65	174	144	19	39	12	1	3	20	0	0	28	32	.271	.385	.431	.816
1979	32	MON	NL	29	53	42	5	12	4	0	1	7	0	0	11	16	.286	.434	.452	.886
1979	32	TOR	AL	36	121	102	14	27	8	1	2	13	0	0	17	16	.265	.364	.422	.785
7 Yrs				525	1554	1316	164	336	66	1	50	203	2	8	214	345	.255	.357	.421	.778

RON BLOMBERG

Year	Age	Tm	Lg	G	PA	AB	R	H	2B	3B	HR	RBI	SB	CS	BB	SO	BA	OBP	SLG	OPS
1969	20	NYY	AL	4	7	6	0	3	0	0	0	0	0	0	1	0	.500	.571	.500	1.071
1971	22	NYY	AL	64	216	199	30	64	6	2	7	31	2	4	14	23	.322	.363	.477	.840
1972	23	NYY	AL	107	341	299	36	80	22	1	14	49	0	2	38	26	.268	.355	.488	.843
1973	24	NYY	AL	100	338	301	45	99	13	1	12	57	2	0	34	25	.329	.395	.498	.893
1974	25	NYY	AL	90	301	264	39	82	11	2	10	48	2	1	29	33	.311	.375	.481	.856
1975	26	NYY	AL	34	119	106	18	27	8	2	4	17	0	0	13	10	.255	.336	.481	.817
1976	27	NYY	AL	1	2	2	0	0	0	0	0	0	0	0	0	0	.000	.000	.000	.000
1978	29	CHW	AL	61	169	156	16	36	7	0	5	22	0	0	11	17	.231	.280	.372	.652
8 Yrs				461	1493	1333	184	391	67	8	52	224	6	7	140	134	.293	.360	.473	.832

CLINT HURDLE

Year	Age	Tm	Lg	G	PA	AB	R	H	2B	3B	HR	RBI	SB	CS	BB	SO	BA	OBP	SLG	OPS
1977	19	KCR	AL	9	28	26	5	8	0	0	2	7	0	0	2	7	.308	.357	.538	.896
1978	20	KCR	AL	133	481	417	48	110	25	5	7	56	1	3	56	84	.264	.348	.398	.746
1979	21	KCR	AL	59	204	171	16	41	10	3	3	30	0	1	28	24	.240	.343	.386	.729
1980	22	KCR	AL	130	438	395	50	116	31	2	10	60	0	0	34	61	.294	.349	.458	.807
1981	23	KCR	AL	28	89	76	12	25	3	1	4	15	0	0	13	10	.329	.427	.553	.980
1982	24	CIN	NL	19	37	34	2	7	1	0	0	1	0	1	2	6	.206	.270	.235	.506
1983	25	NYM	NL	13	35	33	3	6	2	0	0	2	0	0	2	10	.182	.229	.242	.471
1985	27	NYM	NL	43	97	82	7	16	4	0	3	7	0	1	13	20	.195	.313	.354	.666
1986	28	STL	NL	78	184	154	18	30	5	1	3	15	0	0	26	38	.195	.311	.299	.610
1987	29	NYM	NL	3	3	3	1	1	0	0	0	0	0	0	0	1	.333	.333	.333	.667
10 Yrs				515	1596	1391	162	360	81	12	32	193	1	6	176	261	.259	.341	.403	.745

KIRK GIBSON

Year	Age	Tm	Lg	G	PA	AB	R	H	2B	3B	HR	RBI	SB	CS	BB	SO	BA	OBP	SLG	OPS
1979	22	DET	AL	12	39	38	3	9	3	0	1	4	3	3	1	3	.237	.256	.395	.651
1980	23	DET	AL	51	189	175	23	46	2	1	9	16	4	7	10	45	.263	.303	.440	.743
1981	24	DET	AL	83	313	290	41	95	11	3	9	40	17	5	18	64	.328	.369	.479	.848
1982	25	DET	AL	69	294	266	34	74	16	2	8	35	9	7	25	41	.278	.341	.444	.785
1983	26	DET	AL	128	467	401	60	91	12	9	15	51	14	3	53	96	.227	.320	.414	.734
1984	27	DET	AL	149	611	531	92	150	23	10	27	91	29	9	63	103	.282	.363	.516	.879
1985	28	DET	AL	154	670	581	96	167	37	5	29	97	30	4	71	137	.287	.364	.518	.882
1986	29	DET	AL	119	521	441	84	118	11	2	28	86	34	6	68	107	.268	.371	.492	.863
1987	30	DET	AL	128	568	487	95	135	25	3	24	79	26	7	71	117	.277	.372	.489	.861
1988	31	LAD	NL	150	632	542	106	157	28	1	25	76	31	4	73	120	.290	.377	.483	.860
1989	32	LAD	NL	71	292	253	35	54	8	2	9	28	12	3	35	55	.213	.312	.368	.679
1990	33	LAD	NL	89	359	315	59	82	20	0	8	38	26	2	39	65	.260	.345	.400	.745
1991	34	KCR	AL	132	540	462	81	109	17	6	16	55	18	4	69	103	.236	.341	.403	.744
1992	35	PIT	NL	16	60	56	6	11	0	0	2	5	3	1	3	12	.196	.237	.304	.541
1993	36	DET	AL	116	454	403	62	105	18	6	13	62	15	6	44	87	.261	.337	.432	.769
1994	37	DET	AL	98	382	330	71	91	17	2	23	72	4	5	42	69	.276	.358	.548	.906
1995	38	DET	AL	70	265	227	37	59	12	2	9	35	9	2	33	61	.260	.358	.449	.808
17 Yrs				1635	6656	5798	985	1553	260	54	255	870	284	78	718	1285	.268	.352	.463	.815

JAY BUHNER

Year	Age	Tm	Lg	G	PA	AB	R	H	2B	3B	HR	RBI	SB	CS	BB	SO	BA	OBP	SLG	OPS
1987	22	NYY	AL	7	23	22	0	5	2	0	0	1	0	0	1	6	.227	.261	.318	.579
1988	23	TOT	AL	85	299	261	36	56	13	1	13	38	1	1	28	93	.215	.302	.421	.723
1988	23	NYY	AL	25	76	69	8	13	0	0	3	13	0	0	3	25	.188	.250	.319	.569
1988	23	SEA	AL	60	223	192	28	43	13	1	10	25	1	1	25	68	.224	.320	.458	.778
1989	24	SEA	AL	58	226	204	27	56	15	1	9	33	1	4	19	55	.275	.341	.490	.831
1990	25	SEA	AL	51	185	163	16	45	12	0	7	33	2	2	17	50	.276	.357	.479	.835
1991	26	SEA	AL	137	471	406	64	99	14	4	27	77	0	1	53	117	.244	.337	.498	.834
1992	27	SEA	AL	152	629	543	69	132	16	3	25	79	0	6	71	146	.243	.333	.422	.755
1993	28	SEA	AL	158	675	563	90	153	28	3	27	98	2	5	100	144	.272	.379	.476	.855
1994	29	SEA	AL	101	436	358	74	100	23	4	21	68	0	1	66	63	.279	.394	.542	.936
1995	30	SEA	AL	126	539	470	86	123	23	0	40	121	0	1	60	120	.262	.343	.566	.909
1996	31	SEA	AL	150	667	564	107	153	29	0	44	138	0	1	84	159	.271	.369	.557	.926
1997	32	SEA	AL	157	665	540	104	131	18	2	40	109	0	0	119	175	.243	.383	.506	.889
1998	33	SEA	AL	72	286	244	33	59	7	1	15	45	0	0	38	71	.242	.344	.463	.807
1999	34	SEA	AL	87	343	266	37	59	11	0	14	38	0	0	69	100	.222	.388	.421	.809
2000	35	SEA	AL	112	430	364	50	92	20	0	26	82	0	2	59	98	.253	.361	.522	.883
2001	36	SEA	AL	19	53	45	4	10	2	0	2	5	0	0	8	9	.222	.340	.400	.740
15 Yrs				1472	5927	5013	797	1273	233	19	310	965	6	24	792	1406	.254	.359	.494	.852

Bold season totals indicate player led league. *Italic* season totals indicate player led major leagues.

GREGG JEFFERIES

Year	Age	Tm	Lg	G	PA	AB	R	H	2B	3B	HR	RBI	SB	CS	BB	SO	BA	OBP	SLG	OPS
1987	19	NYM	NL	6	6	6	0	3	1	0	0	2	0	0	0	0	.500	.500	.667	1.167
1988	20	NYM	NL	29	118	109	19	35	8	2	6	17	5	1	8	10	.321	.364	.596	.961
1989	21	NYM	NL	141	559	508	72	131	28	2	12	56	21	6	39	46	.258	.314	.392	.706
1990	22	NYM	NL	153	659	604	96	171	40	3	15	68	11	2	46	40	.283	.337	.434	.771
1991	23	NYM	NL	136	539	486	59	132	19	2	9	62	26	5	47	38	.272	.336	.374	.711
1992	24	KCR	AL	152	657	604	66	172	36	3	10	75	19	9	43	29	.285	.329	.404	.733
1993	25	STL	NL	142	612	544	89	186	24	3	16	83	46	9	62	32	.342	.408	.485	.894
1994	26	STL	NL	103	447	397	52	129	27	1	12	55	12	5	45	26	.325	.391	.489	.880
1995	27	PHI	NL	114	521	480	69	147	31	2	11	56	9	5	35	26	.306	.349	.448	.797
1996	28	PHI	NL	104	446	404	59	118	17	3	7	51	20	6	36	21	.292	.348	.401	.749
1997	29	PHI	NL	130	531	476	68	122	25	3	11	48	12	6	53	27	.256	.333	.391	.724
1998	30	TOT	MLB	144	592	555	72	167	28	3	9	58	12	3	29	32	.301	.333	.411	.744
1998	30	PHI	NL	125	520	483	65	142	22	3	8	48	11	3	29	27	.294	.331	.402	.733
1998	30	ANA	AL	19	72	72	7	25	6	0	1	10	1	0	0	5	.347	.347	.472	.819
1999	31	DET	AL	70	225	205	22	41	8	0	6	18	3	4	13	11	.200	.258	.327	.585
2000	32	DET	AL	41	160	142	18	39	8	0	2	14	0	2	16	10	.275	.344	.373	.717
14 Yrs				1465	6072	5520	761	1593	300	27	126	663	196	63	472	348	.289	.344	.421	.765

Bold season totals indicate player led league.

RUBEN RIVERA

Year	Age	Tm	Lg	G	PA	AB	R	H	2B	3B	HR	RBI	SB	CS	BB	SO	BA	OBP	SLG	OPS
1995	21	NYY	AL	5	1	1	0	0	0	0	0	0	0	0	0	1	0	0	0	0
1996	22	NYY	AL	46	106	88	17	25	6	1	2	16	6	2	13	26	.284	.381	.443	.824
1997	23	SDP	NL	17	22	20	2	5	1	0	0	1	2	1	2	9	.250	.318	.300	.618
1998	24	SDP	NL	95	204	172	31	36	7	2	6	29	5	1	28	52	.209	.325	.378	.703
1999	25	SDP	NL	147	475	411	65	80	16	1	23	48	18	7	55	143	.195	.295	.406	.701
2000	26	SDP	NL	135	479	423	62	88	18	6	17	57	8	4	44	137	.208	.296	.400	.696
2001	27	CIN	NL	117	290	263	37	67	13	1	10	34	6	3	21	83	.255	.321	.426	.747
2002	28	TEX	AL	69	186	158	17	33	4	0	4	14	4	2	17	45	.209	.302	.310	.612
2003	29	SFG	NL	31	55	50	6	9	2	0	2	4	1	0	5	14	.180	.255	.340	.595
9 Yrs				662	1818	1586	237	343	67	11	64	203	50	20	185	510	.216	.307	.393	.701

MIKE TROUT

Year	Age	Tm	Lg	G	PA	AB	R	H	2B	3B	HR	RBI	SB	CS	BB	SO	BA	OBP	SLG	OPS
2011	19	LAA	AL	40	135	123	20	27	6	0	5	16	4	0	9	30	.22	.281	.390	.672
2012	20	LAA	AL	139	639	559	*129*	182	27	8	30	83	*49*	5	67	139	.326	.399	.564	.963
2013	21	LAA	AL	157	716	589	*109*	190	39	9	27	97	33	7	110	136	.323	.432	.557	.988
2014	22	LAA	AL	157	705	602	*115*	173	39	9	36	111	16	2	83	184	.287	.377	.561	.939
2015	23	LAA	AL	159	682	575	104	172	32	6	41	90	11	7	92	158	.299	.402	.590	.991
2016	24	LAA	AL	159	681	549	*123*	173	32	5	29	100	30	7	*116*	137	.315	.441	.550	.991
2017	25	LAA	AL	114	507	402	92	123	25	3	33	72	22	4	94	90	.306	.442	.629	*1.071*
2018	26	LAA	AL	140	608	471	101	147	24	4	39	79	24	2	*122*	124	.312	.46	.628	1.088
2019	27	LAA	AL	134	600	470	110	137	27	2	45	104	11	2	110	120	.291	*.438*	.645	*1.083*
2020	28	LAA	AL	53	241	199	41	56	9	2	17	46	1	1	35	56	.281	.390	.603	.993
2021	29	LAA	AL	36	146	117	23	39	8	1	8	18	2	0	27	41	.333	.466	.624	1.090
2022	30	LAA	AL	119	499	438	85	124	28	2	40	80	1	0	54	139	.283	.369	.630	.999
12 Yrs				1407	6159	5094	1052	1543	296	51	350	896	204	37	919	1354	.303	.415	*.587*	1.002

Bold season totals indicate player led league. *Italic* season totals indicate player led major leagues.
Italic career totals indicate actice cereer leader.

BRYCE HARPER

Year	Age	Tm	Lg	G	PA	AB	R	H	2B	3B	HR	RBI	SB	CS	BB	SO	BA	OBP	SLG	OPS
2012	19	WSN	NL	139	597	533	98	144	26	9	22	59	18	6	56	120	.270	.340	.477	.817
2013	20	WSN	NL	118	497	424	71	116	24	3	20	58	11	4	61	94	.274	.368	.486	.854
2014	21	WSN	NL	100	395	352	41	96	10	2	13	32	2	2	38	104	.273	.344	.423	.768
2015	22	WSN	NL	153	654	521	118	172	38	1	42	99	6	4	124	131	.330	*.460*	*.649*	*1.109*
2016	23	WSN	NL	147	627	506	84	123	24	2	24	86	21	10	108	117	.243	.373	.441	.814
2017	24	WSN	NL	111	492	420	95	134	27	1	29	87	4	2	68	99	.319	.413	.595	1.008
2018	25	WSN	NL	159	695	550	103	137	34	0	34	100	13	3	*130*	169	.249	.393	.496	.889
2019	26	PHI	NL	157	682	573	98	149	36	1	35	114	15	3	99	178	.260	.372	.510	.882
2020	27	PHI	NL	58	244	190	41	51	9	2	13	33	8	2	*49*	43	.268	.420	.542	.962
2021	28	PHI	NL	141	599	488	101	151	*42*	1	35	84	13	3	100	134	.309	.429	*.615*	*1.044*
2022	29	PHI	NL	99	426	370	63	106	28	1	18	65	11	4	46	87	.286	.364	.514	.877
11 Yrs				1382	5908	4927	913	1379	298	23	285	817	122	43	879	1276	.280	.390	.523	.913

Bold season totals indicate player led league. *Italic* season totals indicate player led major leagues.

ENDNOTES

INTRODUCTION

1. *Sports Illustrated*, June 21, 1965
2. *The Decline and Fall of the New York Yankees* by Jack Mann, p. 17
3. *Sports Illustrated*, June 21, 1965
4. Ibid.
5. *The Sporting News*, July 27, 1974

CHAPTER 1: THE CURSE OF TALENT AND THE BURDEN OF POTENTIAL

1. *Ninety Percent Mental*, Bob Tewksbury and Scott Miller, p. 108
2. *Baseball Digest*, January-February 2013
3. *Ninety Percent Mental*, p. 132
4. *Newport Daily News*, March 23, 1951
5. *The Crowley Post Standard*, March 1, 1952
6. *The Sporting News*, January 18, 1956
7. *Baseball Digest*, March 1969
8. www.SABR.org
9. *Detroit Free Press*, April 13, 1980
10. *The Sporting News*, September 24, 1981
11. *Times Herald*, October 2, 1984
12. *Sports Illustrated*, June 4, 2020
13. www.peakperformancesports.com
14. *Miami News*, October 12, 1984

CHAPTER 2: MICKEY MANTLE: THE GOLD STANDARD

1. *Mickey Mantle: Rookie in Pinstripes* by Fred Glueckstein, p.45
2. *Newport Daily News*, March 23, 1951
3. *Arizona Republic*, April 18, 1951
4. *Newport Daily News*, March 23, 1951
5. *Daily News*, April 1, 1951
6. *Mickey Mantle: The Indispensable Yankee* by Dick Schaap, p. 73
7. Ibid.
8. *My Favorite Summer 1956* by Mickey Mantle with Phil Pepe, p. 157
9. Ibid.
10. Ibid.
11. www.cooperstownexpert.com
12. *The Crowley Post Standard*, March 1, 1952
13. *Arizona Daily Star*, October 8, 1952
14. *Chicago Tribune*, February 13, 1953
15. *The Sporting News*, April 22, 1953
16. *The Daily News*, May 29, 1954
17. *The Sporting News*, April 29, 1953
18. *The Sporting News*, June 10, 1953
19. *Daily News*, May 29, 1954
20. *The Sporting News*, June 30, 1954
21. *The Sporting News*, March 16, 1955
22. *The Sporting Nerws*, April 6, 1955

23. *Clarion Ledger*, August 12, 1955
24. *Lexington Herald Ledger*, March 29, 1956
25. *Mickey Mantle: The Indispensable Yankee*, p. 114
26. *The Sporting News*, January 18, 1956
27. *Lexington Herald Ledger*, March 29, 1956
28. *Hartford Couant*, April 5, 1956
29. *The Sporting News*, September 5, 1956
30. *The Sporting News*, October 10, 1956
31. *The Sporting News*, October 31, 1956
32. *My Favorite Summer 1956*, p. 207
33. *The Tennessean*, January 25, 1957
34. *The Sporting News*, July 17, 1967
35. *The Sporting News*, October 2, 1957

CHAPTER 3: TOM TRESH: THE FIRST NEXT MICKEY MANTLE

1. *The Sporting News*, May 16, 1962
2. *The Sporting News*, July 28, 1962
3. *The Sporting News*, September 1, 1962
4. Ibid.
5. *The Yankees of the Early 1960s* by William Ryczek, p. 105
6. *The Sporting News*, November 5, 1962
7. *The Sporting News*, September 29, 1962
8. *The Sporting News*, November 5, 1962
9. *The Sporting News*, October 6, 1962
10. *Burlington Free Press*, October 11, 1962
11. *The Daily Press*, October 17, 1962
12. *The Times Dispatch*, May 10, 1963
13. Ibid.
14. *The Sporting News*, April 25, 1963
15. *The Sporting News*, August 21, 1965
16. Ibid.
17. http:..dannypeary.blogspot.com
18. www.sabr.org
19. *The Baltimore Sun*, June 29, 1969
20. *The Sporting News*, August 27, 1967
21. *The Sporting News*, April 6, 1968
22. www.sabr.org
23. *The Baltimore Sun*, June 29, 1969
24. *The Yankees in the Early 1960s*, p. 209
25. *New York Daily News*, October 15, 2008
26. Ibid.

CHAPTER 4: JOE PEPITONE: THE PLAYER WHO WAS HIS OWN WORST ENEMY

1. *The Sporting News*, August 30, 1969
2. *The Sporting News*, March 7, 1962
3. *Ptess and Bulletin*, February 8, 1962
4. *The Sporting News*, February 21, 1962
5. *The Sporting News*, March 28, 1962
6. *The Sporting News*, April 6, 1963
7. Ibid.
8. *Miami News*, March 9, 1964
9. Ibid.
10. *Miami News*, April 8, 1964
11. Ibid.

12. *Joe, You Coulda Made Us Proud* by Joe Pepitone and Berry Stainback, p. 133
13. *Herald Statesman*, July 17, 1965
14. *Joe, You Coulda Made Us Proud*, p. 144
15. Ibid. p. 145
16. *New York Daily News*, December 2, 1965
17. *Press and Sun Bulletin*, February 3, 1966
18. *The Daily Messenger*, January 19, 1966
19. *News-Press*, February 15, 1968
20. *Asbury Park Press*, February 16, 1966
21. *The Sporting News*, June 22, 1968
22. *Miami Herald*, April 19, 1969
23. *Oneonta Star*, December 10, 1969
24. *Tampa Bay Times*, December 11, 1969
25. *El Paso Times*, July 22, 1970
26. *The Sporting News*, August 8, 1970
27. *The Sporting News*, August 22, 1970
28. Ibid.
29. *Philadephia Inquirer*, July 17, 1971
30. *The Pantagraph*, May 3, 1972
31. Ibid.
32. *Joe, You Coulda Made Us Proud*, p. 246
33. *Miami Herald*, March 24, 1985
34. *The Yankees in the Early 1960s*, p. 4
35. Ibid.
36. *Joe, You Coulda Made Us Proud*, p. 258

CHAPTER 5: ROGER REPOZ: THE QUICK STARTER

1. *Baseball Digeest*, September 1965
2. *The Sporting News*, June 26, 1965
3. Ibid.
4. *The Yankees in the Early 1960s* by William Ryczek, p. 209
5. *Sports Illustrated*, June 26, 1965
6. *The Daily News*, July 10, 1965
7. *The Yankees in the Early 1960s*, p. 210
8. *Where Have All the Yankees Gone?* By Brian Jensen, p. 202
9. *The Yankees in the Early 1960s*, p. 210
10. *The Sporting News*, Sept 5, 1965
11. *Daily News*, February 27, 1966
12. *Star Press*, August 22, 1967
13. *The Sporting News*, May 11, 1968
14. Ibid.
15. *Independent Press-Telegram*, May 5, 1968
16. *The Sporting News*, June 6, 1970
17. Ibid.
18. *San Bernardino County Sun*, July 9, 1970
19. *The Sporting News*, December 6, 1970
20. *The Yankees in the Early 1960s*, p. 211

CHAPTER 6: RICK REICHARDT: THE $200,000 BONUS BABY

1. *Pensacola News*, June 25, 1964
2. *Sports Illustrated*, July 5, 1964
3. *The Sporting News*, July 4, 1964
4. *The Sporting News*, April 11, 1970
5. *Pensacola News*, Jjune 25, 1965

6. Ibid.
7. *Indianapolis Star*, July 26, 1964
8. Ibid.
9. *Independent Press-Telegram*, April 4, 1965
10. *Sports Illustrated*, July 7, 1965
11. *Grit*, March 27, 1966
12. *Baseball Digest*, August 1966
13. *Los Angeles Times*, May 28, 2007
14. *Janesville Daily Gazette*, June 17, 1966
15. *The Sporting News*, October 15, 1966
16. *The York Dispatch*, May 9, 1967
17. Ibid.
18. *The Sporting News*, May 20, 1967
19. Ibid.
20. Ibid.
21. Ibid.
22. *Minneapolis Star*, September 27, 1967
23. *Independent Press-Telegram*, March 8, 1968
24. Ibid.
25. *The Sporting News*, March 30, 1968
26. *Baseball Digest*, February 1968
27. *The Sporting News*, July 13, 1968
28. *Independent Press-Telegram*, March 6, 1969
29. *Independent Press-Telegram*, May 9, 1969
30. *The Sporting News*, June 9, 1969
31. Ibid.
32. *Los Angeles Times*, June 24, 1969
33. *Independent Press-Telegram*, August 14, 1969
34. *The Baltimore Sun*, August 21, 1969
35. *Miami Herald*, April 27, 1970
36. *Kenosha News*, May 1, 1970
37. *Sann Francisco Examiner*, May 13, 1970
38. *The Sporting News*, March 13, 1971
39. *The Perry County Times*, March 18, 1971
40. *The Sporting News*, March 13, 1971
41. *Independent Press-Telegram*, June 27, 1971
42. Ibid.
43. *The Sporting News*, October 2, 1971
44. *The Spokesman-Review*, May 9, 1973
45. *The Sporting News*, June 16, 1973
46. Mamievandoreninsideout.org
47. *Los Angeles Times*, May 27, 2007
48. *Los Angeles Times*, June 17, 1985
49. Ibid.
50. Ibid.

CHAPTER 7: BOBBY MURCER: THE OTHER OKLAHOMA KID

1. *Baseball Digest*, July 1969
2. www.OKlahomaHOF.com
3. *The Sporting News*, February 6, 1966
4. *The Daily News*, April 2, 1966
5. *The Sporting News*, May 31, 1969
6. *Yankee for Life* by Bobby Murcer and Glen Waggoner, p. 54
7. *Ludington Daily News*, April 19, 1969
8. *Kansas City Star*, June 1, 1969

9. Ibid.
10. *News Press*, March 18, 1970
11. *The Sporting News*, October 10, 1970
12. *Cncinnati Enquirer*, December 20, 1970
13. *The Sporting News*, April 24, 1971
14. *The Sporting News*, July 10, 1971
15. Ibid.
16. *The Sporting News*, December 25, 1971
17. *The Daily News*, February 29, 1972
18. Ibid.
19. *Montgomery Advertiser*, March 7, 1973
20. *The Sporting News*, May 11, 1974
21. *The Sporting News*, June 22, 1974
22. *Daily News*, September 24, 1974
23. *Yankee for Life*, p. 94
24. *Kingston Daily Freeman*, November 18, 1974
25. *The Sporting News*, November 9, 1974
26. *The Sporting News*, July 12, 1975
27. *The Sporting News*, July 31, 1976
28. *The News-Herald*, September 3, 1976
29. *The Sporting News*, May 7, 1977
30. *Capital Times*, March 30, 1979
31. *Chicago Tribune*, May 6, 1979
32. *Capital Times*, May 6, 1979
33. *Chicago Tribune*, May 6, 1979
34. *The Sporting News*, April 21, 1979
35. *The Sporting News*, July 14, 1979
36. Ibid.
37. *Times-Tribune*, Sept 6, 1980
38. *The Journal News*, March 23, 1981
39. *Miami News*, August 18, 1982
40. *Daily News*, June 22, 1983

CHAPTER 8: STEVE WHITAKER: THE HOT-TEMPERED SLUGGER

1. *Tampa Bay Times*, September 18, 1966
2. *Baseball Digest*, January-February 1967
3. *The Yankees in the Early 1960s* by William Ryczek, p. 121
4. *The Yankees in the Early 1960s*, p. 213
5. *Fort Lauderdale News*, March 15, 1967
6. *Tampa Bay Times, September 18, 1966*
7. *The Sporting News, June 17, 1967*
8. *The Yankees in the Early 1960s, p. 214*
9. *Baseball Digest*, December-January 1967
10. *The Sporting News*, April 6, 1968
11. *IBaseball Digest*, December-January 1967
12. *The Yankees ib the Early 1960s,* p. 214
13. Ibid.
14. *The Sporting News,* March 22, 1969
15. *The Oshkosh Northwestern*, December 4, 1968
16. *The Miami News*, June 24, 1975
17. *The Yankees in the Early 1960s*, p. 216
18. *The Gaffney Ledger*, March 13, 1967
19. Ibid.

CHAPTER 9: BILL ROBINSON: THE BLACK MICKEY MANTLE

1. *Baseball Digest*, March 1969
2. www.SABR.org
3. *Herald and Review*, February 9, 1967
4. *Where Have All the Yankees Gone?* By Brian Jensen, p. 223
5. *The Sporting News*, May 20, 1967
6. *The Record*, July 15, 1967
7. *Where Have All the Yankees Gone?* p. 223
8. *The Sporting News*, October 21, 1967
9. *The Sporting News*, October 26, 1968
10. *Baseball Digest*, March 1980
11. *The Sporting News*, June 26, 1969
12. *The Sporting News*, December 6, 1969
13. *Baseball Digest*, March 1980
14. www.SABR.org
15. *Baseball Digest*, March 1980
16. Ibid.
17. *The Sporting News*, September 8, 1973
18. *The Sporting News*, May 4, 1974
19. *The Sporting News*, June 7, 1975
20. *The Sporting News*, January 29, 1977
21. *The Sporting News*, August 13, 1977
22. *The Sporting News*, September 24, 1977
23. *The Sporting News*, April 22, 1978
24. *Baseball Digest*, March 1980
25. *The New York Times*, October 20, 2003

CHAPTER 10: TONY SOLAITA: THE POWERFUL SAMOAN

1. *The Daily Times-News*, March 8, 1969
2. *The Sporting News*, July 27, 1974
3. *Fort Lauderdale News*, June 12, 1967
4. *The Miami Herald News*, March 4, 1969
5. *Fort Lauderdale News*, August 18, 1968
6. *The Miami Herald*, March 4, 1969
7. *The Sporting News*, June 5, 1971
8. *The Gazette*, March 22, 1978
9. *The Sporting News*, July 27, 1974
10. *Kansas City Star*, September 1, 1974
11. *The Sporting Ness*, December 22, 1974
12. *Kansas City Star*, July 9, 1974
13. *The Sporting News*, July 27, 1974
14. *Lansing State Journal*, May 14, 1975
15. Ibid.
16. *The Sporting News*, June 7, 1975
17. *Fort Myers News-Press*, June 21, 1975
18. *Kansas City Star*, September 8, 1975
19. *Independent News-Post*, April 19, 1977
20. *News-Pilot*, July 3, 1978
21. *The Gazette*, March 22, 1978

CHAPTER 11: RON BLOMBERG: THE OFTEN-INJURED JEWISH HERO

1. *Moments in the Sun* by Mark McGuire and Michael Sean Gormley, p. 91
2. *Esquire*, Summer 1970

3. *Fort Lauderdale News*, July 18, 1967
4. *Designated Hebrew* by Ron Blomberg as told to Dan Schlossberg, p. 38
5. *Baseball Digest*, March 1969
6. *Designated Hebrew*, p. 41
7. Ibid.
8. *Moments in the Sun*, p. 91
9. *Courier News*, June 1, 1973
10. *Edwardsville Intelligencer*, June 5, 1973
11. Ibid.
12. *The St. Louis Jewish Light*, Aug 1, 1973
13. *Courier News*, June 1, 1973
14. *Edwardsville Intelligencer*, June 5, 1973
15. *Poughkeepsie Journal*, July 7, 1973
16. *The Sporting News*, June 15, 1974
17. *The Sporting News*, September 6, 1975
18. *The Sporting News*, March 12, 1976
19. *Designated Hebrew*, p. 101
20. *The Dispatch*, November 15, 1977
21. Ibid.
22. *The Red Deer Advocate*, April 8, 1978
23. *Herald and Review*, March 31, 1979
24. *Designated Hebrew*, p. 142
25. *Moments in the Sun*, p. 95
26. Ibid.

CHAPTER 12: CLINT HURDLE: THE CAN'T-MISS KID

1. *The Sporting News*, March 31, 1979
2. *Sports Illustrated*, March 20, 1978
3. Ibid.
4. Ibid.
5. *Florida Today*, June 12, 1975
6. *Philadelphia Inquirer*, April 5, 1978
7. Ibid.
8. *The Tampa Times*, March 3, 1982
9. *Journal Gazette*, June 20, 1978
10. *Des Moines Register*, July 25, 1978
11. *Journal Gazette*, June 20, 1978
12. *Des Moines Register*, July 25, 1978
13. *The Sporting News*, August 5, 1978
14. *The Sporting News*, September 7, 1978
15. *Press and Sun Bulletin*, September 16, 1978
16. *The Sporting News*, November 11, 1978
17. Ibid.
18. Ibid.
19. *The Sporting News*, March 31, 1979
20. Ibid.
21. Ibid.
22. *The Record*, June 10, 1979
23. Ibid.
24. *Sacramento Bee*, July 6, 1978
25. *Lincoln Star*, July 2, 1979
26. *The Sporting News*, January 12, 1980
27. *Miami Herald*, March 13, 1980
28. *Detroit Free Press*, April 13, 1980
29. Ibid.

30. Ibid.
31. *Florida Today*, May 24, 1982
32. *Press Sun Bulletin*, July 10, 1983
33. *The Gazette*, April 28, 1985
34. Ibid.
35. *Florida Today*, December 1, 1987
36. *The Journal News*, December 21, 1986

CHAPTER 13: KIRK GIBSON: THE HARD-NOSED IMPACT PLAYER

1. *Akron Beacon Journal*, October 7, 1984
2. *Lansing State Journal*, May 20, 1978
3. *Bottom of the Ninth* by Kirk Gibson with Lynn Henning, p. 50
4. *Detroit Free Press*, June 9, 1978
5. Yahoo Sports, March 22, 2017
6. *Bottom of the Ninth*, p. 53
7. *Detroit Free Press*, April 16, 1979
8. *Detroit Free Press*, August 17, 1995
9. *Petoskey News Review*, September 18, 1979
10. *Sports Illustrated*, March 24, 1980
11. *Detroit Free Press*, January 24, 1980
12. *Sports Illustrated*, March 24, 1980
13. *The Sporting News*, May 17, 1980
14. *The Sporting News*, September 26, 1981
15. *The Sporting News*, September 19, 1981
16. *Detroit Free Press*, September 9, 1981
17. *The Sporting News*, September 10, 1981
18. *Tampa Bay Times*, January 8, 1982
19. *The Tennessean*, March 12, 1982
20. *Bottom of the Ninth*, p. 4
21. *The Sporting News*, February 28, 1983
22. *Bottom of the Ninth*, p. 4
23. *Detroit Free Press*, August 3, 1983
24. *Bottom of the Ninth*, p. 79
25. *Bottom of the Ninth*, p. 80
26. *The Sporting News*, September 24, 1984
27. *Times Herald*, October 2, 1984
28. *The Sporting News*, December 9, 1985
29. *Detroit Free Press*, March 2, 1986
30. *The Sporting News*, September 8, 1986
31. Ibid.
32. *Detroit Free Press*, March 2, 1986
33. *The Sporting News*, February 29, 1988
34. *San Bernardino County News*, August 21, 1988
35. *The Sporting News*, November 28, 1988
36. *Bottom of the Ninth*, p. 133
37. *St. Louis Post Dispatch*, October 6, 1991
38. *Detroit Free Press*, August 13, 1995
39. Ibid.
40. *Detroit Free Press*, August 17, 1995
41. *Detroit Free Press*, May 2, 1994
42. *Miami News*, October 15, 1994

CHAPTER 14: JAY BUHNER: THE UNDERAPPRECIATED PROSPECT

1. *The Miami Herald*, April 12, 1985
2. Ibid.

3. Ibid.

4. *Fort Lauderdale News*, May 9, 1985

5. Ibid.

6. *Pittsburgh Press*, June 30, 1985

7. *Fort Lauderdale News*, May 9, 1985

8. *The Record*, August 8, 1986

9. *The Daily News*, June 26, 1987

10. *Hartford Courant*, August 30, 1988

11. *Burlington Free Press*, April 15, 1988

12. *The Journal News*, June 19, 1988

13. *The Daily News*, August 11, 1988

14. *The Daily News*, July 22, 1988

15. *The Spokesman-Review*, August 27, 1988

16. *The Press and Sun Bulletin*, September 6, 1988

17. www.youtube.com

18. *Calgary Herald*, April 6, 1989

19. *The Sporting News*, July 3, 1989

20. *Press and Sun Bulletin*, August 21, 1989

21. *Sports Illustrated*, March 18, 1996

22. Ibid.

23. Ibid.

24. *Baltimore Sun*, December 23, 1994

25. *Miami Herald*, March 14, 1997

26. *Kitsap Sun*, December 20, 2001

CHAPTER 15: GREGG JEFFERIES: THE WUNDERKIND

1. *Clarion Ledger*, April 5, 1987

2. *Sports Illustrated*, March 21, 1088

3. Ibid.

4. *Cincinnati Enquirer*, October 6, 1988

5. *The Sporting News*, April 11, 1988

6. *Sports Illustrated*, March 21, 1988

7. *The Bad Guys Won* by Jeff Pearlman, p. 5

8. *St. Louis Post Dispatch*, April 2, 1989

9. *Palm Beach Post*, March 17, 1989

10. *Philadelphia Inquirer*, March 27, 1989

11. *Green Bay Press Gazette*, June 16, 1989

12. *St. Louis Post Dispatch*, June 26, 1990

13. *The Sporting News*, June 26, 1989

14. *The Sporting News*, September 11, 1989

15. *Sports Illustrated*, April 20, 1989

16. *The Bad Guys Won*, p. 268

17. *Southern Illinoisan*, March 22, 1990

18. *Los Angeles Times*, June 28, 1990

19. *The Journal News*, May 21, 1991

20. www.johnstrubel.com

21. *Daily Record*, May 25, 1991

22. *The Courier News*, June 30, 1991

23. *Daily News*, December 13, 1991

24. *Kansas City Star*, February 13, 1993

25. *The Sporting News*, December 26, 1994

26. *Philadelphia Inquirer*, August 29, 1995

27. *Wilmington News Journal*, July 30, 1998

28. *Philadelphia Inquirer*, November 1, 1997

29. *Philadelphia Daily News*, August 29, 1998

30. www.stltoday.com
31. *The Des Moines Register*, August 31, 1998
32. www.nationalreview.com

CHAPTER 16: RUBEN RIVERA: THE COLOSSAL MYSTERY

1. *New York Post*, July 11, 2015
2. *Baseball America*, December 25, 1994
3. *Daily News*, November 17, 1994
4. *Baseball America*, December 25, 1994
5. *Daily News*, November 17, 1994
6. Ibid.
7. *Herald News*, September 3, 1995
8. *Daily News*, November 17, 1994
9. *Central New Jersey Home News*, May 19, 1995
10. *Herald News*, September 3, 1995
11. *Daily News*, May 23, 1996
12. Ibid.
13. *Daily News*, May 24, 1996
14. *Daily News*, May 28, 1996
15. *Daily News*, May 29, 1996
16. *Daily News*, August 27, 1996
17. *Asbury Park Press*, January 19, 1997
18. Ibid.
19. *Star Gazette*, April 27, 1997
20. *The Sporting News*, May 5, 1997
21. *Latrobe Bulletin*, June 19, 1999
22. *North County Times*, December 20, 2000
23. *North County Times*, March 14, 2001
24. Ibid.
25. *Dayton Daily News*, April 20, 2001
26. Ibid.
27. *Hartford Courant*, March 7, 2002
28. Ibid.
29. *The Sporting News*, March 25, 2002
30. *Sports Illustrated*, March 26, 2001
31. *New York Post*, July 11, 2015
32. Ibid.

CHAPTER 17: MIKE TROUT: THE COMPLETE PACKAGE

1. *Baseball Digest*, July/August 2015
2. *The Des Moines Register*, July 17, 2018
3. www.espn.com
4. *Philadelphia Inquirer*, July 17, 2018
5. *Courier Post*, May 16, 2010
6. *The Daily Journal*, Jyuly 7, 2010
7. *The Daily Journal*, October 11, 2011
8. *Baseball Digest*, January/February 2013
9. *The Daily Journal*, November 16, 2012
10. Ibid.
11. *Philadelphia Daily News*, December 23, 2012
12. www.espn.com
13. *Star Tribune*, July 13, 2014
14. *The Daily Journal*, November 14, 2014
15. *Springfield News-Sun,* July 15, 2015

16. *Baseball Digest*, July/August 2015
17. *The Daily Journal*, December 31, 2015
18. *Los Angeles Times*, September 30, 2016
19. *Los Angeles Times*, November 18, 2016
20. Ibid.
21. Ibid.
22. *Philadelphia Inquirer*, April 9, 2017
23. *USA Today*, July 17, 2018
24. Ibid.
25. *Orange County Register*, July 20, 2018
26. *Democrat and Chronicle*, March 20, 2019
27. *Baseball Digest*, November/December 2019
28. *Philadelphia Inquirer*, November 14, 2015
29. Ibid.
30. *The Sporting News*, December 17, 2019
31. *Los Angeles Times*, November, 15, 2019

CHAPTER 18: BRYCE HARPER: THE TEEN DESTINED TO BE A STAR

1. *Sports Illustrated*, June 8, 2009
2. *Associated Press*, June 7, 2010
3. *Florida Today*, February 23, 2011
4. *Asheville Citizen-Times*, February 23, 2011
5. *Philadelphia Inquirer*, May 15, 2011
6. *The Austin American-Statesman*, June 9, 2011
7. *The Daily News*, June 12, 2001
8. *The Baltimore Sun*, July 5, 2011
9. *Anniston Star*, February 26, 2012
10. *Chicago Tribune*, February 1, 2012
11. *Spokane Review*, May 5, 2012
12. *The Journal News*, May 11, 2011
13. Ibid.
14. *Phenom: The Making of Bryce Harper* by Rob Miech, p. 345
15. *The Herald*, May 25, 2012
16. *Kansas City Star*, November 13, 2012
17. *USA Today*, March 28, 2013
18. Ibid.
19. *Baseball Digest*, September/October 2013
20. *Daily Press*, April 22, 2014
21. www.sbnation.com
22. *The Tennessean*, May 11, 2015
23. *The Daily Sentinel*, May 22, 2015
24. *The Daily Item*, February 23, 2016
25. *The Herald*, May 13, 2016
26. *The Gazette*, July 10, 2017
27. *The Springfield News-Leader*, July 17, 2018
28. *Messenger Inquirer*, March 9, 2019
29. *Philadelphia Inquirer*, July 23, 2020
30. Ibid.
31. *Philadelphia Inquirer*, November 18, 2021

ACKNOWLEDGMENTS

Writers often ask themselves questions and then answer them through research. This book is the result of that process. As a 13-year-old baseball fan, I remember Tom Tresh, a 23-year-old switch-hitter and 1962 American League Rookie of the Year, being referred to as the "next Mickey Mantle." Tresh and a long line of highly touted prospects could never fill Mantle's shoes.

I wondered why that was. Did they lack the ability? Did they get an opportunity to prove themselves? Were they managed correctly? What were their weaknesses? Did the pressure of being the 'next Mickey Mantle' crush them?

After initial research and conversations with longtime baseball fans, I compiled a list of players who had been tabbed "the next Mickey Mantle." The list doesn't include every player ever referred to as the next Mickey Mantle. But that's not the goal of this book.

In researching the players, I read more than 1,500 articles. I am thankful for the archived copies of *The Sporting News*, www.newspapers.com, the Society for American Baseball Research website and its player biographies, www.baseball-reference.com, www.baseballalmanac.com, and various other websites.

I am indebted to John Coulson, author of *Wee Willie Sherdel* and a SABR member who read my initial manuscript. His perspective and suggestions were invaluable.

Early feedback from Joel Fish, Ph.D., director of the Center for Sports Psychology in Philadelphia, about my approach and several sample chapters convinced me I was on the right track. It made moving ahead much easier.

I am thankful for countless sportswriters, from Joe Falls of *The Sporting News* and Pat Jordan, author of *A False Spring,* to Frank Fitzpatrick of the *Philadelphia Inquirer* and Thomas Boswell of the *Washington Post*, who have inspired me over the years. I am particularly indebted to Bill Mowbray, former sports editor of the *Cambridge (Md.) Daily Banner*, who gave me a chance to write for the newspaper in 1970. He was a valuable mentor and role model.

Finally, I thank my wife, Ann, the one person who truly understands the time and effort that has gone into this book. She knows that writing a book is a marathon, not a sprint.

BIBLIOGRAPHY

MAGAZINES AND PERIODICALS
Baseball Digest
Esquire
Sports Illustrated
The Sporting News

BOOKS
Allen, Maury. *Yankees, Where Have You Gone?* Sports Publishing, New York, N.Y., 2004.

Appel, Marty. *Casey Stengel: Baseball's Greatest Character*, Doubleday, New York, N.Y., 2017.

———. *The Pinstripe Empire: The New York Yankees from Before the Babe to After the Boss*, Bloomsbury, New York, N.Y., 2012.

Blomberg, Ron as told to Schlossberg, Dan. *Designated Hebrew: The Ron Blomberg Story*, Sports Publishing L.L.C., Champaign, Ill., 2006.

Cohen, Robert. *The Lean Years of the New York Yankees, 1965-1975*, McFarland & Co., Jefferson, N.C., 2004.

Dorfman, H.A. and Kuehl, Karl. *The Mental Game of Baseball*, Diamond Communications, Lanham, Md., 2002.

Fader, Jonathan, Ph.D. *Life as Sport*, Da Capo Press, Boston, Mass., 2016.

Falkner, David. *The Last Hero: The Life of Mickey Mantle*, Simon & Schuster, New York, N.Y., 1995.

Frommer, Harvey. *The New York Yankees Encyclopedia*, MacMillan Co., New York, N.Y., 1997.

Gibson, Kirk with Henning, Lynn. *Bottom of the Ninth*, Sleeping Bear Press, Chelsea, Mich., 1997.

Glueckstein, Fred. *Mickey Mantle: Rookie in Pinstripes*, iUniverse, Inc., New York, N.Y., 2008.

Gormley, Michael and McGuire, Mark. *Moments in the Sun: Baseball's Briefly Famous*, McFarland & Co., Jefferson, N.C., 1999.

Jensen, Brian. *Where Have All Our Yankees Gone?* Taylor Trade Publishing, New York, N.Y., 2004.

Leavy, Jane. *The Last Boy: Mickey Mantle and the End of America's Childhood*, HarperCollins, New York, N.Y., 2010.

Mann, Jack. *The Decline and Fall of the New York Yankees*, Simon and Schuster, New York, N.Y., 1967.

Mantle, Mickey. *The Education of a Baseball Player*, Simon and Schuster, New York, N.Y., 1967.

Mantle, Mickey with Gluck, Herb. *The Mick*, Doubleday & Company, Garden City, N.Y., 1985.

Miech, Rob. *Phenom: The Making of Bryce Harper*, Thomas Dunne Books, New York, N.Y., 2012.

Murcer, Bobby with Waggoner, Glen. *Yankee for Life*, HarperCollins, New York, N.Y., 2008.

Pearlman, Jeff. *The Bad Guys Won*, Perennial Currents, New York, N.Y., 2004.

Pepitone, Joe with Stainback, Barry. *Joe, You Coulda Made Us Proud*, Dell Publishing Co., New York, N.Y., 1976.

Ryczek, William. *The Yankees in the Early 1960s*, McFarland & Co., Jefferson, N.C., 2007.

Tewksbury, Bob and Scott Miller. *Ninety Percent Mental*, Da Capo Press, New York, N.Y., 2018.

Weiner, Dave, Gutman, Bill and Heiman, Lee. *When the Cheering Stops . . . Former Major Leaguers Talk about Their Game & Their Lives*, MacMillan Publishing Co., New York, N.Y., 1990.

White, Roy with Berger, Darrell. *"Then Roy Said to Mickey . . ." The Best Yankee Stories Ever Told*, Triumph Books, Chicago, Ill., 2009.

NEWSPAPERS

Akron Beacon Journal
Anniston Star
Arizona Republic
Arizona Daily Star
Asbury Park Press
Ashville Citizen Times
Austin American Statesman
Baltimore Sun
Burlington Free Press
Calgary Herald
Capital Times (Madison, Wis.)
Central New Jersey Home News
Chicago Tribune
Cincinnati Enquirer
Clarion-Ledger
Courier News
Courier Post
Crowley Post-Standard
Daily Messenger (Canandaigua, N.Y.)
Daily News (New York)
Daily Sentinel
Daily Times-News (Danbury, Conn.)
Dayton Daily News
Democrat and Chronicle
Des Moines Register
Detroit Free Press
Dispatch (Moline, Ill.)
Edwardsville Intelligencer
El Paso Times
Florida Today
Fort Lauderdale News
Fort Myers News-Press
Gaffney Ledger
Gazette (Cedar Rapids, Iowa)
Green Bay Press-Gazette
Grit
Hartford Courant
Herald Statesman
Independent News-Press
Independent Press-Telegram (Long Beach, Calif.)
Indianapolis Star

Janesville Daily Gazette
Journal Gazette (Ft. Wayne, Ind.)
Journal News (Westchester, N.Y.)
Kansas City Star
Kenosha News
Kingston Daily Freeman
Kitsap Sun
Latrobe Bulletin
Lansing State Journal
Lexington Herald-Leader
Lincoln Star
Los Angeles Times
Ludington Daily News
Messenger-Inquirer (Owensboro, Ken.)
Miami Herald
Miami News
Minneapolis Star
Montgomery Advertiser
Newport Daily News
News-Press (Ft. Myers, Fla.)
New York Post
New York Times
North County Times (Escondido, Calif.)
Oneonta Star
Orange County Register
Oshkosh Northwestern
Palm Beach Post
Pantagraph (Bloomington, Ill.)

Pensacola News
Perry County Times
Petoskey News-Review
Philadelphia Daily News
Philadelphia Inquirer
Pittsburgh Press
Poughkeepsie Journal
Press and Sun-Bulletin
Record (Bergen, N.J.)
Red Deer Advocate
Sacramento Bee
San Bernardino County News
San Francisco Examiner
Southern Illinoisan
Springfield News-Sun
Spokesman-Review
Star Gazette
Star Press
Star Tribune
St. Louis Post-Dispatch
Tampa Bay Times
Tennessean
Times-Dispatch (Richmond)
Times Herald (Port Huron, Mich.)
Times-Tribune (Scranton, Pa.)
Wilmington News Journal
USA Today
York Dispatch

WEBSITES AND BLOGS

www.SABR.org
www.baseball-reference.com
www.baseballalmanac.com
www.peakperformance.com
www.cooperstownexpert.com
www.OklahomaHOF.com
www.yahoosports.com
www.stltoday.com

www.nationalreview.com
www.espn.com
www.sbnation.com
www.johnstrubel.com
https://dannypeary.blogspot.com
https://mamievandoreninsideout.word
   press.com

INDEX

A

Adcock, Joe, 65
Addie, Bob, 17
Albom, Mitch, 152
Alomar, Roberto, 181
Anderson, Dave, 126
Anderson, Marlon, 215
Anderson, Sparky, 8, 145–48, 150, 157–58
Arbuckle, Mike, 202
Autry, Gene, 62–63

B

Babe, Loren, 93
Baker, Dusty, 221–22
Baseball America, 170–71, 186–87, 200–201, 204, 206, 213, 216
Baseball Digest, 11, 124
Bauer, Hank, 68
Baylor, Don, 204
Beane, Billy, 206
Bench, Johnny, 82, 221–23
Berg, Ted, 209
Berra, Yogi, 19, 22–23, 27, 32, 42, 205
Blefary, Curt, 46, 115
Blomberg, Ron, 121–30
Blue, Vida, 221
Bonds, Barry, 185, 189, 205, 210, 216, 226
Bonds, Bobby, 84, 129
Boros, Scott, 224
Boswell, Thomas, 217, 219
Bouton, Jim, 3
Bowa, Larry, 202
Bowden, Jim, 194, 216
Boyer, Clete, 3, 25, 28, 32, 40–41, 55, 103
Boyer, Cloyd, 123
Brett, George, 136, 157, 180
Brookover, Bob, 182
Brown, Bobby, 14
Brown, Gates, 8, 151

Buhner, Jay, 159–68
Burke, Joe, 135, 137
Burke, Mike, 96

C

Cabrera, Miguel, 202–203
Campbell, Jim, 152
Camilli, Dolph, 113
Carew, Rod, 128, 180
Carey, Harry, 73
Carreon, Mark, 184
Cashman, Brian, 195–96
Cepeda, Orlando, 27, 29, 223
Chambliss, Chris, 163
Clines, Gene, 166
Cobb, Ty, 10, 197, 201, 209
Coffey, Wayne, 215
Cohn, Patrick, 6
Coleman, Jerry, 7, 20, 26, 38
Conigliaro, Tony, 64, 217–18, 224
Corcoran, Paul, 71
Crosetti, Frank, 15
Cubbage, Mike, 179
Cuyler, Kiki, 180

D

Daley, Arthur, 46
Davis, Willie, 41, 105
Del Chiaro, Brent, 200
Dent, Bucky, 161–62
Dexter, Charles, 100
Dickey, Bill, 6, 10, 16
Didier, Mel, 144, 155
Dilbeck, Steve, 154
DiMaggio, Joe, 2, 6, 9, 11, 13, 15–16, 18–19, 22, 25, 36, 38–39, 44–45, 50, 82, 91, 187, 197, 203
Dorfman, H.A., 5–6, 8
Daubach, Brian, 215
Durocher, Leo, 47–49
Durso, Joseph, 54

E

Eckersley, Dennis, 155–56, 188
Eppler, Billy, 206, 209
Erskine, Carl, 17

F

Falls, Joe, 36, 146
Feeney, Chub, 49
Finley, Charlie, 62
Finley, Steve, 192–93
Fischer, Bill, 7, 132
Flores, Abe, 200
Ford, Whitey, 18, 31, 39–40, 77
Foxx, Jimmie, 16, 23, 197, 205, 207, 217
Francona, Terry, 183
Frandsen, Kevin, 225
Franks, Herman, 86–87
Fregosi, Jim, 182
Frey, Jim, 137–38

G

Gammons, Peter, 146–47
Garagiola, Joe, 65
Garner, Phil, 183
Gehrig, Lou, 2, 16, 21
Gehringer, Charlie, 150
Giannones, John, 188
Gibson, Kirk, 142–58
Gooden, Dwight, 172, 218
Gordon, Joe, 57, 98
Gossage, Goose, 145, 151
Gorman, Lou, 140
Green, Dallas, 133
Green, Jerry, 158
Greenwade, Tom, 9, 75–76
Grienke, Zack, 198
Griffey, Ken Jr., 166–67, 181, 185, 187, 189, 191, 204, 216, 219
Griffith, Coleman, 8
Gwynn, Tony, 151, 180, 194

H

Hamey, Roy, 39
Haney, Fred, 67
Harazin, Al, 174, 179
Harmon, Merle, 55
Harper, Bryce, 212–26
Harrelson, Bud, 178
Hawkins, Jim, 7, 138
Hemond, Roland, 62, 71
Henrich, Tommy, 10
Hernandez, Keith, 172–73, 177
Heron, Chico, 186
Hershiser, Orel, 172–73
Hertzel, Bob, 8, 158
Herzog, Whitey, 134–37, 141
Hodges, Gil, 21–22
Holcomb, Stu, 73
Holland, John, 48–49
Horner, Bob, 144
Hornsby, Rogers, 209
Houk, Ralph, 9, 25–27, 30, 32, 38, 40, 43, 45–46, 56, 62
Howser, Dick, 88
Hunter, Torii, 201–202
Hurdle, Clint, 131–41

J

Jackson, Reggie, 56, 68, 87–88, 187–89, 195
Jameson, Pete, 162
Jefferies, Gregg, 169–85
Jeter, Derek, 26, 186–88, 195, 203
Johnson, Darrell, 171
Johnson, Davey, 140, 171, 174–78, 216–17, 219
Johnson, Jimmy, 188
Johnson, Johnny, 2, 54
Justice, Richard, 205

K

Kaline, Al, 19, 21, 27, 65, 145, 208
Kamzic, Nick, 61
Kapler, Gabe, 226
Keene, Johnny, 42–43, 32, 55, 77
Kennedy, Bob, 87

King, Clyde, 163
Killebrew, Harmon, 64, 69, 117–18
Kiner, Ralph, 16
Kingman, Dave, 86, 118
Klein, Moss, 163–64
Krause, Jerry, 144
Kubek, Tony, 3, 25, 28, 40, 55
Kuehl, Karl, 5–6, 8

L

Lachmann, Rene, 140
Lacques, Gabe, 220
Lajoie, Bill, 152–53
Larsen, Don, 21
LaRussa, Tony, 147
Lasorda, Tommy, 155
Lau, Charlie, 73, 133–45
Lauder, Scott, 225
Law, Keith, 202
Lefebvre, Jim, 165
Lemon, Bob, 64
Lewis, Buddy, 19
Leyland, Jim, 144–45, 157
Leyritz, Jim, 196
Leyva, Nick, 177
Lindbergh, Ben, 220
Linz, Phil, 25
Litwhiler, Danny, 143
Livesey, Bill, 187
Lockman, Whitey, 49
Lopez, Al, 9
Lynn, Fred, 5

M

Machado, Manny, 208–209
MacMullen, Jackie, 140
MacPhail, Lee, 104, 122, 130
Madden, Bill, 187
Maddon, Joe, 211
Maddox, Elliott, 83
Madlock, Bill, 85–86
Manfred, Rob, 207–208
Mann, Jack, 2
Mantle, Mickey, 1–28, 30–31, 34–35, 37, 41–42, 44, 46, 52–57, 62, 64–65, 66, 68, 74–82, 88, 90, 95–96, 99, 101–102, 104,

111–12, 114, 122–24, 142, 144, 147–48, 151, 158–59, 161–62, 170, 174, 179, 184–87, 196, 199, 206, 208, 210–11, 214, 216, 219, 222
Mantle, Mutt, 12, 14–15
Maris, Roger, 1, 23, 26–27, 30–31, 34, 41, 43, 54–56, 96, 132
Martin, Billy, 18
Mathews, Eddie, 50
Mayberry, John, 116–19, 125, 133–34
Mayo Clinic, 65, 67, 146
Mays, Willie, 13, 18, 27, 63, 65
McCoy, Hal, 157
McDougald, Gil, 13
McDowell, Roger, 154, 176–77
McGuff, Joe, 132
McIlvaine, Joe, 173
McKeon, Jack, 73, 114, 116
McRae, Hal, 157
Melvin, Bob, 210
Merrill, Stump, 189
Milkes, Marvin, 98
Molitor, Paul, 180
Monaghan, Tom, 154
Monday, Rick, 56, 63
Morhardt, Greg, 199
Moses, Wally, 34, 39–40, 53–54
Munson, Thurman, 87
Murcer, Bobby, 75–90
Murtaugh, Danny, 107
Musial, Stan, 64, 126, 197, 205

N

Newhan, Ross, 69
Newhouse, Hal, 23
Nigro, Ken, 69
Nippon Ham Fighters, 119
Normadin, Marc, 220

O

Ogle, Jim, 101
Oglivie, Ben, 193

Oh, Sadahuru, 119
Ojeda, Bob, 177, 179
Ott, Mel, 197, 205, 207, 217–18

P
Passan, Jeff, 203
Patterson, Pat, 25
Patterson, Red, 16
Peak Performance Sports, 6, 8
Pearlman, Jeff, 173
Pepe, Phil, 50, 84, 90
Pepitone, Joe, 36–51
Phelps, Ken,163–65
Phillips, Lefty, 58, 69–70
Picking, Ken, 118
Pinella, Lou, 79, 98, 162–63, 166–67
Pope, Edwin, 136
Povich, Shirley, 19, 76
Pujols, Albert, 203, 223

Q
Quinn, Bob, 164

R
Raybourn, Herb, 186
Reagins, Tony, 200
Reed, Jack, 93–94
Reichardt, Rick, 60–74
Reichler, Joe, 17
Repoz, Roger, 52–59
Reynolds, Bob, 62–63
Richardson, Bobby, 3, 20, 28–29, 35, 40, 78
Richardson, Spec, 47
Riggleman, Jim, 215–16
Rigney, Bill, 56–57, 63, 65–66, 68–69, 74, 95
Rivera, Mariano, 186, 188, 191–92
Rivera, Ruben, 185–96
Rizzo, Mike, 215–16, 218, 220, 222
Robinson, Bill, 100–110
Robinson, Jackie, 3, 15
Rodriguez, Alex, 167, 209, 224
Roeder, Jack, 200

Rogers, Darryl, 143
Rose, Pete, 144, 174, 181, 219
Ruth, Babe, 2, 6, 11, 16, 20–22, 226

S
Sauer, Hank, 98
Schmidt, Mike, 224
Schuerholz, John, 137
Scioscia, Mike, 198, 203, 205–206
Scully, Vin, 155
Seinfeld, 164, 168
Sheehy, Pete, 78
Shore, Ray, 133
Showalter, Buck, 187–88
Sievers, Roy, 22–23
Skaggs, Tyler, 209–210
Skowron, Bill, 28, 39
Smith, Mayo, 34
Snyder, Paul, 144
Snyder, Jim, 164
Solaita, Tony, 11–12
Souchock, Steve, 38, 98, 113
Sports Illustrated, 8, 127, 131, 145–46, 170, 196, 202, 207, 213
Stafford, Bill, 3
Stargell, Willie, 108–109, 160
Stanton, Giancarlo, 223–24
Stark, Jayson, 142, 202
Stearns, John, 186
Steinbrenner, George, 82, 84, 89, 140, 161–62, 164
Stengel, Casey, 11, 16, 19, 21, 23
Stobbs, Chuck, 16
Strawberry, Darryl, 170, 172–73

T
Tallis, Cedric, 98
Tanner, Chuck, 63, 68, 72–73, 107, 109, 160
Tebbetts, Birdie, 2–3
Terry, Ralph, 28–29
Tewksbury, Bob, 5–6

The Sporting News, 61, 66, 68, 80, 127–28, 146–57, 192, 205, 210
Thomas, Lee, 181
Thornton, Andre, 50
Thrift, Syd, 116
Torre, Joe, 180, 189–90, 195
Towers, Kevin, 192, 194
Tresh, Tom, 24–35
Trimble, Joe, 17
Trout, Mike, 197–211

V
Vecsey, George, 110
Veeck, Bill, 129–30
Verdi, Frank, 53–54, 115, 124
Virdon, Bill, 83, 127–28

W
Wade, Ed, 183
Wagner, Dick, 139
Walker, Harry, 46–47
Walsh, Dick, 57–59
Wathan, John, 157
Watson, Bob, 188, 190
Wertz, Vic, 21
Westrum, Wes, 84
Whicker, Mark, 208
Whitaker, Steve, 91–99
White, Bill, 125
White, Jack, 61
Williams, Dick, 118, 151
Williams, Ted, 19–21, 23, 59, 70–72, 124, 126, 197, 203, 205, 221
Wrigley, Philip K., 8

Y
Yakult Atoms, 50
Yakult Swallows, 59
Yost, Ned, 204
Young, Dick, 16

Z
Zernial, Gus, 18
Zimmer, Don, 147
Zimmerman, Ryan, 216–17, 221

ABOUT THE AUTHOR

BARRY SPARKS has written about baseball for more than 50 years. His first article was published in the July 1970 *Baseball Digest*. He has written for more than 70 national and regional publications, including the *Baltimore Sun, Philadelphia Inquirer, Wall Street Journal, National Pastime, Sports Collectors Digest, Sports Parade, Phillies Report, 50 Plus Life,* and many others. He is the author of *Frank "Home Run" Baker: World Series Hero and Hall of Famer*.

He is a longtime member of Society for American Baseball Research (SABR) and a regular contributor to *The Baltimore Chop*, the quarterly newsletter for SABR's Baltimore Babe Ruth Chapter. Sparks also has made presentations at Bob Davids and Connie Mack SABR chapters. He wrote a weekly baseball column for several years for *The York (Pa.) Sunday News*.

Sparks is a member of the Eastern Shore (Md.) Baseball Hall of Fame. He was inducted in the sportswriter category.

www.ingramcontent.com/pod-product-compliance
Lightning Source LLC
Chambersburg PA
CBHW031245090426
42742CB00007B/317